The Jurassic Ammonite Zones of the Soviet Union

Edited by

G. Ya. Krymholts
Geological Faculty
Leningrad University
University emb. 7/9, 199034 Leningrad, U.S.S.R.

M. S. Mesezhnikov
VNIGRI
Liteiny 39, 191104 Leningrad, U.S.S.R.

G.E.G. Westermann
Department of Geology
McMaster University
1280 Main Street West
Hamilton, Ontario L8S 4M1, Canada

SPECIAL PAPER

223

Translated from the Russian by T. I. Vassiljeva
The Jurassic Zones of the USSR
Edited by G. Ya. Krymholts and M. S. Mesezhnikov
Interdepartmental Stratigraphic Committee of the USSR
Transactions, Volume 10
Originally published by
Nauka Publishers, Leningrad, 1982
(Revised 1986)

Authors' addresses:
G. Ya. Krymholts, Geological Faculty, Leningrad University, University emb. 7/9, 199034, Leningrad, U.S.S.R.
M. S. Mesezhnikov and Ju S. Repin, VNIGRI, Liteiny 39, 191104, Leningrad, U.S.S.R.
N. I. Fokina and V. A. Vakhrameev, Geological Institute of Academy of Sciences of the U.S.S.R., Pyzhevsky 7, 119107 Moskva, U.S.S.R
V. I. Iljina and S. V. Meledina, Institute of Geology and Geophysics, 630090 Novosibirsk, U.S.S.R.
E. D. Kalacheva, VSEGEI, Sredny av. 74, 199026 Leningrad, U.S.S.R.

Published by The Geological Society of America, Inc.
3300 Penrose Place, P.O. Box 9140, Boulder, Colorado 80301

Printed in U.S.A.

GSA Books Science Editor Campbell Craddock

Library of Congress Cataloging-in-Publication Data

Zony iurskoi sistsemy v. SSSR. English.
  The Jurassic ammonite zones of the Soviet Union.

  (Special paper ; 223)
  Translation of: Zony iurskoi sistemy v SSSR.
  Bibliography: p.
  1. Geology, Stratigraphic—Jurassic. 2. Geology—
Soviet Union. I. Krymgol'ts, G. IA. II. Mesezhnikov,
Mikhail Semenovich. III. Westermann, Gerd Ernst Gerold,
1927–   . IV. Title. V. Series: Special papers
(Geological Society of America) ; 223.
QE681.Z6613   1988   551.7'66'0947   88-22954
ISBN 0-8137-2223-3

10 9 8 7 6 5 4 3 2

Cover photo: Berdjinka River, Ural River Basin, Upper Callovian and Oxfordian.

Contents

Contents

Preface

In August 1984, at the Moscow meeting of the International Geological Congress, I met with Drs. Krymholts and Mesezhnikov and suggested that their important work, *The Jurassic Zones of the USSR* (in Russian), should be translated into English. Translation would make the large amount of data compiled in that book available to the world community of Jurassic workers. As members of the International Commission on Jurassic Stratigraphy and of Project 171, Circum-Pacific Jurassic, of the International Geological Correlation Program, all three of us were particularly aware of the need to publish an English synthesis of the large, pertinent Russian literature from the several past decades, which unfortunately, has been available to only a few in the non-Russian-speaking world.

Agreement in principle with Drs. Krymholts and Mesezhnikov on a revised edition in English was the result of my negotiations with the Books Editor of the Geological Society of America, Dr. C. Craddock, and of application to the copyright commission in the Soviet Union.

I received the English version of the revised typescript, translated by Mr. Vassiljeva, in December 1986. Considerable technical and scientific editing as well as redrafting of tables was required before the final typescript could be submitted to the GSA Books Editor. Internal consistency had suffered under the varying degrees of revision of the Russian original carried out by the different authors, such as the difficulty in tracing the Bajocian/Bathonian boundary in the Boreal Realm. Another basic problem is the definition of the Middle/Upper Jurassic boundary, which Soviet authors consistently place at the base of the Callovian; the rest of the world, as far as I know, follows the ruling of the International Subcommission on Jurassic Stratigraphy (IVGS Commission on Stratigraphy) drawing the boundary above the Callovian. Since the Soviet decision cannot be altered by us, I have attempted to bypass this problem by omitting the use of the formal Series, writing instead "lower/middle/upper part of the Jurassic." I have also introduced the different spelling of standard and biozones by capitalizing the species epithet for the former, following contemporary English and North American practice.

Gerd E. G. Westermann
McMaster University, Hamilton, Canada
January 1988

Foreword

In the past few decades, due to intensive geological investigations, much attention was given to stratigraphic studies of certain regions, constructing defined stratigraphic schemes, and restructuring the theory of stratigraphy. Geological surveys and other geological investigations have become more detailed, and hence, require a more precise stratigraphic basis. At the same time, problems of correlation, both within certain regions and over the entire country, have become more complicated. There is an increasing need to create a standard that allows correlations for entire continents and the entire Earth's surface. This has required the construction of a general, well-grounded stratigraphic standard, i.e., the Standard (International) Stratigraphic Scale, compiled in maximum detail. The present zonal scheme serves as such a standard for the Phanerozoic.

The Commission on the Jurassic System of the USSR analyzed and summarized the data available and recommended a standard scale for subdivision of this system as the basis for studying Jurassic deposits in the USSR. Documents of specialized international meetings (e.g., Luxemburg, 1962, 1967; Moscow, 1967; Budapest, 1969; Lyon-Neuchatel, 1973; Stuttgart, 1977; Novosibirsk, 1977; and others) resulted from studies of type sections and their fossils, as well as other investigations, in the USSR. The latter were synthesized at inter-departmental regional stratigraphic meetings (Russian Platform, 1958; Caucasus, 1977; Baltic area, 1976; Urals, 1977; western Siberia, 1976; central Siberia, 1978; North-east, 1975; Far East, 1978; central Asia, 1971; Kazakhstan, 1967).

The results of these conferences are summarized herein. They were prepared by a group of authors and discussed and accepted by the plenary session of the commission. Also considered are the results of discussions on certain problems of Jurassic stratigraphy, which were carried out by the commission and published in *Resolutions of the Interdepartmental Stratigraphic Committee and Its Commissions.* We present the results obtained at different times. A brief history is presented of the origin and subdivisions of each stage, its stratotype, and the composition and fauna of some of its units; problems are discussed, and data are given on structural patterns of deposits in the main Jurassic regions in the USSR. Data on the seven separate Jurassic regions are presented separately from the structural-historical discussions. Each region has its own development of the Jurassic. Within each region, where possible, an area is chosen with the most complete, best studied, and most reliably subdivided section. In some cases, however, more or less remote parts of a region have to be used to characterize a certain stage. The following regions were chosen as being the most characteristic (Fig. 1): 1, Russian Platform; 2, Northern Caucasus, with the most complete and best studied section of the Mediterranean Geosynclinal Belt within the USSR; 3, Turan Plate, with the Kugitangtau area at its southeastern margin; 4, Western Siberian Plate; 5, Siberian Platform; and 6, the eastern parts of the USSR belonging to the Pacific Geosynclinal Belt. The northeastern and southern parts of the Far East of the Soviet Union are discussed separately.

The section dealing with the Upper Jurassic is somewhat different from the other parts. Due to marked provincialism, no common stratigraphic scheme can be used. In order to establish the correlation between the zonations of the Tethyan and Boreal realms and northwestern Europe, I have considered abundant evidence, including fossils; this has resulted in certain changes from the previous zonal correlations and a different interpretation of the Jurassic/Cretaceous boundary in the Boreal Realm.

In the characterization of sections, ample use is made of data from the volume on *Stratigraphy of the USSR Jurassic System* (Krymholts, 1972b) and other summaries and original papers. We show that, in some cases, it is possible to distinguish both local and the standard zones in the Jurassic of the USSR.

The zonal subdivision was discussed at the Plenary Meeting of the Commission on the Jurassic System of the USSR and was published in its preliminary form by Krymholts (1978). During the years that followed, some changes and additions were introduced. The subdivisions are based on ammonoid ranges, an archistratigraphic fossil group of great significance for the Mesozoic.

In stratigraphic studies and their application, other groups of organisms are, of course, also used: above all, these include the foraminifers. These small fossils are of major significance for subdivision and correlation of subsurface deposits, since in boreholes, core fossils are rare and usually fragmented. The Upper Jurassic foraminifers have been studied most thoroughly, and the subdivisions based on evolution of their assemblages are comparable to the biostratigraphic units in the Upper Jurassic based on ammonites.

Some bivalves are used successfully in marine Jurassic stratigraphy. Among them are *Buchia (Aucella* auct.), which are among the most common fossils in the Upper Jurassic, particularly in the northern USSR. *Mytiloceramus* is common in the Middle Jurassic of the eastern USSR, where ammonites are rare, and is equally important. Bivalves are mostly benthic and reflect the conditions in paleobasins to a greater degree than cephalopods. Thus, they are useful not only in stratigraphy but also for facies and biogeographic analysis.

It should be emphasized that during the Jurassic, biogeographical isolation of certain areas within the USSR underwent a significant evolution. At the beginning of the period, isolation in the seas was practically absent. At the end of the Early Jurassic, the differences had become evident, particularly in the composition of molluscs from the southern seas connected with Tethys and northern Boreal seas. Provincialism became more pronounced in the Middle Jurassic. The extreme provincialism that occurred in the Late Jurassic seas, particularly at the end of the period, is the main reason for distinguishing different stratigraphic schemes for certain basins, even when abundant fossils are present.

Extensive areas of the USSR were covered by land in Jurassic time. The recognition of standard zones for continental deposits is, of course, impossible, and it is often difficult to establish the stage to which certain parts of the section belong. In many cases, however, correlation with pairs (or triplets) of stages can be made on the basis of plant remains, mainly leaves, spores, and pollen.

Eight specialists have prepared this volume, each being responsible for a section, according to his or her specialization. Despite a common outline and editing, each section has retained its individuality, but during preparation the authors exchanged ideas and suggestions concerning the improvement of the presentation.

Many new data have become available to Soviet geologists since publication of the Russian version of this volume in 1982. Supplementary investigation of the Middle Jurassic of Siberia and the Far East suggests, for example, that the boundaries of the Bajocian and Bathonian in these regions are very close to the boundaries used in such regions as East Greenland and Canada.

We are grateful to A. I. Zhamoida, I. V. Polubotko, E. L. Prozorovskaja, K. O. Rostovtsev, and I. I. Sey for reading the manuscript, and for their useful advice and remarks.

G. Ya. Krymholts, M. S. Mesezhnikov, 1986

Geological Society of America
Special Paper 223
1988

The Jurassic Ammonite Zones of the Soviet Union

INTRODUCTION
G. Ya. Krymholts and M. S. Mesezhnikov

The Jurassic Period and its deposits in the Soviet Union are well known to specialists. The system has been the subject of a number of general works, such as the compilation and reconstruction of the first paleogeographic and paleobiogeographic maps, past climates, the notion of facies, the foundation of detailed stratigraphy, and the distinction of stages and of smaller stratigraphic units such as zones. The Jurassic is widespread with diverse deposits, and above all, it contains the remains of ammonites. Ammonoids belong to the few groups of fossil organisms that were both widely distributed in old seas and evolved rapidly. Their shells vary greatly in shape, ornamentation, and other characteristics, permitting relatively easy recognition of taxa.

Concerning the history and problems of Jurassic stratigraphy, we emphasize the role of the outstanding French paleontologist-stratigrapher Alcide d'Orbigny (1802–1875). Not only was he the first to formulate the concept that "stage units are manifestations of boundaries drawn by nature, but have nothing arbitrary" (d'Orbigny, 1842–1851, p. 603), but he was also the first to subdivide the Jurassic System into 10 stages (d'Orbigny, 1842–1851), seven of which are used today.

D'Orbigny (1852) listed a locality or area for each of the stages where the type section is located (i.e., stratotype) and after which it is named. He also listed other characteristic sections (parastratotypes) in France, England, Switzerland, and West Germany, and he indicated the types of deposits (e.g., coastal, shallow, or deeper water). He published a list of fauna for each stage, with numerous representatives of different fossil groups, primarily cephalopods and, of these, mainly ammonites. D'Orbigny (1842–1851) described the ammonites in a classic monograph and determined the total number of characteristic species for the Jurassic as 3,731 (d'Orbigny, 1850), thus defining a stage by stratotypes and parastratotypes as well as by fossils.

D'Orbigny prepared the three mentioned works simultaneously (1842–1851, 1850, 1852), so that discrepancies have arisen among historians concerning the date when the stages were established. The preferred date is 1850, when the stratigraphic section of the monograph on Jurassic cephalopods was published (d'Or-

bigny, 1850, p. LIX); it is made up of lists of the characteristic species for each Jurassic stage. A more detailed description of the stages was later published (d'Orbigny, 1852). Some stage names used by d'Orbigny, however, go back to earlier authors, e.g., Bathonian refers back to d'Omalius d'Halloy, 1843; Oxfordien, to Brogniart, 1829; and Kimmeridgian, to Thurman, 1833.

Arkell (1933) enumerated 120 Jurassic stage names used at different times. In order to avoid disagreement in assigning priority, he proposed (Arkell, 1946) accepting the year 1850 as marking the beginning of the stage concept (this is similar to zoology, where 1758, the year of publication of the 10th edition of Linné's *Systema Naturae,* is designated as a beginning of binominal nomenclature). In the *Stratigraphic Code of the USSR,* the year 1881 was chosen for the application of priority right for general stratigraphic units (Stratigraphic Code, 1977, Article IX.6).

In England at the time of d'Orbigny's work, a number of local units/strata were distinguished by their composition, which corresponded to parts of the Jurassic System, e.g., Portland Rock, Coral Rag, Cornbrash. These lithostratigraphic units are used by geologists working in the British Isles up to the present day.

In Germany, F. A. Quenstedt (1809–1889), publishing in the years of d'Orbigny's work, greatly advanced the triple subdivision of the Jurassic System proposed by L. von Buch (1837), as a result of studies in the Swabian Alb. In each of the Lower (or Black), Middle (Brown), and Upper (White) Jurassic, Quenstedt distinguished six lithostratigraphic units, which he characterized by ammonites and other taxa and denoted by letters of the Greek alphabet (alpha to zeta). The rank of these subdivisions was not, however, indicated by Quenstedt or his followers; they correspond more or less in their magnitude to the stages as presently used. These notations are used even today by German geologists in local descriptions.

Quenstedt's pupil, A. Oppel (1831–1865), was the first to successfully correlate units of the Jurassic System adopted in England, France, and southwestern Germany (Oppel, 1856–1858). He used d'Orbigny's stages as the framework for new units distinguished in England and adopted in West Germany, a major

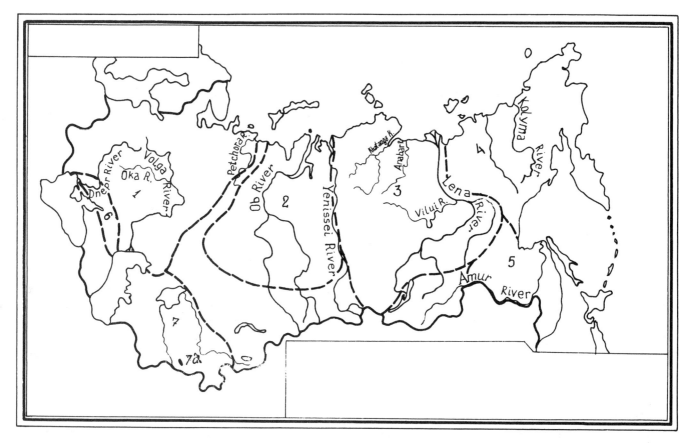

Figure 1. Index map of the Soviet Union: major Jurassic sedimentary basins (Scale, 1:60,000,000). 1, Russian Platform; 2, west Siberia; 3, Siberian Platform; 4, Northeast; 5, Far East; 6, north Caucasia; 7, Turan Plate (7a, Kugitangtau Range).

advance in the studies of Jurassic deposits in Western Europe. Even more significant was his subdivision of the Jurassic stages into zones, the smallest biostratigraphic unit of the standard scale. The term zones, however, had been used previously by d'Orbigny in a different sense. "Zone ou étage," sensu d'Orbigny (1842–1851, p. 602), is a stage named after its characteristic fauna, e.g., Toarcian or *Lima gigantea* and *Ammonites bifrons* Zone; Bajocian or *Trigonia costata* and *Ammonites interruptus* Brug. (*Parkinsoni* Sow.) Zone; and Callovian or *Ammonites jason* and *retractus, Ostrea dilatata* Zone.

In the present work, we follow the definition of zone in the Stratigraphic Code of the USSR (Strat. Code, 1977). Although most of d'Orbigny's stages are retained in the present standard scale of the Jurassic, none of them has retained its initial meaning. More recent studies on Jurassic deposits, including stratotypes, required changes in the interpretation of stages, their boundaries, subdivision, and faunal assemblages.

A very important summary on the Jurassic System of all continents was written by W. Arkell (1956). He showed that it was possible to apply the Western European standard zones as accepted by him to other more remote areas of the globe. Valua-

ble contributions to Jurassic zonations have been made by the English authors W. Dean, D. Donovan, and M. Howarth (Cope and others, 1980a,b), and by groups of English and French geologists (Mouterde and others, 1971). These and other studies were summarized at two international colloquia on the Jurassic, held in Luxembourg in 1962 and 1967, which resulted in agreements on the stage boundaries (Resolutions au Luxembourg, 1964; Resolutions, 1970).

We provide the basis for the zonal subdivisions of certain stages as adopted by the Commission on the Jurassic of the USSR, and characterize these features in the major areas of the Soviet Union. We also discuss historical problems of some biostratigraphic units.

It should be noted that we retain in certain cases, in parentheses, the original spelling of generic names such as *Ammonites* of d'Orbighy, Oppel. This also indicates their generic classification according to present systematics.

It is sometimes difficult to find the reference for the stratotype definition of a zonal unit, for example, if the respective parts of the sections were initially called "beds." In other cases, subzones are named the same as zones: confusing nomenclature, but this is not the place to introduce changes into a historically evolved system. In these cases, we make reference to both the index species and the author who named the zone.

Radiometric data available for the Jurassic Period differ greatly. For example, according to Harland and others (1981), the Jurassic was determined to have begun at 213 Ma and ended at 144 Ma, a duration of 69 m.y. According to Odin (1982), however, the dates are 204 and 130 Ma, a duration of 74 m.y.

HETTANGIAN
Ju. S. Repin

HISTORY AND STANDARD ZONES

The stage name Hettangian was proposed by Renevier (1864)* for the *Ammonites [Psiloceras] planorbis* and *Am. [Schlotheimia] angulatus* Zones as interpreted by Oppel, i.e., the lower part of the Sinemurian stage of d'Orbigny. The stage was named after a quarry near Hettang–Grande Village in Lorraine, 22 km south of Luxembourg. This stratotype, however, is "unfavourable for establishing the succession of ammonite assemblages. The whole stage is represented by sandstone, more or less calcareous, in places resting on Rhaetian beds, and in places on Keuper marls. The lower part, except for occasional oysters, contains no fossils; found above are accumulations of *Cardinia* and *Lima* together with a rich and well-preserved gastropod fauna" (Arkel, 1956, p. 68). For all practical purposes, the succession of ammonoid assemblages was established in sections of other areas of France, England, and West Germany. For instance, Oppel, when describing the *Am. planorbis* Zone (Oppel, 1856–1858), pointed to characteristic sections on the Dorset coast near Lyme Regis, quarries near Uplume, and Watchet sections in Somerset. The last area was proposed as the stratotype for a lower zone of the Hettangian by an English scientist (Morton, 1974).

Regarding the lower boundary of the Hettangian, and of the Jurassic System, the following should be noted. In the sections of England, the Jurassic begins within the "Blue Lias"† shale members, where the first *Psiloceras* appears only in the middle part of the section. The lower part of the Blue Lias section ("paper" shale member) is characterized by *Ostrea liassica* and *Pleuromya tatei;* lacking ammonites, it was distinguished by Richardson (1911) as Pre-Planorbis Beds. Donovan (1956) included these beds in the *Psiloceras planorbis* Subzone at the base of the Jurassic.

The Rhaetian section in the Austrian Alps, 15 km west of Bad-Ischl in the upper Kendlbach stream, consists of massive siliceous limestone between a clay member (12 m) with *Choristoceras marshi* Hauer (*Choristoceras marshi* Zone) and Hettangian limestone with *Psiloceras* ex. gr. *planorbis* (Sow.). It is not

yet clear whether this siliceous limestone member belongs to the Rhaetian or to the basal Jurassic (Zhamoida, 1975; Tollmann, 1976).

Commonly, in sections of marine Hettangian, the first ammonites are representatives of *Psiloceras* with smooth shells, viz. *P. planorbis* (Sow.), *P. erugatum* (Phill.), *P. psilonotum* (Qu.). However, in the Omolon Basin (North-East USSR), ribbed psiloceratids now assigned to *Primapsiloceras* occur below (Polubotko Repin, 1981). Initially named *Psiloceras (Franziceras ?) primulum* Repin (Field Atlas, 1968; Polubotko and Repin, 1972), it defines a level at the base of the *Psiloceras planorbis* Zone in the North-East USSR. Recently, remains of small *"Schlotheimia"* were found in Luxembourg, below the level with *P. planorbis* (Guerin-Franiatte and Müller, 1978). Judging by their description and illustrations, these *"Schlotheimia"* resemble small representatives of the Asian *Primapsiloceras* and probably belong to this genus.

The above facts allowed workers to regard beds containing *Primapsiloceras* (Polubotko and Repin, 1981; Repin, 1983) as an independent and lowermost Hettangian zone. The range corresponds to Pre-Planorbis Beds in England, equivalents of these beds with small *"Schlotheimia"* in Belgium and beds with *Primapsiloceras primulum* in northeast Asia.

In 1962, Hoffmann proposed to distinguish the *Neophyllites antecedens* Subzone at the base of the *Psiloceras psilonotum* (=*planorbis*) zone in northern Germany. The systematic status of *Neophyllites* is vague. Some workers have acknowledged it as a genus (Lange, 1941), whereas others regard it as a junior synonym of *Psilophyllites* (Arkell, in Moore, 1957) or *Psiloceras* (Cope and others, 1980a). Its stratigraphic position is also not quite clear. Distinguishing *N. antecedens,* Lange noted only that it was found below the *Schlotheimia angulata* Zone. Hoffmann found both *N. antecedens* and *P. psilonotum* in the same 0.65-m-thick layer, which he assumed to be condensed.

Bloos, in a guide to the excursion in Franconia, gave a scheme of the stratigraphic range of Hettangian ammonites in northwest and southern West Germany. He distinguished two subzones within the *planorbis* Zone: a lower *antecedens* and an upper *planorbis* subzone. *Neophyllites antecedens,* found only in the upper half of the subzone bearing that name, ranges through the *planorbis* Subzone.

Due to an inadequate systematic and stratigraphic definition of *Neophyllites,* an independent zonal unit on its basis is poorly grounded. On the other hand, this attempt to distinguish beds

---

*A. Leymerie (1838) proposed the term Infra-Lias for the deposits almost equivalent to the present Hettangian; later, this name was also used for the underlying Rhaetian formations. It is now rejected.

†Oppel also included "White Lias," underlying Blue Lias limestone, in the Jurassic. Now the White Lias is known to belong to the Rhaetian (Morton, 1974).

with *Psiloceras planorbis* below the level of other older ammonites is highly instructive.

Initially, Oppel distinguished two zones, viz., *Ammonites [Psiloceras] planorbis* (below) and *Ammonites [Schlotheimia] angulatus* (above) in deposits of the Hettangian. Collenot (1896) proposed a triple subdivision of the Hettangian and distinguished the *Alsatites liasicus* Zone in its central part. Subdivision of the Hettangian into three zones was supported by Lange (1941) and is now universally accepted. An attempt at a more detailed subdivision of the Hettangian was made by the French geologists Elmi and Mouterde (1965). Proceeding from the studies of sections in southeastern France (Ardeche), they proposed subdividing the Hettangian into five zones; however, the same scientists (Mouterde and others, 1971; Elmi and others, 1974) later decided that it would be more logical to accept only three zones, reducing their *Caloceras johnstoni* and *Waehneroceras portlocki* Zones to the rank of subzones.

As for grouping the Hettangian zones into substages, there is no universally accepted viewpoint. German workers (Lange, 1941, 1951; Hölder, 1964; Urlichs, 1977a), proceeding from the scheme for the Lower Jurassic of southwestern West Germany worked out by Quenstedt (1843), subdivided the Hettangian into two substages. The lower substage corresponds to the Black Jurassic $\alpha 1$ (*Psiloceras planorbis* and *Alsatites liasicus* Zones); and the upper one, to the Black Jurassic $\alpha 2$ (*Schlotheimia angulata* Zone), i.e., it corresponds to local lithologic units. Arkell, subdividing the Hettangian into substages, preferred paleontologic features, i.e., grouping successive ammonite levels on the basis of their common characteristics or differences. According to this author (Arkell, 1933), the Lower Hettangian corresponds to the *Psiloceras planorbis* Zone and the Upper Hettangian to the rest of the stage.

Following Arkell and taking into account new data, we take Lower Hettangian as comprising two successive levels: *Primapsiloceras* and *Psiloceras.* The Upper Hettangian in this case corresponds to the development of representatives of Schlotheimiidae and Arietitidae, viz., *Waehneroceras, Alsatites,* and *Schlotheimia.*

Zonal subdivision can be based on the division of the Hettangian in Western Europe (Dean and others, 1961), with the *Primapsiloceras primulum* Zone distinguished at the base of the Jurassic.

Lower Hettangian

1. *Primapsiloceras primulum* Zone. Polubotko & Repin, 1981. Index species—*P. primulum* (Repin). Range zone of *Primapsiloceras;* in England coeval to Pre-Planorbis Beds and their stratigraphic equivalents.

2. *Psiloceras planorbis* Zone. Oppel, 1856-1858. Index species—*P. planorbis* (Sow.). Generally, range zone of *Psiloceras* s. str. and *Caloceras.* (a) *Psiloceras planorbis* Subzone. Trueman, 1922. Two levels are distinguished: the lower one with smooth *Psiloceras planorbis* (Sow.), *P. erugatum* (Phill.), *P. psilonotum* (Qu.), and the upper one with distinctly plicate *Psiloceras plicatu-*

lum (Qu.). (b) *Caloceras johnstoni* Subzone. Trueman, 1922. Index species—*C. johnstoni* (Sow.). Base defined by appearance of genus *Caloceras* and the index species. *Caloceras belcheri* (Simps.) and *C. bloomfieldense* Donovan pass into the base of the overlying zone.

Upper Hettangian

3. *Alsatites liasicus* Zone. Collenot, 1896. Index species—*A. liasicus* (Orb.). Defined by appearance and flourish of *Waehneroceras;* upper half dominated by *Alsatites.* (a) *Waehneroceras portlocki* Subzone. Lange, 1941. Index species—*W. portlocki* (Wright). Characteristic are species of *Waehneroceras;* in certain sections also rare *Alsatites.* (b) *Alsatites laqueus* Subzone. Reynes, 1879. Index species—*A. laqueus* (Qu.). Base defined by appearance of index and species of *Saxoceras.* Some *Waehneroceras* pass into subzone. Generally, two successive *Alsatites* levels are present, a lower level with *Alsatites laqueus* (Qu.), and an upper level with *Alsatites liasicus* (Orb.). Upper Hettangian.

4. *Schlotheimia angulata* Zone. Oppel, 1856-1858. Index species—*S. angulata* (Schloth.). Range zone of *Schlotheimia.* (a) *Schlotheimia extranodosa* Subzone. Donovan, 1956. Index species—*S. extranodosa* (Waehner.). Range subzone. (b) *Schlotheimia complanta* Subzone. Spath, 1942. Index species—*S. complanata* Koenen; *Schlotheimia similis* Spath.

SOVIET UNION

In the Soviet Union, marine Hettangian deposits are not widespread. Mainly they are found in the north and east of the country; rare deposits are recorded within the Mediterranean Geosynclinal Belt (Fig. 2). On the Russian Platform, the Hettangian has not been recorded, although some authors so dated the upper part of the Novorajskoe Formation at the northwestern margin of the Donets folded structure (Krymholts, 1972b).

Mediterranean Geosynclinal Belt

Hettangian deposits occur in the Crimea. Part of the Upper Tauride Group, they are composed of dark gray clay shale with interbeds of siltstone and quartz sandstone (50–150 m). The discovery of *Schlotheimia angulata* (Schloth.) at the Bodrak River establishes this upper Hettangian zone (Krymholts, 1972b). In the northern Caucasus, there are no paleontologically confirmed Hettangian deposits.

On the Turan Plate, Lower Jurassic continental and weathering-crust deposits are recorded. It is impossible to distinguish stages in these sections, which often are characterized only by plant remains. In Kugitangtau, deposition of the thin Sandzhar Formation possibly continued into the early Jurassic with breccias, red mudstone, and siltstone (Resolutions, 1977).

West Siberian Plain

On the West Siberian Plain, the lower part of the Jurassic consists mainly of the limnic Lower Tyumen Member, with only

Stage	EUROPEAN STANDARD ZONES		RUSS. PLAT.	N. CAUCA.	KUNI- TANGTAU RANGE	W. SIBERIA	SIBERIAN PLATFORM	NORTH-EAST		FAR EAST
	Zones	Subzones								
HETTANGIAN — U	ANGULATA	COMPLANATA	(unknown)	(absent)	Sandzhar Form. (part.): breccias, mudstone, siltstone. — 20 m	Lower Tyumen Member (lower): sandstone, mudstone — 60-100 m	Mudstone with "*Pseudomyt.*" *sinuosus* ., *Kolymon. staeschei*, *Meleagrin. subolifex*	mudstone — 55 m	*S. angulata* Zone	(unknown)
		EXTRANODOSA								
	LIASICUS	LAQUEUS							*A. liasicus* Zone	
		PORTLOCKI								
HETTANGIAN — L	PLANORBIS	JOHNSTONI					*P. olenekense* beds		*P. planorbis* Zone	
		PLANORBIS								
	PRIMULUM						100-120 m		*P. primulum* Zone	

Figure 2. The Hettangian of the major regions of the U.S.S.R.

spore-pollen assemblages. The major part (60 to 100 m) of this member, made up of sandstone, siltstone, and mudstone, is presumed to belong to the Hettangian and Sinemurian.

Siberian Platform

On the Siberian Platform, marine Hettangian occurs on the northeastern and eastern margins (Lena-Anabar and Cis-Verkhoyanye Troughs). The rare faunal remains permit dating as Hettangian only. In the inner zone of the Cis-Verkhoyanye Trough (Undyulyung, Begidzhan, Mengkere, Dzhardzhan Rivers), part of the formations (Tarynnakh, Setegei) at the base of the Jurassic section belong to the Hettangian, which is characterized by *Pseudomytiloides sinuosus* Polub., *Kolymonectes* ex gr. *staeschei* Polub. Its thickness is estimated at 100 to 120 m. The only indication of the *Psiloceras planorbis* Zone is the find in the Ust-Olenek area of an ammonite described as *Psiloceras jacuticum* A. Dagis (Dagis and Vozin, 1972; Discovery . . ., 1978). The author of this species later (Discovery . . ., 1978) placed it as junior synonym in *Psiloceras olenekense* (Kipar.), which was initially regarded as a Triassic *Japonites* (Kiparisova, 1937). Besides these ammonites, *Pseudomytiloides sinuosus* Polub. and *Dimyodon* sp. were also collected.

In the Viluj Syneclise, the Hettangian is presumably continental (lower Ukugut and Irelyakh Formations).

Northeast

The Marine Lower Jurassic is widespread and rather well characterized by bivalves, brachiopods, and ammonites. Four

Hettangian zones can be recognized as in the standard sequence and therefore have been given similar names. Their ammonite assemblages are characterized by diverse genera and, usually, low species diversity.

The lower Jurassic outcrops are classified into two major types, subplatform and geosynclinal.

The reference section of subplatform-type Hettangian in the area is a section along the Kedon River in the Omolon Massif (Polubotko and Repin, 1972; Strat. Jurassic System, 1976). The Hettangian is represented by fine alternated mudstone, siliceous mudstone, and tuffaceous mudstone, with a total thickness of 53 to 55 m. All four standard zones are present.

1. *Primapsiloceras primulum* Zone, with the index species (9 m).

2. *Psiloceras planorbis* Zone, with the index species and *P. viligense* Chud. et Polub., *P. suberugatum* Chud. et Polub., *P. plicatulum* (Qu.) (8 m).

3. *Alsatites liasicus* Zone, with *Waehneroceras portlocki* (Wright) at the base, and *Alsatites* cf. *corogonensis* (Sow.), *Discamphiceras* sp. indet., *Psilophyllites* sp. indet. in upper part (35 m).

4. *Schlotheimia angulata* Zone, established by *S.* ex gr. *angulata* (Schloth.) (3 m).

In addition to ammonites, the Hettangian of this section also yields the bivalves *Oxytoma* ex gr. *sinemuriense* Orb., *Otapiria originalis* (Kipar.), *Meleagrinella subolifex* Polub., *Kolymonectes staeschei* Polub., *Pseudomytiloides* ex gr. *rassochaensis* Polub., and the brachiopod *Ochotorhynchia omolonensis* Dagys.

The most representative Hettangian section of geosynclinal-type in this region is in the Viliga Basin (northern Okhotsk area)

(Strat. Jurassic System, 1976), where it consists of mudstone 270 to 300 m thick. Established on ammonites are (1) *Primapsiloceras primulum* Zone, with index species; (2) *Psiloceras planorbis* Zone, with *P.* cf. *planorbis* (Sow.), *P. viligense* Chud. et Polub., *P. suberugatum* Chud. et Polub., *P. plicatulum* (Qu.); and (3) *Alsatites liasicus* Zone, with *A.* cf. *coregonensis* (Sow.) and *Schlotheimia* ? sp. A bivalve assemblage in this section is represented by *Otapiria originalis* (Kipar.), *O. pseudooriginalis* Zakh., *Pseudomytiloides sinuosus* Polub., and *P. latus* Polub.

In the Far East, there is no evidence for the Hettangian.

SUMMARY

From the above data, it follows that Hettangian deposits are relatively restricted on USSR territory. On the Russian Platform, West Siberian Plate, and central and southern Siberian Platform, they are in continental facies, with identification of the Hettangian in the Jurassic sections conventional and not always well grounded. In marine facies, the Hettangian occurs in geosynclinal structures of the Pacific Belt and adjacent areas of the Siberian Platform. It is presumably present in some areas of the Mediterranean Belt. In spite of single finds of ammonites in these regions, a zonal division of the stage is impossible. Zonation has been accomplished only in the northeast USSR, where typical Hettangian ammonite assemblages are represented by a depauperated set of European genera. These assemblages comprise index species or their vicariants, either facilitating correlation with Hettangian standard zones of Western Europe or allowing a similar zonal division. Within most of the northeastern USSR zones, "beds" or biohorizons can be distinguished which correspond to subzones of the European standard zones. This indicates a similar succession in the evolution of Hettangian ammonites. Generally, species differentiation of Hettangian ammonoids in the Northern Hemisphere was only slight, pointing to gradual climatic zonation and free connections among water areas of Europe, northeast Asia, and the Pacific.

SINEMURIAN
Ju. S. Repin

HISTORY AND STANDARD ZONES

D'Orbigny distinguished the Sinemurian stage at the base of the Jurassic. Subsequently, when its lower part was separated as an independent Hettangian stage, the Sinemurian acquired its present range. The stage was named after the town of Simur (lat. Sinemurium) in the Cote d'Or department (France). There, according to d'Orbigny, "the best type of deposits is found which I regard as a standard for comparison purposes" (d'Orbigny, 1842–1858).

The subdivision was made by Oppel (1956–1858), who distinguished five zones. Subsequently, slight corrections included the replacement of the *Pentacrinus tuberculatus* Zone of Oppel—named after an echinoderm—by the *Caenisites turneri* ammonite Zone (Wright, 1869), and the distinction of the upper part of the *Arietites bucklandi* Zone, Oppel's Beds with *Ammonites geometricus,* as an independent *Arnioceras semicostatum* Zone (Judd, 1875). Oppel also grouped zones into substages. According to him, Upper Sinemurian comprises three zones, i.e., *Ammonites* (=*Asteroceras*) *obtusum, Am.* (=*Oxynoticeras*) *oxynotum,* and *Am.* (=*Echioceras*) *raricostatum.*

Haug (1910) distinguished the Lorraine, including the Upper Sinemurian of Oppel, plus the *Asteroceras turneri* Zone of the Lower Sinemurian. Erroneously, Spath (1942) showed the Lorraine as coeval to the Upper Sinemurian only. Later, some French and German geologists, following Haug, used the Lorraine as an independent stage after reducing the Sinemurian by two lower zones, *Arietites bucklandi* and *Arnioceras semicostatum.* Other workers used the term Lotaringian (Gignoux, 1950) as an upper substage of Sinemurian. At the colloquium on the Jurassic System held in Luxembourg in 1962 (Resolution àu Luxembourg, 1964), the range of the Sinemurian was restricted from the *Arietites bucklandi* Zone, below, to the *Echioceras raricostatum* Zone, above. It was recommended to draw the Lower/ Upper Sinemurian boundary between the *Arnioceras semicostatum* and *Caenisites turneri* Zones.

Thus, the principle of priority, i.e., the initial grouping of zones by Oppel, was not taken into account at the colloquium. The use of the term Lorraines in the general scale should be rejected, and it should be left as a local unit. The subdivision should remain as the Upper and Lower Sinemurian, as understood by Oppel, as was justly done in the summary on the Lower Jurassic zones in northwestern Europe (Dean and others, 1961).

In the type area (the vicinity of Sinemurium), the Lower Sinemurian has several breaks and consists of gray semicrystalline limestone, interbedded with clay with ripple marks on the bedding surface and filled with *Gryphaea arcuata* shells. The total thickness of the Lower Sinemurian is 6.2 m. The following biostratigraphic levels are distinguished (in ascending order) (Mouterde and Tintant, 1964):

1. Coroniceras rotiforme Zone. (a) below (0.70 m), horizon with *Vermiceras cordieri* Canav., *Coroniceras haueri* Waehner, *O. westfalicum* Lange var. *elegantula* Lange; (b) above (1.10 m), horizon with *Coroniceras rotiforme* (Sow.)

2. Arietites bucklandi Zone (2.0 m). (a) below, horizon with *Megarietites meridionalis* (Reynes), *Arnioceras densicostata*(?) Qu., *A. kridioides* Hyatt; (b) above, horizon with *Arietites bucklandi* (Sow.), *A.* aff. *sinemuriensis* (Orb.), *Arnioceras ceratitoides* Qu.

3. Arnioceras semicostatum Zone. (a) below (1.0 m),

horizon with *Agassiceras scipionianum* (Orb.), *Arnioceras* sp.; (b) (0.40 m), horizon with *Euagassiceras sauzeanum* (Orb.) [=*E. resupinatum* (Simps)], *Metarnioceras* sp.; (c) above (1.0 m), horizon with *Arnioceras semicostatum* (Y. et B.), *A. miserabile* (Qu.), *Pararnioceras* sp., *Angulaticeras* cf. *lacunata*(J. Buckm.), *Sulciferites sulcifera* S. Buckm., *S. miscellus* (Opp.).

The Upper Sinemurian zones of *Asteroceras obtusum, Oxynoticeras oxynotum,* and *Echioceras raricostatum* are represented in the stratotype by a condensed horizon of phosphorite nodules about 25 cm thick; the stratotype does not show the succession of ammonite assemblages. These shortcomings of the stratotype are made up by more complete and ammonite-rich sections in the Swabian Alb (e.g., Quenstedt, 1882–1885; Oppel, 1856–1858; Hoffman, 1964) and England (Arkell, 1933; Dean and others, 1961). On the basis of the succession of ammonite levels in these regions, Spath (1942) compiled a scheme of zonation for the Sinemurian, later amplified by Donovan (Dean and others, 1961). This scheme is presently used for worldwide correlation of the Lower Jurassic; the Sinemurian has 16 zones and 17 subzones; the zones are grouped in substages as understood by Oppel.

Lower Sinemurian

1. *Arietites bucklandi* Zone. Oppel, 1856-1858. Index species—*A. bucklandi* (Sow.). Characterized by *Coroniceras, Arietites, Arnioceras, Pararnioceras, Vermiceras,* and *Charmasseiceras.* (a) *Coroniceras conybeari* Subzone. Tutcher, 1918. Index species—*C. (Metophioceras) conybeari* (Sow.). The appearance of the subgenus *Metophioceras* marks the base of the Sinemurian throughout the entire Northwest European Province. In addition to the index species, *C. (Metophioceras) longidomum* (Qu.) and *C. (M.) brevidorsale* (Qu.), and *Vermiceras scylla* (Reynes) are also common. (b) *Coroniceras rotiforme* Subzone. Collenot, 1879. Index species—*C. rotiforme* (Sow.). Lower boundary marked by appearance of subgenus *Coroniceras.* The ammonite assemblage comprises also *Coroniceras schloenbachi* (Reynes), *C. (C.) caprotinum* (Orb.), and *C. (C.) rotiforme* (Sow.). In southwestern Germany, *C. (C.) hyatti* (Donovan) passes into the overlying subzone and is found together with *Arietites bucklandi* (see Urlichs, 1977a). (c) *Arietites bucklandi* Subzone. Besides the index species occur *Epammonites,* and, probably, the first *Arnioceras.*

2. *Arnioceras semicostatum* Zone. Judd, 1875. Index species—A. semicostatum (Y. et B.). The assemblage comprises *Arnioceras, Coroniceras, Paracoroniceras, Metarnioceras,* and *Euagassiceras.* (a) *Coroniceras reynesi* Subzone. Dononvan, 1961. Index species—*C. reynesi* (Spath). Also found are *Paracoroniceras gmuendense* (Opp.) and *Pararnioceras meridionale* (Reynes). (b) *Agassiceras scipionianum* Subzone. Tutcher, 1918. Index species—*A. scipionianum* (Orb.). Also common are *Arnioceras acuticarinatus* (Simps.), *Agassiceras nodosaries* (Qu.), and subgenus *Metophioceras.* (c) *Euagassiceras sauzeanum* Sub-

zone. Tutcher, 1923. Index species—*E. sauzeanum* (Orb.). With *Euagassiceras* spp. and *Pararnioceras alcinoe* (Qu.).

3. *Caenisites turneri* Zone. Wright, 1860. Index species—*C. turneri* (Sow.). Lower part characterized by *Caenisites,* certain species of which range higher; upper half dominated by *Microderoceras* and *Promicroceras.* (a) *Caenisites brooki* Subzone. Lange, 1914. Index species—*C. brooki* (Sow.). Also with *C. preplotti* Spath and *C. costariformis* Spath. (b) *Microderoceras birchi* Subzone. Collenot, 1869. Index species—*M. birchi* (Sow.). Range zone of *Microderoceras; Caenisites* has disappeared and *Promicroceras capricornoides* (Qu.) is common.

Upper Sinemurian

4. *Asteroceras obtusum* Zone. Oppel, 1856–1858. Index species—*A. obtusum* (Sow.). Characterized by the Asteroceratinae *Asteroceras, Aegasteroceras, Epophioceras,* and, in the upper part, *Eparietites;* also with the Eoderoceratidae *Promicroceras, Xipheroceras,* and the last *Arnioceras.* Subzones reflect the trend in Asteroceratinae evolution toward increased whorl compression and decreased umbilical walls. (a) *Asteroceras obtusum* Subzone. Characteristic also is *Asteroceras stellare* (Sow.); common, but also found above are *Promicroceras planicosta* (Sow.) and *Xipheroceras dudressieri* (Orb.). (b) *Asteroceras stellare* Subzone. Buckman, 1910. Index species—*A. stellare* (Sow.). Range zone. (c) *Eparietites denotatus* Subzone. Buckman, 1919. Index species—*E. denotatus* (Simps.). Characteristic are *Eparietites* species.

5. *Oxynoticeras oxynotum* Zone. Oppel, 1856–1858. Index species—*O. oxynotum* (Qu.). Most characteristic of this zone are *Oxynoticeras, Gagatyceras, angulaticeras, Palaeoechioceras, Bifericeras, Slatterites,* and *Cheltonia.* On the basis of succession of *Oxynoticeras* species, two subzones are distinguished. (a) *Oxynoticeras simpsoni* Subzone. Spath, 1942. Index species—*O. simpsoni* (Simps.). Also with *Gagatyceras gagateum* (Y. et B.) and *Cheltonia* spp. but also range higher. (b) *Oxynoticeras oxynotum* Subzone. Range zone. Also found are *Bifericeras bifer* (Qu.), *Angulaticeras,* and *Palaeoechioceras* spp.

6. *Echioceras raricostatum* Zone. Oppel, 1856. Index species—*E. raricostatum* (Zieten). *Paltechioceras* and *Eoderoceras* range zone. Common in lower part are *Bifericeras, Crucilobiceras, Echioceras,* and *Gleviceras.* (a) *Crucilobiceras densinodulum* Subzone. Lange, 1926. Index species—*C. densinodulum* Buckm. Base at appearance of *Crucilobiceras* and *Paltechioceras;* also common are *Eoderoceras bispinigerum* (Buckm.) and *E. armatum* (Sow.); *Gleviceras* appears. (b) *Echioceras raricostatum* Subzone. Base at first appearance of *Echioceras,* i.e., *E. raricostatum* (Zieten), *E. aeneum* Truem. et Will; also *Bifericeras, Crucilobiceras,* and *Epideroceras.* (c) *Leptechioceras macdonnelli* Subzone. Lange, 1926. Index species—*L. macdonnelli* (Portlock). *Leptechioceras* range zone, with different Echioceratidae, and, to a lesser degree, Eoderoceratidae. (d) *Paltechioceras aplanatum* Subzone. Lange, 1926. Index species—*P. aplanatum* (Hyatt). Range zone.

Stage	European Standard Zones	European Standard Subzones	RUSSIAN PLATFORM	N. CAUCAUSUS	KUGI-TANGTAU RANGE	WEST SIBERIA	SIBERIAN PLATFORM	NORTH-EAST	FAR EAST
SINEMURIAN (U)	RARICOSTATUM	APLANATUM	(unknown)	**Bugunzha Form.: mudst., sandst.** *Echioceras declivus, Oxynotic. oxynotum, Microderoc. birchi* — 130-170 m	Sandzhar Form. (part): breccies, mudst., siltst. — 200 m	Lower Tyumen Member (lower): sandst., siltst., mudst. — 60-100 m	**Siltst.** *Otapiria limaeformis,* "*Pseudomytil. rassochaensis*" — 200 m	Mudstone — 70 m; *Angulatic. kolymicum* Zone	**Siltst.** *Angulatic. ochoticum, Oxynoticeras sp., Otapiria limaeformis,* "*Pseudomytil. rassochaensis*" — 300 m
		MACDONNELLI							
		RARICOSTATUM							
		DENSINODULUM							
	OXYNOTUM	OXYNOTUM							
		SIMPSONI							
	OBTUSUM	DENOTATUS							
		STELLARE							
		OBTUSUM							
	TURNERI	BIRCHI							
		BROOKI							
SINEMURIAN (L)	SEMICOSTATUM	SAUZEANUM						*Coroniceras siverti* Zone	
		SCIPIONIANUM							
	BUCKLANDI	REYNESI							
		BUCKLANDI						*BUCKLANDI ZONE*	
		ROTIFORME							
		CONYBEARI							

Figure 3. The Sinemurian of the major regions of the U.S.S.R.

SOVIET UNION

Marine Sinemurian occurs mainly in northern Siberia, the Far East, and Northeast, as well as within the Mediterranean Geosynclinal Belt. On the Russian Platform, marine sediments are absent (Fig. 3). Previous authors assumed that the upper Novorajskoe Formation at the northwestern margin of the Donets Folded Structure was Sinemurian.

Mediterranean Geocynclinal Belt

Marine Sinemurian deposits, widespread in this belt, are characterized by ammonites. In the Carpathians, Crimea, northern and southern slopes of the Great Caucasus, Minor Caucasus, and Southern Pamirs, index or guide species of certain standard zones are found. In the northern Caucasus, the marine Sinemurian is most complete in the Laba Basin (Bugunzha Formation), at the base of the Jurassic section, resting unconformably on Paleozoic and Triassic rocks. The formation is divisible into two parts: below, massive sandstone with conglomerate and gritstone lenses (Veriyut horizon of V. N. Robinson, 1932), 10 to 20 m thick; above, a sequence of silty mudstone (120 to 150 m). This formation contains *Microderoceras birchi* (Sow.), *Arietites pseudospiralis* Vad., *Oxynoticeras oxynotum* (Qu.), and *Echioceras declivis* Truem. et Will., indicative of Turneri, Oxynotum, and Raricostatum Zones (Beznosov, 1973; Resolutions, 1984).

On the southern slope of the Great Caucasus, in the Mzymta and Shakhe Basins, the Sinemurian comprises the Eskisadok Formation. This is a sequence of banded clay shale with sandstone and comglomerate interbeds, which yields *Arietites* cf. *bucklandi* (Sow.) and *A. grossi* (Wright) (Krymholts, 1972b).

Central Asia

In most areas, the Sinemurian is continental and cannot be distinguished as an independent unit. In Kugitangtau, it includes the upper Sandzhar Formation (Resolutions, 1977).

West Siberian Plate

The Sinemurian is present in the Lower Tyumen Member (see under Hettangian).

In northern Siberia and northeast USSR, Sinemurian deposits are known from Anabar Bay in the west, to the Okhotsk and Bering Sea coasts in the east. In this area, the marine Sinemurian is almost ubiquitous and can locally be recognized if fauna is present. In other places, it is presumably present but cannot be distinguished, as on the Anabar Bay coast, where undivided Hettangian-Sinemurian yields *Meleagrinella* cf. *subolifex* Polub. and *Otapiria* sp.

Northeast

Platform-type sediments (Kedon, Vizual'naya rivers) (Strat. Jurassic System, 1976; Polubotko and Repin, 1972, 1974) represent the Sinemurian, with 70 m of finely alternating mudstone, tuff mudstone, and tuffite. Three zones are distinguished on the basis of ammonite assemblages:

1. The lower zone corresponds in its range to the Bucklandi Zone of the Standard Scale and retains this name; the two upper ones are local units.

2. The assemblage of the *Coroniceras siverti* Zone yields also *C. reynesi* Spath, *C.* cf. *bisulcatum* (Brug.), and *Paradasyceras*(?) sp.

3. The *Angulaticeras* (*Gydanoceras*) *kolymicum* Zone is the range zone of the local subgenus *Gydanoceras,* with *A.* (*G.*) *kolymicum* Repin and *A.* (*G.*) *ochoticum* Repin. Correlation of these zones (lonas) with the standard zones, and the position of the boundary between them, are rather uncertain and based on convention; however, representatives of the ammonite assemblages are rather widespread, from Verkoyanye to Beringia.

Far East

The Sinemurian is reported from the south Bureya Trough, Sikhote-Alin, and Southern Primorye. The siltstones are characterized by *Angulaticeras* (*Gydanoceras*) cf. *ochoticum* Repin, *Oxynoticeras* sp., *Otapiria limaeformis* Zakh., and *Pseudomytiloides rassochaensis* Polub. Possibly, the Sinemurian comprises the upper part of the Kiselevka Formation, in the Lower Amur River, from which *Juraphyllites amurensis* (Kipar.), various *Cardinia, Chlamys textoria* (Schloth.), and other bivalves were described.

SUMMARY

The distributional pattern of the continental and marine Sinemurian is similar to that of the Hettangian. With the beginning of the Sinemurian age, the transgression extended over most of the Mediterranean Belt, as shown by ammonite finds in the Carpathians, Crimea, northern Caucasus, Transcaucasus, and Pamirs. The ammonites belong to Western European genera and indicate the presence of most standard zones.

In boreal areas of the USSR, the depauperated assemblage of Sinemurian ammonites is represented by *Arietites, Coroniceras, Paracoroniceras, Eparietites, Paradasyceras,* and *Angulaticeras.*

PLIENSBACHIAN
Ju. S. Repin

HISTORY AND STANDARD ZONES

The term Pliensbachian was proposed by Oppel (1856–1858) to replace Lias (*étage liasien*), which had no geographic base in the scheme of d'Orbigny (1842–1851). The stage was named after the village of Pliensbach (Geppingen, Baden-Württemberg, West Germany). The stratotype is 35 km southeast of the town of Stuttgart, in the Swabian Alb. Along the Pliensbach stream are a number of small outcrops, which, together with excavations for a water pipe, made it possible to compile a complete composite section of this stage (Schlatter, 1977; Urlichs, 1977a). The fossil character of the Lower Pliensbachian is amplified by ammonites from the Nürtingen section 15 km to the southeast. Fossils from the type area of Pliensbachian have long attracted the attention of investigators. In the first description of the natural history of Württemberg, published in 1602, numerous ammonites were described and illustrated, and in Württemberg, Quenstedt and Oppel carried out their studies.

Charmouthian, Carixian, and Domerian stages were at different times distinguished within the Pliensbachian. The Charmouthian (Charmouthien) of Renevier (1864) is a later synonym of Pliensbachian and was not used further. Carixian, derived from Carixia (=Charmouth), was distinguished by Lang (1913) and corresponded to the Lower Pliensbachian of Oppel. The Domerian was proposed by Bonarelli (1894) and corresponded to the Upper Pliensbachian.

The Colloquium on Jurassic Stratigraphy, held in Luxembourg in 1962 (Resolution, 1964), used Carixian and Domerian in its recommendations as Pliensbachian substages. However, use of these names in the standard scale seems unwarranted, since they only duplicate the Lower and Upper Pliensbachian. The use of the term Domerian in the general scale is also a cause for objection: in distinguishing the Upper Pliensbachian, Oppel noted that it corresponded to the range of Amaltheidae (see also Bonarelli, 1894). However, in the stratotype named after San Domaro Mount in the Lombardian Alps (Brescia Province, Italy), Amaltheidae are practically absent. The lower boundary of the Domerian in the stratotype has not been traced, and its upper boundary is rather arbitrary.

The stratotype of the Pliensbachian consists, below, of massive marl and flag-like limestone, the Numismalis Marl (Numismalismergel) or Lias-gamma (Black Jurassic γ, according to Quenstedt); above, it consists of clay and marly clay (Amaltheenthone) of Lias-delta (Black Jurassic δ), crowned by a 2-m-thick marl bed. The thicknesses are approximately 12 and 24 m, respectively (Urlichs, 1977a).

Oppel subdivided Pliensbachian into zones and substages, and regarded the Numismalis Marl (except for the upper 3 m) as Lower Pliensbachian, comprising the three zones of *Ammonites* [*Uptonia*] *jamesoni*, *Am.* [*Tragophylloceras*] *ibex*, and *Am.* [*Prodactylioceras*] *davoei*. He placed the uppermost Numismalis Marl

and the overlying Amaltheus Clay into the Upper Pliensbachian and subdivided it into the three zones of lower *Ammonites* [*Amaltheus*] *margaritatus*, upper *Am.* [*Amaltheus*] *margaritatus*, and *Am.* [*Pleuroceras*] *spinatus*. Since the time of Oppel, no changes have been introduced into the subdivision of Lower Pliensbachian. All workers who have recently studied the problems of zonal stratigraphy of the Pliensbachian regard this subdivision as quite satisfactory and rational. There are only certain differences at subzonal level. They concern the number of subzones distinguished by different authors, and sometimes the choice of the index species. The two *A. margaritatus* zones of Oppel are now regarded as a single zone (Spath, 1942), with the three subzones of *A. stokesi*, *A. subnodosus*, and *A. gibbosus* (Howarth, 1955, 1958–1959; Dean and others, 1961).

In 1971, French stratigraphers proposed elevating the lower subzone of the Margaritatus Zone, without the index, to a full zonal rank (Mouterde and others, 1971), which seems reasonable. Although the Stokesi Zone is stratigraphically small, it is widely recognized in the Northern Hemisphere. Besides the North-West European Zoogeographic Province, the index species is recorded from Bulgaria; the Caucasus; the north USSR-Anabar and Begidzhan (right tributary of the Lena) Rivers; the Sededema, Bolshoi Anyuj, Gizhiga, and Omolon Basins (northeast USSR); the Far East; the Transbaikal area; and Japan (Kyushu Island), Alaska, and Canada. Thus, the increase in rank of the Stokesi Subzone to a zone is justified. This is particularly important for correlating Upper Pliensbachian in boreal areas of the USSR and North America, where zonal subdivision of the entire Upper Pliensbachian is based on a succession of species of *Amaltheus*. It existed in this region throughout Late Pliensbachian, whereas *Pleuroceras* was locally restricted.

The stratotype of Pliensbachian is best shown among those of the Lower Jurassic stages, and its abundant fossils made possible Oppel's zonation. Later, many European scientists worked out a scheme of Pliensbachian subzones, based on the succession of ammonite assemblages in Western Europe.

Lower Pliensbachian

1. *Uptonia jamesoni* Zone. Oppel, 1856. Index species—*U. jamesoni* (Sow.). In the stratotype 5 m thick and comprising five subzones, in contrast to the scheme of Donovan (Dean and others, 1961), which combines the Masseanum Subzone and Ibex Zone. (a) *Phricodoceras taylori* Subzone. Spath, 1923. Index species—*P. taylori* (Sow.). Base in stratotype defined by appearance of *Apoderoceras nodogigas* (Qu.); index species appears in the upper part of the subzone. (b) *Polymorphites polymorphus* Subzone. Spath, 1923. Index species—*P. polymorphus* (Qu.). Base defined by appearance of *Radstockiceras* (=*Metoxynoticeras*) and index species. Other species of *Polymorphites* appear in upper part of subzone and persist to middle part of next subzone.

Characterized by abundant *Tragophylloceras numismale* (Qu.), which account for about two-thirds of all ammonites; also single *Epideroceras, Microderoceras, Hyperderoceras,* and *Coelodero-cas*(?), ranging from the base of Pliensbachian; first Liparocerati-dae also appear, e.g., *Liparoceras (Parinodiceras) reineckii* (Qu.). (c) *Platypleuroceras brevispina* Subzone. Spath, 1922. Index species—*P. brevispina* (Sow.). In the stratotype (~0.8 m) *Platy-pleuroceras* is rare; base defined (Nürtingen section) by the index species *Crucilobiceras submuticum* (Opp.) and *C. rotundum* (Qu.). In the middle of the subzone, a 3- to 7-cm-thick bed is filled with *Polymorphites lineatus* (Qu.), *P. mixtus* (Qu.), etc. (d) *Uptonia jamesoni* Subzone. Base defined by appearance of *Uptonia* with index species passing through entire subzone; 20 cm below top in the Pliensbach section, a layer (15 cm) yields numer-ous *Coeloceras pettos* (Qu.), *C. pettos grenouillouxi* (Orb.), *C. pettos planula* (Qu.), and rare *C. pettos pinguecostatum* Bremer; *Polymorphites* is found more rarely than below. (e) *Tropidoceras masseanum* Subzone. Spath, 1923. Index species—*T. masseanum* (Orb.). Appearance of *Tropidoceras masseanum* and similar spe-cies marks lower boundary in stratotype; *Uptonia* is also found. At Pliensbach and Nürtingen, *Tropidoceras* passes into beds with *Acanthopleuroceras valdani* (Orb.). The *jamesoni/masseanum* subzonal transition is marked by appearance of *Tragophylloceras undulatum* (Smith).

2. *Tragophylloceras ibex* Zone. Oppel, 1856. Index species—*T. ibex* (Qu.). (a) *Acanthopleuroceras valdani* Subzone. Spath, 1942. Index species—*A. valdani* (Orb.). Base in stratotype marked by appearance of *Acanthopleuroceras maugenesti* (Orb.), *A. arietiforme* (Oppel), and similar species. The index species appears higher, but *Tragophylloceras ibex* (Qu.) is common here and occurs with single specimens also below. The upper part of the subzone also yields *Beaniceras centaurus* (Orb.), *Liparoceras zieteni* (Qu.), and *L. bronni* Spath. (b) *Beaniceras luridum* Sub-zone. Dean and others, 1961. Index species—*B. luridum* (Simps.). Stratotype with poorly preserved *Beaniceras luridum* (Simps.), *B. costatus* Buckm., and *B. rotundum* Buckm.

3. *Prodactylioceras davoei* Zone. Oppel, 1856. Index species—*P. davoei* (Sow.). Varying numbers of subzones, with different names, have been proposed. Based on the stratotype, we accepted two subzones: (a) *Androgynoceras maculatum–capri-cornus* Subzone. Schlatter, 1977. Index species—*A. maculatum* (Y. et B.) and *A. capricornus* (Schloth.). Also characteristic are *A. henleyi* (Sow.), *A. heterogenes* (Y. et B.), *A. infracapricornus* (Qu.), *A. sparsicosta* (Truem.), *A. lataecosta* (Sow.), and *Liparoc-eras divaricosta* (Truem.), etc. In England, where the index spe-cies occur at successive levels, Donovan (Dean and others, 1961) separates two subzones, Maculatum and Capricornus. However, on the continent, in West Germany (stratotype), and in France, these and associated species originated from the same beds. (b) *Oistoceras figulinum* Subzone. Lange, 1936. Index species—*O. figulinum* (Simps.). Base marked by appearance of *Oistoceras,* together with *Prodactylioceras davoei* (Sow.). Also characteristic are *Oistoceras angulatum* (Qu.), *O. curvicorne* (Schloenb.), *O. wrighti* Spath, and *O. omissum* (Simps.).

Upper Pliensbachian

4. *Amaltheus stokesi* Zone. Lange, 1936. Index species—*A. stokesi* (Sow.). In stratotype (~1.4 m) characterized also by *Protogrammoceras monestieri* Fischer. In Western Europe, this zone also yields *Amaltheus bifurcus* How., *A. wertheri* (Lange), *A. evolutus* Buckm., and *Amauroceras ferrugineum* (Simps.).

5. *Amaltheus margaritatus* Zone. Oppel, 1856* emend. Mouterde et al., 1971. Index species—*A. margaritatus* (Mont-fort). (a) *Amaltheus subnodosus* Subzone. Howarth, 1955 (=*nodifer* Subzone, Spath, 1942). Index species—*A. subnodosus* (Y. et B.). In stratotype (8.6 m), the base is at appearance of index species. The lower half also yields *Amaltheus gloriosus* Hyatt, *Lytoceras fimbriatum* (Sow.), *Derolytoceras tortum* (Qu.). *Amal-theus striatus* How., *A. margaritatus* Montf., *Amauroceras fer-rugineum* (Simps.), and *Sowerbyceras tortisulcoides* (Qu.) pass through the entire subzone and into the next subzones. (b) *Amal-theus gibbosus* Subzone. Kuhn, 1935. Index species—*A. gibbosus* (Schloth.). Base of subzone (14 m) at appearance of index spe-cies. Besides index species and ammonites, ranging upward from (a), also common *Amaltheus laevigatus* How., *Cymbites centri-globus centriglobus* (Opp.), *C. centriglobus nanus* Schindewolf, *Fuciniceras compressum* (Monestier), *Protogrammoceras depres-sum* (Qu.).

6. *Pleuroceras spinatum* Zone. Oppel, 1856. Index species—*P. spinatum* (Bruguiere). (a) *Pleuroceras apyrenum* Subzone. Spath, 1942. Index species—*P. apyrenum* Buck. In stratotype (2.8 m), base marked by appearance of *Pleuroceras transiens* (Frentzen); also *Amaltheus gibbosus* (Schloth.) and *Amauroceras ferrugineum* (Simps.), ranging upward from the Margaritatus Zone. (b) *Pleuroceras hawskerense* Subzone. Spath, 1942. Index species—*P. hawskerense* (Y. et B.). In stratotype (1 m), *P.* cf. *hawskerense* occurs, which defines lower boundary; also *Pleuroceras* cf. *spinatum* (Brug.) characteristic of the upper half.

SOVIET UNION

The marine Pliensbachian, especially Upper Pliensbachian, is more widespread than Hettangian and Sinemurian (Fig. 4); but Pliensbachian is unknown from the Russian Platform.

Mediterranean Geosynclinal Belt

In the northern Caucasus, the Pliensbachian makes up the upper part of the Khumara Formation, and the base of the Sebel'da Series comprises several formations (Beznosov, 1973; Resolutions, 1984).

Lower Pliensbachian deposits are characterized by brachio-pods, bivalves, and foraminifers; ammonites are rare. At the

*Retention of the name of the zone by the French workers, while changing its range appreciably, is unfortunate. However, we have no opportunity to propose a different solution (eds.).

Stage	EUROPEAN STANDARD Zones	EUROPEAN STANDARD Subzones	RUSSIAN PLATFORM	N. CAUCAUSUS	KUGI-TANGTAU RANGE	WEST SIBERIA	SIBERIAN PLATFORM	NORTH-EAST	FAR EAST
PLIENSBACHIAN (U)	SPINATUM	HAWSKERENSE	(unknown)	Mudst., sandst. *Amaltheus margaritatus* — 200 m	Sandzhar Formation (part): breccias, siltst., mudst. — 20 m	Lower Tyumen Member (upper): sandst., siltst., mudst. — 40 m	Siltst. — 120-180 m; Amaltheus Beds	Siltst., sandst. — 80 m; Amaltheus viligaensis Zone	Siltst. — 580 m; Amaltheus gr. viligaensis "Paltarpites" Beds
PLIENSBACHIAN (U)	SPINATUM	APYRENUM							
PLIENSBACHIAN (U)	MARGARITATUS	GIBBOSUS		Limest. *Tropidoceras* — 2 m			*A. margaritatus* Zone	*A. talrosei* Zone	*A. margaritatus* Zone
PLIENSBACHIAN (U)	MARGARITATUS	SUBNODOSUS							
PLIENSBACHIAN (U)	STOKESI			Sebelda Series (lower)			*A. stokesi* Zone	*A. stokesi* Zone	*A. stokesi* Zone
PLIENSBACHIAN (L)	DAVOEI	FIGULINUM		Sandst. *Uptonia ignota, Tropidoceras flandrini* — 100-200 m			Sandst. *Peregrinelloidea, Kolymonectes ex gr. staeschei* — 250-300 m	Siltst. *Kolymonectes ex gr. staeschei, Harpex nodosus, Polymorphites sp.* — 60 m	(unknown)
PLIENSBACHIAN (L)	DAVOEI	CAPRICORNUS							
PLIENSBACHIAN (L)	IBEX	LURIDUM							
PLIENSBACHIAN (L)	IBEX	VALDANI							
PLIENSBACHIAN (L)	IBEX	MASSEANUM							
PLIENSBACHIAN (L)	JAMESONI	JAMESONI							
PLIENSBACHIAN (L)	JAMESONI	BREVISPINA							
PLIENSBACHIAN (L)	JAMESONI	POLYMORPHUS							
PLIENSBACHIAN (L)	JAMESONI	TAYLORI							

Figure 4. The Pliensbachian of the major regions of the U.S.S.R.

Bol'shaya Laba-Zelenchuk interfluve, single finds of *Uptonia ignota* (Simps.) and *Tropidoceras flandrini* (Dum.) were made, which date the upper part of the sandy-silty Khumara Formation as the Jamesoni Zone. Resting on top with the erosional surface is a limestone (2 m) at the base of the Sebel'da Series (the Chuba and other formations). The limestone contains *Tragophylloceras huntoni* (Simps.), *T. anonymium* Haas, *Tropidoceras ellipticum* (Sow.), *T. flandrini* (Dum.), and *T. obtusum* Futterer, indicating the Ibex Zone, and probably also the Davoei Standard Zone.

The Upper Pliensbachian of the northern Caucasus consists of several formations in the lower Sebel'da Series, mainly mudstone (as much as 200 m) with siltstone interbeds, locally with sandstone horizons (sandstones of Mount Akhyzyrta and Bodetskoe Santstone). These strata are characterized by rather abundant Amaltheidae; the lower part yields *Androgynoceras oblongum* (Qu.), characteristic of Davoei Zone. The most complete Amaltheidae assemblages are recorded at the Belaya-Kyafar and Ardon-Urukh conferences. Often found are *Amaltheus margaritatus* Montf., *A. striatus* Howard, *A. evolutus* Buckm., and *A. subnodosus* (Y. et B.). Stankevich (1964) also described *A. stokesi* (Sow.) from the Laba Basin. These mudstones correspond to most of the Upper Pliensbachian. No ammonites characteristic of Spinatum Zone have been found here.

In the Caucasus, the boundary between the Boreal Realm and Tethys is well worked out. Particularly, Upper Pliensbachian deposits of the Bokovoi Range in the Eastern Caucasus (Andijskoe Kojsu River) yield an excellent ammonite assemblage. Among them, the following forms were defined: *Fuciniceras bonarelli* (Fuc.), *Arieticeras algovianum* (Opp.), *Grammoceras* cf. *normannianum* (Orb.), *Harpoceras* cf. *falciplicatum* Fuc., *Arieticeras bertrandi* Kill., and *A.* cf. *retrocostatum* (Opp.) (Beznosov, 1973).

In the territory of Kugitangtau, deposition of red mudstone and siltstone of the Sandzhar Formations continued in the Pliensbachian under continental conditions (Resolutions, 1977).

Western Siberia

Continental deposits prevailed here. The upper part (40 m) of the Lower Tyumen Member, mostly inequigranular sandstone with siltstone and mudstone interbeds, may be Pliensbachian.

Siberian Platform

Pliensbachian (mostly upper) marine deposits form parts of troughs and depressions surrounding the platform along its northern and eastern margins. Along the Anabar River, Upper Pliensbachian clays, silts, and sandstones (150 m) contain bivalves and foraminifers; they yielded single *Amaltheus* cf. *stokesi* (Sow.), *A.* cf. *margaritatus* Montf., and *A. brodnaensis ventrocalvus* Repin., suggesting the presence of two lower zones of the Upper Pliensbachian in the northeastern USSR, i.e., the *Amaltheus stokesi* and *A. talrosei* Zones (Strat. Jurassic System, 1976).

In the inner zone of the Cis-Verkhoyanye Foredeep (the right bank of the Lena River, from the Kele River to the Begidzhan River), the Pliensbachian is represented mostly by sandstone (as much as 300 m), below, and siltstone (as much as 200 m), above. The lower part is characterized by such species as *Eopecten viligaensis* (Tuchk.) and *Harpax spinosus* (Sow.); the upper, in addition to bivalves, yields single *Amaltheus stokesi* (Sow.), *A.* cf. *talrosei* Repin, and *A. striatus asiaticus* Repin, establishing the *A. stokesi* and *A. talrosei* Zones (Zinchenko and others, 1978; Slastenov, 1978).

In the outer zone of the foredeep, Pliensbachian deposits of the Motorchun Formation are maximally 80 m. The main ammonites are *Amaltheus articus* Kosch., *A. brodnaensis vetrocalvus* Repin, and *A.* cf. *margaritatus* Montf. (Kirina and others, 1978).

Northeast

Reliably identified Lower Pliensbachian is known from the Upper Bolshoi Anyui River, where 70-m-thick volcanomictic inequigranular sandstones yielded *Chlamys vurguveemensis* Mil., *Plagiostoma bilibini* Mil., and *Polymorphites* sp. In other parts of the extensive Northeast region, the Lower Pliensbachian occurs in continuous sections containing brachiopods and bivalves, but ammonoids are absent (Polubotko and Repin, 1974; Resolutions, 1978). Lower Pliensbachian is generally characterized by bivalves, e.g., *Oxytoma* (*Palmoxytoma*) *cygnipes* (Y. et B.), *Chlamys textoria* (Schloth.), *Ch. vurguveemensis* Mil., *Kolymonectes* aff. *anjuensis* (Mil.), *Eopecten hartzi* Rosenk., *Harpax nodosus* Polub., *H. spinosus* (Sow.), *Lima gizhigensis* Polub., *Plagiostoma bilibini* Mil., and *P. punctata* (Sow.).

The Upper Pliensbachian is usually established on ammonoids reported from many areas of the Northeast, although they consist of monotonous and poorly preserved Amaltheidae assemblages. In the northeastern USSR, similar to the entire Boreal belt, *Amaltheus* is widespread but mainly with endemic species. This, and the absence of other genera, make a precise correlation with the type section rather difficult. The zonal scheme for the Upper Pliensbachian of the northeastern USSR is based on the regional evolution of *Amaltheus* species. The scheme was based on subplatform sections of the Omolon Massif (the Brodnaya, Bulun, Russkaya Rivers), where the Upper Pliensbachian is represented by siltstone and sandstone (80 m), and was supplemented by other sections (the Viliga, Bolshoi Anyui, Sededema Rivers). This is the standard zonation (Field Atlas, 1968; Polubotko and Repin, 1974; Resolutions, 1978) for the entire northern part of the USSR, and some of its elements are also recorded from other regions (Transbaikal area, northern Far East). Three units with zonal rank are distinguished.

1. Below is the *Amaltheus stokesi* Zone (Field Atlas, 1968), which in addition to the index species, is also characterized by *A. bifurcus* How., *Fudirhynchia najahaensis* (Moiss.), *Rimirhynchia*

maltanensis Dagys, *Meleagrinella ansparsicosta* Polub., *Eopecten viligaensis* (Tuchk.), *Harpax spinosus* (Sow.), *Myophoria lingonensis* (Dum.), *Lima philatovi* Polub., and *Pleuromya gataghea* Agass.

2. In the *Amaltheus talrosei* Zone (Polubotko and Repin, 1972), three beds with successive ammonite assemblages are present: (a) beds with *A. subbifurcus* Repins and *A. brodnaensis ventrocalvus* Repin; (b) beds with *A. talrosei* Repin, *A. striatus asiaticus* Repin, and *A. brodnaensis ventrocalvus* Repin; and (c) above, beds with *A. talrosei* Repin and *A. bulunensis* Repin. *Talrosei* Zone is commonly characterized by *Meleagrinella ptchelincevae* Polub., *Radulonectites hayamii* Polub., *R. japonicus* Hayami, *Chlamys* (*Ochotochlamys*) spp., *Harpax laevigatus* (Orb.), and *Pleuromya galathea* Agass.

3. In the *Amaltheus viligaensis* Zone (Dagis, 1975), at the top of the Pliensbachian, two ammonite assemblages are distinguished: (a) the lower beds with *A. viligaensis* Tuchk., *A. talrosei* Repin, and *A. brodnaensis* brodnaensis Repin, followed by (b) beds with *A. extremus* Repin and *Arieticeras* (?) aff. *algovianum* (Opp.). Besides ammonites, this zone also contains *Rudirhynchia najahaensis* (Moiss.), *Orlovirhynchia viligaensis* (Moiss.), *Veteranella* (*Glyptoleda*) *formosa* (Vor.), *Kolymonectes terekhovi* (Polub.), *Aguilerella kedonensis* Polub., *Harpax laevigatus* (Orb.), *Pholadomya idea* Orb., *Ph. ambigua* Sow., *Tancredia omolonensis* Polub., and *Pleuromya galathea* Agass.

Noteworthy is that the rather abundant bivalve assemblages of the Upper Pliensbachian change up-section, but are connected by transient species. In certain areas, they might be used for subdivision and correlation of sections, although biostratigraphic units common to the entire Northeast cannot be distinguished on the basis of bivalves.

In the Viliga Basin (Northern Okhotsk area), the geosynclinal-type Pliensbachian is recorded and is widespread. The characteristic facies is sedimentary and volcano-sedimentary, attaining considerable thickness (1,000 m).

Far East

The Lower Pliensbachian is not recorded by fossils. The Upper Pliensbachian is reported from the Bureya Trough and southern Sikhote Alin. In the Bureya Basin (the lower part of the Lower Umalta Formation), mainly in siltstone with basal sandstone and conglomerate (580 m), the *Amaltheus stokesi* and *A. margaritatus* Zones are distinguished; above, beds with *A. viligaensis* are placed in the Upper Pliensbachian. In Sikhote Alin (the Izvilinka Basin), a siltstone member (16 m) is also divisible into three units. The lower unit is the *A. stokesi* Zone, which, besides the index species, yielded *Arieticeras japonicum* Mats., *A. aff. algovianum* (Opp.), *Fontanelliceras* cf. *fontanellense* (Gemm.), *Dactylioceras polymorphum* Fuc., *D. simplex* Fuc., and *Protogrammoceras* cf. *serotinum* (Bett.). The middle unit is correlated with the *A. margaritatus* Zone and contains *Amaltheus* sp. ind., *Arieticeras japonicum* Mats., *Montanelliceras* cf. *fontanellense* (Gemm.), and *Protogrammoceras* cf. *serotinum* (Bett.). The upper unit, beds with *Paltarpites* (=*Protogrammoceras*), also contains single *Arieticeras japonicum* and *Protogrammoceras* cf. *serotinum,* which are conventionally placed in the *spinatum* and *viligaensis* zones in the northeastern USSR.

SUMMARY

The Lower Pliensbachian occupied the same areas as the Sinemurian. Characteristic ammonites establish the Jamesoni and Ibex Zones in the Caucasus. Upper Pliensbachian marine deposits are much more extensive. In the south (Caucasus, Transcaucasus, southern Pamirs, southern Sikhote Alin), Western European ammonite species occur. In northwest Asia, Amaltheidae are dominated by endemic species. Their evolution parallels that of the European species, allowing a rather reliable correlation of local zonal units with the standard zones. The Pliensbachian zonation for the northeastern USSR can serve as the basis for the entire Arctic Province of the Boreal Realm.

TOARCIAN
E. D. Kalacheva

HISTORY AND STANDARD ZONES

The Toarcian was proposed by d'Orbigny (1842–1851). The type section is in the southwestern Paris Basin, near the town of Thouars, Department Deux-Sèvres. D'Orbigny also listed parastratotypes in other areas of France, and in England, West Germany, and Switzerland. In the type section, the stage (7 to 8 m) is represented by blue marl with clayey limestone interbeds, yielding abundant fossils. A faunal list given by d'Orbigny (1842–1851, 1850) as characteristic for the Toarcian, comprised 32 ammonite species, among them *Ammonites* [*Pleydellia*] *aalensis,* *Am.* [*Pachylytoceras*] *jurensis,* *Am.* [*Dumortieria*] *levesquei,* *Am.* [*Hildoceras*] *bifrons,* and *Am.* [*Hildaites*] *serpentinus.*

The first subdivision of the Toarcian, by Oppel (1856–1858), has two zones, the *Posidonia bronni* Zone (below) and the *Ammonites* [*Pachylytoceras*] *jurensis* Zone. The range corresponds to the lower and upper substages of the present scale. The lower zone was directly above the uppermost *Pleuroceras* (present nomenclature), and below the appearance of abundant *Dactylioceras.* The top of the upper zone was placed between beds with *Pleydellia aalensis,* below, and *Leioceras opalinum,* above. Oppel began the overlying Bajocian with the *Ammonites* [*Pachylytoceras*] *torulosus* Zone (equal to *L. opalinum* Zone). Thus, the upper boundary of the Toarcian, according to Oppel, coincided with the Lower/Middle Jurassic boundary according to Buch. All scientists drew the lower boundary at the same level; however, the position of the upper boundary was much debated and interpreted differently for more than a century. Contradictory interpretations of this boundary are due to the fact that stratigraphic relations between the Toarcian and Bajocian were not clear to their author. D'Orbigny (1852, p. 469), in a layer-by-layer description of the reference (and only!) section in Thouars, named *Am. jurensis* (Bed 1) as the uppermost ammonite: above (Bed h), no ammonites are found. At the same time, the Toarcian includes "Opalinusthone, partie du jura brun de Schmidt" (d'Orbigny, 1852, p. 464). The list of characteristic Toarcian ammonite species comprises *Ammonites torulosus, Am. primordialis* [*Leioceras opalinum*], and *Am.* [*Graphoceras*] *concavus* (d'Orbigny, 1842–1851, 1850). The Bajocian began with beds containing *Am.* [*Stephanoceras*] *humphriesianum.* The distinction of a new stage, Aalenian, by Mayer-Eymar (1864) did not clarify this matter (see below).

In recommendations of the International Colloquium on the Jurassic System (Resolution du Colloque, 1964), the range of the Toarcian is determined as Tenuicostatum to Levesquei Zones, inclusive. The problem of the range of the Toarcian was thus solved.

An improvement of the zonal subdivision of the Toarcian was accomplished by Reynes (1868), Buckman (1909–1930), Spath (1942), and other workers. The most complete and comprehensive reasoning for Toarcian zones and subzones is given by Dean and others (1961). Their scheme is based on the ammonite successions in the most complete sections of the United Kingdom and on correlations with other Western European countries.

A zonal subdivision of the stratotype (section of Vrines quarry, Tours, Deux-Sèvres) was first accomplished by Welsch (1897), who established eight zones. The Toarcian in the stratotype is almost complete: only the Tenuicostatum Zone, recorded in adjacent areas, is missing. In the stratotype, a thin limestone bed (~10 cm) lacking characteristic fossils corresponds to this zone. Welsch's zones have been retained until now, their range being slightly changed. Not long ago, the type locality was revised in a zonal scheme for the Jurassic of France (Gabilly, 1964; Gabilly and others, 1974; Mouterde and others, 1971).

The zonation for northwestern Europe by Dean and others (1961) was accepted as a zonal standard for the Toarcian; it is close to the zonation of the French authors (Mouterde and others, 1971). Other index species are used in part; more subzones are distinguished, and the uppermost zone is replaced by three zones.

Below is a brief biostratigraphic characterization of the Toarcian zones and subzones, mainly based on Dean and others (1961), and Howarth (1973, 1978). Many units of this scheme are traced in different areas of the world, including the Soviet Union.

Lower Toarcian

1. *Dactylioceras tenuicostatum* Zone. Buckman, 1910. Index species—*D. tenuicostatum* (Y. et B.). Replacing the *Ammonites annulatus* zone of Tate and Blake (1876); *Catacoeloceras annulatus* lies in the Bifrons Zone. Lower boundary at disappearance of *Pleuroceras;* upper boundary at appearance of *Harpoce-*

ras. Dactylioceras (*Orthodactylites*) spp. are characteristics. (a) *Protogrammoceras paltum* Subzone. Howarth, 1973. Index species—*P. paltum* (Buckm.). Characterized by large *P. paltum* and single *Dactylioceras pseudocommune* Fucini. (b) *Dactylioceras clevelandicum* Subzone. Howarth, 1973. Index species—*D.* (*Orthodactylites*) *clevelandicum* Howarth. Also characteristic is *D.* (*O.*) *crosbeyi* (Simp.). (c) *Dactylioceras tenuicostatum* Subzone. Howarth, 1973. Index species—*D.* (*Orthodactylites*) *tenuicostatum* (Y. et B.), which is typically common. (d) *Dactylioceras semicerlatum* Subzone. Howarth, 1973. Index species—*D.* (*Orthodactylites*) *semicelatum* (Simps.), which is characteristically common; also single *D.* (*O.*) *directum* Buckm., and abundant *Tiltoniceras antiquum* (Wright).

2. *Harpoceras falciferum* Zone. Haug, 1885. Index species—*H. falciferum* (Sow.). Oppel (1856–1858) proposed *Ammonites* [=*Hildaites*] *serpentinus* Rein. as index for the *Posidonia bronni* Zone, but Haug regarded *H. falciferum* as most characteristic of this zone; earlier, most *H. falciferum* were erroneously identified as with *H. serpentinum.* Range zone of *Harpoceras.* Also characteristic are *Ovaticeras, Hildaites,* and *Nodicoeloceras.* (a) *Harpoceras exartum* Subzone. Buckman, 1910. Index species—*H. exaratum* (Y. et B.). Lower boundary at appearance of index species; upper, at appearance of *H. falciferum* (Sow.). Characteristic are such species as *H. elegans* (Sow.), *H. serpentinum* (Schloth.), *Hildaites murleyi* (Moxon), *Dactylioceras* (*Orthodactylites*) *semiannulatum* Howarth, and *Nodicoeloceras crassoides* (Simps.). (b) *Harpoceras falciferum* Subzone. Range zone. *Eleganticeras, Hildaites, Dactylioceras* s.s., *Ovaticeras,* and *Polyplectus* are characteristic.

3. *Hildoceras bifrons* Zone. Reynes, 1868. Index species—*H. bifrons* (Brug.). Range zone of *Hildoceras,* which replaces *Harpoceras* and disappears at *Haugia* appearance. (a) *Dactylioceras commune* Subzone. Wright, 1863. Index species—*D. commune* (Sow.). Also characteristic are *D. athleticum* (Simps.), *D. praepositum* Buckm., *Hildoceras bifrons* (Brug.), *H. sublevisioni* Fuc., *Frechiella subcarinata* (Y. et B.), *H. sublevisoni* Fuc., *Frechiella subcarinata* (Y. et B.), *Pseudolioceras lythense* (Y. et B.), and *H. falciferum.* (b) *Peronoceras fibulatum* Subzone. Tompson, 1910. Index species—*P. fibulatum* (Sow.). Also in lower part are *Peronoceras subarmatum* (Y. et B.), *P. perarmatum* (Y. et B.), and *P. turriculatum* (Simps.); the lower and middle parts yield numerous species of *Zugodactylites,* e.g., *Z. braunianus* (Orb.), *Z. pseudobraunianus* (Monestier), *Z. rotundiventer* Buckm., and *Z. thompsoni* Howarth; upper part characterized by different species of *Porpoceras.* Also *Harpoceras subplanulatum* (Opp.), *Hildoceras bifrons* (Brug.), and *Pseudolioceras lythense* (Y. et B.). (c) *Catacoeloceras crassum* Subzone. Howarth, 1978. Index species—*C. crassum* Buckm. Also characterized by *C. dumortieri* Maub. and *Collina* spp.; *Hildoceras semipolitum* Buckm. and *H. bifrons* (Brug.) disappear.

Upper Toarcian

4. *Haugia variabilis* Zone. Buckman, 1888. Index species—*H. variabilis* (Orb.). Lower boundary at appearance of abundant

Phymatoceratinae, particularly *Haugia;* upper below first *Grammoceras.* Appearance of Phymatoceratinae coincides with disappearance of *Hildoceras.* Also *Pseudolioceras,* and last *Dactylioceras* and *Catacoeloceras.*

5. *Grammoceras thouarsense* Zone. Brasil, 1896. Index species—*G. thouarsense* (Orb.). Lower boundary at appearane of *Grammoceras,* i.e., *G. thouarsense* (Orb.) and *G. striatulum* (Sow.), most Phymatoceratinae disappear; upper boundary at appearance of *Phlyseogrammoceras.* (a) *Grammoceras striatulum* Subzone. Buckman, 1988. Index species—*G. striatulum* (Sow.). Lower boundary at appearance of index species; upper, at appearance of first *Pseudogrammoceras.* Characterized by *Grammoceras* spp. and *Pseudolioceras* spp. (b) *Pseudogrammoceras fallaciosum* Subzone. Howarth (in Cope and others, 1980a). Index species—*P. fallaciosum* (Bayle). *P. latescens* (Simps.), *P. pedicum* Buckm., etc.

6. *Dumortieria levesquei* Zone. Benecke, 1901. Index species—*D. levesquei* (Orb.). Lower boundary at appearance of *Phlyseogrammoceras* and *Dumortieria.* Includes range zone of *Dumortieria.* Upper boundary at appearance of *Leioceras.* (a) *Phlyseogrammoceras dispansum* Subzone. Spath, 1942. Index species—*P. dispansum* (Lyc.). Also characterized by *P. metallaricum* (Orb.), *P. orbignyi* Buckm., and *P. dispansiforme* (Wunstorf), and by early *Dumortieria,* i.e., *E. insignissimilis* Brauns and *D. striatulocostata* (Qu.). (b) *Dumortieria levesquei* (Orb.) Subzone. Lower boundary at disappearance of *Phlyseogrammoceras.* Characterized by coarse-ribbed *Dumortieria,* i.e., index species, *D. munieri* (Haug), *D. subsolaris* Buckm., and *D. prisca* Buckm. Upper boundary at appearance of first fine-ribbed *Dumortieria.* (c) *Dumortieria moorei* Subzone. Buckman, 1910. Index species—*D. moorei* (Lyc.). Range zone. Characterized by fine-ribbed species, i.e., *D. radiosa* (Seebach), *D. pseudoradiosa* (Branco), *D. gundershofensis* (Haug), and *D. rhodanica* (Haug); also *Phylloceras* (*Xenophylloceras*) *xeinum* (Buckm.) and *Catulloceras* (*Dactylogammites*) *digitatum* (Buckm.) (d) *Pleydellia aalensis* Subzone. Reynes, 1868. Index species—*P. aalensis* (Ziet.). Base at appearance of index and similar species; upper boundary at first *Leioceras.* Characterized by *Pleydellia costulata* (Zieten), *P. leura* Buckm., and *P. mactra* (Dum.).

SOVIET UNION

Marine Toarcian deposits are known from geosynclinal and platform areas with great diversity in sections and an abundance of fauna. The presence of numerous and diverse ammonites permits extensive correlations, and in certain instances, the recognition of standard zones. In some regions, local biostratigraphic units are distinguished and more or less confidently correlated with the standard scale. We give the main Toarcian reference sections in differnt regions (Fig. 5).

Russian Platform

The marine Toarcian occurs only in the south, at the northwestern margins of the Donets Folded Structure. Toarcian

deposits are transgressive on the Triassic and, locally on the Middle Carboniferous; they consist mainly of about 100 m of clay. In the lower part of the stage are rare *Dactylioceras* sp., *Hildaites serpentinus* (Rein.), and *Hildoceras bifrons* (Brug.). Higher beds comprise *Pseudogrammoceras fallaciosum* (Bayle) and *Hammatoceras* sp. Both Toarcian substages, or at least the Bifrons and Thouarsense Zones, are developed. The Toarcian passes without visible break into the Lower Aalenian, which yields *Leioceras opalinum* (Rein.).

Mediterranean Geosynclinal Belt

Toarcian deposits are reported from the Crimea, northern Caucasus, Minor Caucasus, Carpathians, and Pamirs. The most complete section, yielding the best fauna, is in the northern Caucasus. The composition, thickness, and structure are highly variable due to diverse sedimentation conditions and tectonics. Relations with underlying rocks vary from gradual transitions to unconformities or erosion.

In the western part of the northern slope of the Great Caucasus (Beznosov, 1973; Resolutions, 1984), at the Belaya-Urupa confluence, the Toarcian is represented by the Bagovskaja Formation and part of the Tubinsky Formation. The former consists of alternating sandstone, mudstone, and siltstone layers (750 m), and contains—at different levels—fine ribbed *Dactylioceras tenuicostatum* (Y. et B.) and *D. semicelatum* (Simps.), *Harpoceras falciferum* (Sow.), and *H. exaratum* (Y. et B.); above are also *Hildoceras bifrons* (Brug.), *H.* cf. *levisoni* (Simps.), *H. sublevisoni* (Fuc.), *Dactylioceras commune* (Sow.) and similar species, *Zugodactylites* sp., and rare *Peronoceras subarmatum* (Y. et B.), *P. desplacei* (Orb.), etc. This assemblage indicates all three standard zones of the Lower Toarcian (Tenuicostatum, Falciferum, Bifrons), but they cannot as yet be separated in the section. This sequence was distinguished (Beznosov, 1973) as a local *Dactylioceras-Hildoceras* zone. Upper Toarcian includes most of the lower part of the Tubinsky Formation (600 m), made up of mudstone with siderite and impersistent sandstone interbeds. The lower part yields numerous *Phymatoceras tirolense* Hauer, *Ph. chelussi* Parisch et Viale, and *Haugia* cf. *variabilis* (Orb.), etc., suggesting the lower zone of this substage. Above is the Thouarsense Zone, characterized by various *Grammoceras* and *Pseudogrammoceras* species. Overlying beds yield *Dumortieria munieri* Haug, *D. subundulata* Br., *P. brancoi* Ben., *Pleydellia costulata* (Ziet.), and other ammonites, typical of the Levesquei Zone. In this part of the Upper Toarcian, the *Dumortieria pseudoradiosa* Zone was distinguished earlier (Beznosov, 1973) and correlated with the Levesquei and Aalensis Subzones.

On the *Turan Plate,* terrigenous continental sediments (in places coal-bearing) were deposited in Toarcian time. The entire area, including the adjacent folded structures, is characterized by a more or less common sequence for which the reference section is in the Kugitangtau Range (southwestern spurs of the Gissar). Judging from the succession of spore-pollen and leaf assemblages, the uppermost Sandzhar Formation and the lower member of the

Stage	EUROPEAN STANDARD		RUSSIAN PLATFORM	N. CAUCASUS	KUGITANGTAU RANGE	WEST SIBERIA	SIBERIAN PLATFORM Zones	NORTH-EAST Zones	FAR EAST
	Zone	Subzone							
TOARCIAN (U)	LEVESQUEI	AALENSIS	Silty clay siderite, limest., quartz sandst. *Pseudogram. fallaciosum*	600 m — Tubinsky Form. (lower part): mudst., siderite, sandst. — *Dumortieria*	Gurud Formation, lower member	50-70 m — Siltst., sandst., mudst., coal, plants	20-130 m — Tumen Formation, middle member — Siltst., mudst., few sandst., plants	53 m	400 m — Siltst., sandst.
		MOOREI							
		LEVESQEI							
		DISPANSUM							
	THOUARSENSE	FALLACIOSUM		*Grammoceras. Pseudogram.*					
		STRIATULUM							
	VARIABILIS		50 m	*Haugia* cf. *variabilis, Phymatoceras*				*Pseudolioceras rozenikrantzi*	
TOARCIAN (L)	BIFRONS	CRASSUM	750 m — Bagovskaja Form.: sandst., siltst.	*Hildoceras bifrons*			33 m — Clay	*Porpoceras polare*	*P.* cf. *polare* Beds
		FIBULATUM	Estheria Beds, Lingula Beds, **Clay** *Hildoceras bifrons, Dactylioceras*				*Zugodactylites monestieri*	*Zugodact. monestieri*	*Z. monestieri* Zone
		COMMUNE		*Dactylioc. commune*			*Dactylioceras athleticum*	*Dactylioc. athleticum*	*D. athleticum* Zone
	FALCIFERUM	FALCIFERUM		*Harpoceras exaratum*			*Harpoceras falciferum*	*Harpoceras falciferum*	
		EXARATUM							
	TENUICOSTATUM	SEMICELATUM		*Datylioc. ex gr. tenuicosta.*				*Tiltoniceras propinquum*	
		TENUICOSTATUM							
		CLEVELANDICUM							
		PALTUM	20-40 m						

Figure 5. The Toarcian of the major regions of the U.S.S.R.

Gurud Formation (sandstone, gritstone, and siltstone, 50 to 70 m) may be Toarcian (Resolutions, 1977).

West Siberian Plate

Lower-Middle Jurassic deposits are almost ubiquitous. The lacustrine-alluvial deposits of the Tyumen Formation, of which the middle member is Toarcian, is reported from South Yamal, the Konda Basin, and the lower Lyapina River, as well as from central and southern parts of the lowland. Predominant are siltstone and mudstone, with few sandstone interbeds and coalified plant detritus. The thickness varies between 20 and 130 m.

Siberian Platform

In northern areas, i.e., Ust'-Yenisei, Anabar-Khatanga, and Lena-Vilyuj, the marine facies predominates. The stage is established on ammonites, belemnites, and bivalves. The most complete section of the lower substage (without the lowermost part, the Tenuicostatum Zone) is in the Lena-Vilyuj Depression where, along the Vilyui, Tyung and Markha Rivers, it is mainly represented by about 33 m of clay with sand, pebble, and clayey limestone interbeds. The Falciferum Zone and the local *Dactylioceras athleticum* and *Zugodactylites monestieri* zones are distinguished on the basis of ammonites. The latter are tentatively correlated with the Commune and Fibulatum Subzones, Bifrons Zone, of the Western European scale.

The Upper Toarcian, characterized by the belemnites *Nannobelus nordvikensis* Sachs, *N. erensis* Sachs, *Lenobelus minaevi* Sachs, etc., is established only in the Anabar-Khatanga area. The boundary with the overlying deposits is tentatively drawn at the base of the beds with *Pseudolioceras maclintocki,* a characteristic Aalenian species. In the Ust'-Yenisei area, the Toarcian presumably includes the middle and upper parts of the Dzhangod Formation (120 to 234 m). It consists of a lower clay and mudstone member, with *Meleagrinella substriata* (Goldf.). Predominant in the upper section is sandstone with plants, siltstone, and mudstone interbeds, with *M.* cf. *substriata.*

Northeast

In the northern Pacific Geosynclinal Belt, the Toarcian is characterized by ammonites in practically all structural facies zones. One of the most complete sections is in the Omolon and Korkodon Basin (Omolon Massif) where the Toarcian conformably overlies the Pliensbachian; the section consists of siltstone, mudstone, and sandstone with numerous ammonites. This is the reference section for the Toarcian of the eastern USSR. The lower substage is almost complete, but the upper substage consists only of the local *Pseudolioceras rosenkrantzi* Zone.

1. *Tiltoniceras propinquun* Zone is divisible into two parts: beds with *Kedonoceras comptum* A. Dagis (=*Orthodactylites*),* below, also characterized by *K. asperum* A. Dagis, *K. comptum* A. Dagis, *Tiltoniceras propinquum* (Whit.), and *T. costatum*

---

*Howarth (1978, p. 253) regarded *Kedonoceras* A. Dagis as a possible synonym of *Orthodactylites* Buckm.

Buck.; and beds with *Arctomercaticeras costatum* Repin, above, also with *A. tenue* Repin and *Tiltoniceras propinquum* (Whit.).

2. Falciferum Standard Zone, divisible into three subzones (from below): *Eleganticeras alajaense* Subzone, also characterized by *E. elegantulum* (Y. et B.), *E. connexium* A. Dagis, and *E. confragosum* A. Dagis; *Harpoceras exaratum* Subzone; and *Harpoceras falciferum* Subzone.

3. *Dactylioceras athleticum* Zone, contains also *D. commune* (Sow.), *D. kanense* McLearn, *D.* spp., *Kolymoceras viluense* (Krimh.), *Harpohildoceras grande* Repin, and *H. chrysantemum* (Yok.).

4. *Zugodactylites monestieri* Zone, also characterized by *Z. braunianus* (Orb.), *Z. proprium* (A. Dagis), *Z. manifestum* (A. Dagis), *Pseudolioceras lythense* (Y. et B.), and *P. kedonense* Repin.

5. *Porpoceras polare* Zone, also contains *Collina mucronata* (Orb.), *C. orientalis* A. Dagis, and *Pseudolioceras gradatum* Buckm.

6. *Pseudolioceras rosenkrantzi* Zone, also with *P. compactile* (Simps.).

The presence of many European ammonite genera and species (sometimes index species) allows a rather reliable correlation, particularly in the lower substage, of provincial zones and subzones with the European Standard Zone. The total thickness of these deposits is 53 m.

Far East

In the more southern parts of the Pacific Geosynclinal Belt, the Toarcian is established on ammonites in some areas of the Khabarovsk Territory. In the Uda Trough and the southern Bureya Basin, *Dactylioceras commune* (Sow.), *D.* cf. *athleticum* (Simps.), and *Porpoceras* cf. *spinatum* Freb. are known. The first two species identify the *D. athleticum* Zone; *P.* cf. *polare* indicates a higher level, the upper Fibulatum Standard Subzone of northwestern Europe. In the western Okhotsk area (Tugur Bay), sandy siltstone (70 m), containing large globular calcareous nodules, rests conformably on immature sandstone. It is conditionally Pliensbachian(?)–Lower Toarcian, and yields *Zugodactylites braunianus* (Orb.), *Z. rotundiventer* Buckm., *Pseudolioceras lythense* (Y. et B.), and *P.* ex gr. *kedonense* Repin. This assemblage indicates the *Zugodactylites monestieri* Zone, placed in the middle Bifrons Standard Zone of Europe.

SUMMARY

Toarcian deposits within the USSR are more extensive than those of other Liassic stages. They are known from all major areas of development of the Jurassic System, but are relatively thin, thickening appreciably only in the Caucasus. In most marine facies, the substages, and sometimes zones or subzones, can be distinguished. Despite the presence of zonal index species in some areas of the USSR, the standard zones (Fig. 5) are established only in the Caucasus. As a rule, local biostratigraphic units are distinguished, which, with a different degree of confidence, may be correlated with the standard scale.

AALENIAN
E. D. Kalacheva

HISTORY AND STANDARD ZONES

As a stage unit, "étage aalenien" (Fig. 6) was proposed by Mayer-Eymar (1864) by combining a number of local units (from top): Gingen Beds or beds with *Ammonites sowerbyi;* Cheltenham Beds or beds with *Ammonites murchisonae;* Gundershofen Beds or beds with *Trigonia navis;* and Boll Beds or beds with *Ammonites torulosus.*

This stage was placed between the Toarcian (d'Orbigny) and "Bath-series" (Omalius d'Halloy) and assigned to the Middle Jurassic. In 1874, the same author (Mayer, 1874) determined the range of the Aalenian more precisely by excluding the Gingen locality, which he placed in the Bajocian. Thus, the lower boundary of the new stage coincided with the boundary of the present Opalinum and Levesquei Standard Zones, i.e., with the base of the Brown (Middle) Jurassic as defined by L. Buch. Mayer-Eymar lowered the upper boundary to the base of the Gingen Beds with *Am.* [*Sonninia*] *sowerbyi* (in the Swabian Alb, β/γ boundary of Quenstedt), and he began the Bajocian with the beds bearing ammonites of the *A. sowerbyi* Zone as presently accepted.

The stage was named after the town of Aalen at the northeastern margin of the Swabian Alb, southwestern Germany, where iron ore was mined. The deposits occur in isolated exposures, so that the complete Aalenian can be obtained only by combining separate sections. The Aalenian is therefore a synthetic unit without a single complete type section.

According to the latest work (Dietl and Etzold, 1977) in the Aalen area, the stage comprises the following units of Quenstedt's scheme (from base):

1. Brown Jurassic α. The Opalinus Clay (Opalinus-Ton; 100 to 110 m) with *Leioceras opalinum* (Rein.). At base, clay-shale with *Pachylytoceras torulosum* (Ziet.); at top, sandy limestone (Wasserfallbank; 10 to 20 cm).

2. Brown Jurassic β. Alternating clay-shale and sandstone, with interbeds and layers of oolitic ferruginous sandstone (42 m); with *Leioceras comptum* (Rein.).

3. Oolitic ferruginous layers, alternated with sandstone and clay-shale (18 m); with *Staufenia* (*Staufenia*) *staufensis* (Opp.), *S.* (*Costileioceras*) *sinon* (Bayle), *S.* (*Ancolioceras*) *opalinoides* (Mayer), *Ludwigia haugi* (Douv.), *L. bradfordensis* Buckm., and *L. murchisonae falcifera* Althoff.

4. Sandy clay (2 m) and clay-shale (5 to 6 m), which, judging by ammonites found in the nearby areas, correspond to the Concavum Zone.

The range of the Aalenian was interpreted differently, since it was initially characterized only by reference to different areas from England to Swabia; its boundaries were not drawn precisely, and there was no reference section. Significantly, the Toarcian/Bajocian boundary had not been clearly interpreted by d'Orbigny, the author of these stages. In different areas of France, this boundary was drawn by him at different levels.

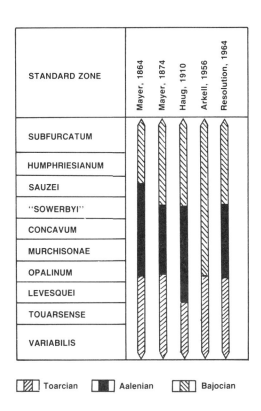

STANDARD ZONE	Mayer, 1864	Mayer, 1874	Haug, 1910	Arkell, 1956	Resolution, 1964
SUBFURCATUM					
HUMPHRIESIANUM					
SAUZEI					
"SOWERBYI"					
CONCAVUM					
MURCHISONAE					
OPALINUM					
LEVESQUEI					
TOUARSENSE					
VARIABILIS					

▨ Toarcian   ▣ Aalenian   ▨ Bajocian

Figure 6. Historical development of the Aalenian stage.

Oppel (1856–1858) distinguished three zones in the lower part of the Middle Jurassic: *Ammonites* [*Pachylytoceras*] *torulosus* Zone, *Trigonia navis* Zone, and *Am.* [*Ludwigia*] *murchisonae* Zone. This scheme was based on the correlation of classical sections of Germany, England, and France, and the boundary between the Lower and Middle Jurassic was drawn as proposed by L. Buch, at the base of the *Ammonites torulosus* Zone (=*L. opalinum* Zone). This corresponded to the Black/Brown Jurassic boundary in southern Germany and the Lias/Lower Oolite boundary in England. Thus, Oppel's boundary between the Lower and Middle Jurassic is coincident with the Toarcian/Bajocian boundary of d'Orbigny.

The Aalenian was accepted by many geologists, Haug (1892) among them. Studying sections and ammonites from the Gundershofen Beds in Alsace, this author concluded that the *Am. torulosus* and *Trigonia navis* zones* were coeval, but belong to

---
*The choice of the index species for the two lower zones of the middle Jurassic by Oppel was unfortunate; both species have greater vertical ranges than assumed.

different facies. He presumed that the Aalenian should begin with the beds containing *Dumortiera,* which occur at the base of Gundershofen Beds; thus, Haug included the upper part of d'Orbigny's Toarcian. Like Mayer-Eymar, Haug first drew the upper boundary of the Aalenian at the top of the *Am. sowerbyi* Zone and subsequently lowered it to its base (Haug, 1910). He also included the Aalenian in the Lower Jurassic, as was common in France and beyond its borders. In the Soviet Union, Nutsubidze (1966), Tsagareli (1962, 1970), and some other specialists of Jurassic of the Caucasus followed Haug's scheme. The problems of the range and position of the Aalenian were also discussed in a number of papers by Krymholts (1942, 1957), Migacheva (1957, 1958), and Beznosov (1978); some authors proposed splitting the Aalenian into two stages, assigning one to the Lower Jurassic, the other to the Middle Jurassic.

In *Jurassic Geology of the World,* W. Arkell (1956) rejected the Aalenian and interpreted it as the lower of three substages of the Bajocian. This decision was based on his formal attitude to the priority of d'Orbigny's stages. Arkell's viewpoint was, until quite recently, adhered to by some workers in England, the United States, and Canada.

The Aalenian was discussed at the colloquia of the Stratigraphic Commission held in Luxembourg in 1962 and 1967. Considering that in most areas of the world an interval corresponding to the Aalenian could be defined, marked by a characteristic group of ammonites, the Graphoceratidae, as well as for practical reasons, the Commission recommended (Resolution, 1964, 1970) that the Aalenian be retained as an independent stage, with the range from the Opalinum Zone to Concavum Zone inclusive. However, the recommendation was ambiguous with respect to the position of the stage. The Aalenian was included in the "Dogger," while the boundary of the Lower and Middle Jurassic was drawn at the base of the *Sonninia sowerbyi* Zone, i.e., the base of the Bajocian. The Commission for the Jurassic System of the USSR (Resolution, 1963) regarded such a decision as erroneous and recommended drawing the boundary between the Lower and Middle Jurassic at the base of the Opalinum Zone, following Oppel and Buch according to the priority principle and geological practice. The same conclusion was drawn by Westermann (1979). Finally, in 1980, the International Subcommission for Jurassic Stratigraphy, at a meeting during the XXVI Session of the International Geological Congress in Paris, decided to assign the Aalenian to the Middle Jurassic.

The history concerning significant range changes for the Aalenian is shown in Figure 6 (see also Rieber 1977).

In the scheme of standard zones for northwestern Europe, Arkell (1956) used English zones for the Aalenian part of the Middle Jurassic, i.e., *Leioceras opalinum, Tmetoceras scissum,* and *Ludwigia murchisonae* Zones. The present zonal standard, which includes the *L. opalinum, L. murchisonae,* and *G. concavum* Zones, is based on the succession of genera (*Leioceras, Ludwigia,* and *Graphoceras*) of the Graphoceratidae in sections of the type locality, recently studied by German scientists (Rieber, 1963, 1977; Dietl and Etzold, 1977). Recent works by French geolo-

gists (Dubar and others, 1974; Mouterde, 1961) revealed the same succession of ammonite assemblages in France, and it is also recorded in other areas of Europe. Below are brief characteristics of the Aalenian zones, based on the work of the authors mentioned. In the USSR, the Aalenian is divided into two substages (see *Jurassic Stratigraphy of the USSR,* 1972; Westermann, 1967).

Lower Aalenian

1. *Leioceras opalinum* Zone. Buckman, 1887. Index species—*L. opalinum* (Rein.). Range zone of *Leioceras.* (a) *Leioceras opalinum* Subzone. Also characteristic are *Leioceras costosum* (Qu.), *L. opaliniformis* (Buckm.), *L. lineatum* Buckm., *Pseudammatoceras subinsigne* (Opp.), and *Pseudolioceras beyrichi* (Schloenb.). (b) *Leioceras comptum* Subzone. Rieber, 1963. Index species—*L. comptum* (Rein.). Also common are *Leioceras striatum* Buckm., *L. crassicostatum* Rieb., and *L. paucicostatum* Rieb.; in the upper part, *Tmetoceras scissum* (Ben.) and frequent *Hammatoceras* spp.

In England, the zone is divided into the Opalinum and Scissum Subzones.

Upper Aalenian

2. *Ludwigia murchisonae* Zone. Oppel, 1856. Index species—*L. murchisonae* (Sow.). Characterized by species including *Ludwigia haugi* Douv., *L. bradfordensis* Buckm., *L. subtuberculata* Rieber, *L. crassa* Horn., *L. umbilicata* (Buckm.), *Staufenia* (*Costileioceras*) *opalinoides* (Mayer), *S.* (*C.*) *sinon* (Bayle), *S.* (*Staufenia*) *discoidea* (Qu.), and *S.* (*S.*) *staufensis* (Oppel). In France, also *Pseudammatoceras rugatum* (Buckm.), *Planammatoceras planiforme* Buckm., and *Erycites fallifax* Arkell.

In West Germany (Dietl, 1977; Rieber, 1977), the zone is divisible into four subzones: Sinon, Sehndense, Discoidea, and Bradfordensis; in France, into three subzones: Haugi, Murchisonae, and Bradfordensis (Mouterde and others, 1971); and in England into four subzones: Haugi, Murchisonae, Bradfordensis, and Gigantea (Cope and others, 1980).

3. *Graphoceras concavum* Zone. Buckman, 1888. Index species—*G. concavum* (Sow.). Lower boundary at appearance of first *Graphoceras.* Characterized also by *G. cornu* (Buckm.), *G. rudis* (Buckm.), *G. formosus* (Buckm.), and *G. fallax* (Buckm.). In France, the zone also yields *Pseudammatoceras diadematoides* (Mayer), *P. mouterdei* Elmi, *Euaptetoceras dorsatum* (Merla), *E. imetoceras* (Buckm.), *E. klimakomphalum* (Vaceck), and abundant *Haplopleuroceras.* Upper boundary at disappearance of *Graphoceras* and *Euaptetoceras,* and appearance of *Sonninia* and *Hyperlioceras.* In France, this zone is divisible into two subzones—Concavum and Formosum-Limitatum (Mouterde and others, 1971)—and in England, into Concavum and Formosum Subzones (Cope and others, 1980).

SOVIET UNION

Aalenian (Fig. 7) is recorded in most areas, but only in the northern Caucasus is it possible to recognize the standard zones.

Russian Platform

In the northwestern Donets Folded Structures, undivided Upper Toarcian–Lower Aalenian deposits are recognized on the basis of *Leioceras opalinum* in the upper part of the section. Presumably, Upper Aalenian deposits are eroded and Bajocian is preceded by a break (Krymholts, 1972b).

Mediterranean Geosynclinal Belt

In the south of the Soviet Union, the Aalenian is recorded in the Carpathian, the Crimea, on the northern and southern slopes of the Great Caucasus, in the Minor Caucasus, and in the Pamirs. These deposits are best studied and most complete in the northern Caucasus (Beznosov, 1973; Resolutions, 1984). In its western part, at the Belaya-Urupa interfluve, the Aalenian comprises the upper part of the Tubinsky Formation. (For the Toarcian, see above.) Mudstone with siderite nodules (60 m) has yielded Lower Aalenian *Leioceras opalinum* (Rein.), and, in more complete sections, *Leioceras comptum* (Rein.), *Tmetoceras scissum* (Ben.), and also *Ludwigia bradfordensis* Buckm., indicating the Upper Aalenian.

Continuous, thick Aalenian sections, yielding abundant fossils, are recorded in the eastern part of the northern Caucasus, in Daghestan. They are a basis for Aalenian subdivision in the Mediterranean Belt of the USSR. The Aalenian comprises most of the Karakh and the conformable Igatly Formation.

The Karakh Formation consists of thick-bedded sandstone and interbedded sandstone, siltstone, and mudstone, locally (central Dagestan) with coal. The Aalenian portion attains roughly 1,500 to 1,800 m. In the lower part of the formation, above Toarcian ammonites, *Pseudolioceras beyrichi* (Schloenb.), *Leioceras opalinum* (Rein.), *L. comptum* (Rein.), *L. gotzendorfense* Dorn, and *L. costosum* (Qu.), etc., indicating most of the lower Opalinum Zone. The upper part of the formation yields *Tmetoceras scissum* (Ben.), *Leioceras acutum* (Qu.), *L. costosum* (Qu.), *Staufenia* (*Costileioceras*) *sinon* (Bayle), and *Ludwigia murchisonae* (Sow.).

The Igatli Formation consists of alternating mudstone, siltstone, and sandstone members (300 to 700 m); locally, siderite nodules form interbeds and conglomerate-like accumulations. *Ludwigia murchisonae* (Sow.), *L. bradfordensis* Buckm., *L. aperta* Buckm., and *Holcophylloceras submontanum* Besn. are found in the lower part, indicating the Murchisonae Zone. Higher up, species including *Graphoceras concavum* (Sow.), *G. casta* Buckm., and *G. rudis* Buckm. occur, which indicates the Concavum Zone. At the top of the formation, some early Bajocian ammonites are present (Kazakova, 1978; see next section).

On the *Turan Plate* (Kugitang Range), Aalenian deposits

(130–150 m) and the Toarcian were tentatively distinguished. They consist of alternating continental sandstone, siltstone, mudstone, and coal; ankerite lenses are present at the top middle part of Gurud Formation (Resolutions, 1977). This part of the section is characterized by abundant remains of plants, insects, and freshwater bivalves.

West Siberian Plate

The Aalenian is present in the Upper Tyumen Member (Aalenian, 30–80 m). Similar to the Toarcian in the lower part of the section, they are lacustrine-alluvial. Sandstone with gritstone lenses and interbeds and plant remains predominates.

Siberian Platform

In the Anabar-Khatanga and Lena-Vilyui areas, the Aalenian is characterized by ammonites, belemnites, and bivalves, and is divisible into substages. The Lower Aalenian is represented by the *Pseudolioceras maclintocki* Zone, with the basal beds with *P. (P.) alienum;* the Upper Aalenian by the *Pseudolioceras tugurense* Zone. The *P. maclintocki* Zone is traced along the coasts of the Anabar Bay and Anabar Gulf, the Uryung-Tumus Peninsula, the Lower Olenek River (Kelimyar River), left tributaries of the Lena River–Molodo, Syungyuyud, Motorchun, and at the Lena River. At the Vilyuj, Markah, and Tyunga Rivers, the zone consists of alternating clay, siltstone, and sandstone (20–86 m). Characteristic are *Pseudolioceras alienum* A. Dagis, *P. (Tugurites) maclintocki* (Haugh.), and *P. sp.; the belemnites *Pseudodicoelites, Sachsibelus, Rhabdobelus,* and *Hastites;* and bivalves including *Arctotis lenaensis* (Lah.) and *Oxytoma jacksoni* (Pomp.). (For review of *Pseudolioceras* taxonomy and evoltuion, see Sey and others, 1986.)

The upper substage, the *Pseudolioceras tugurense* Zone, is traced more extensively with the guide fossils among ammonites, i.e., the subgenus *Tugurites,* and the bivalve *Mytiloceramus,* as well as with the aid of a belemnite assemblage. The zone or substage is recorded in Franz Josef Land (Northbrook, Hooker, and Rainer Islands); eastern Taimyr and Chernokhrebetnaya River; on the coasts of Anabar Bay and Anabar Gulf; on the Uryung-Tumus Peninsula, Lower Olenek, and left tributaries of the Lena-Molodo, Syungyuyud, and Motorchun; and on the western slope of the Verkhoyanye Range. It consists of mudstone, siltstone, clay, and sandstone, with gritstone at the base (6–89 m).

Northeast

The Aalenian here is also divisible into two substages. The Lower Aalenian is again represented by the *Pseudolioceras maclintocki* Zone, with basal beds containing *P. (P.) replicatum;* the upper Aalenian by the *P. tugurense* Zone. The *P. maclintocki* Zone is traced in most structural facies zones: Alazeya Highland, Bolshoi Anyui Basin, Omolon Massif, Anadyr Basin, Taigonos Peninsula, Munugudzhak Basin, and Viliga Basin. This part of the

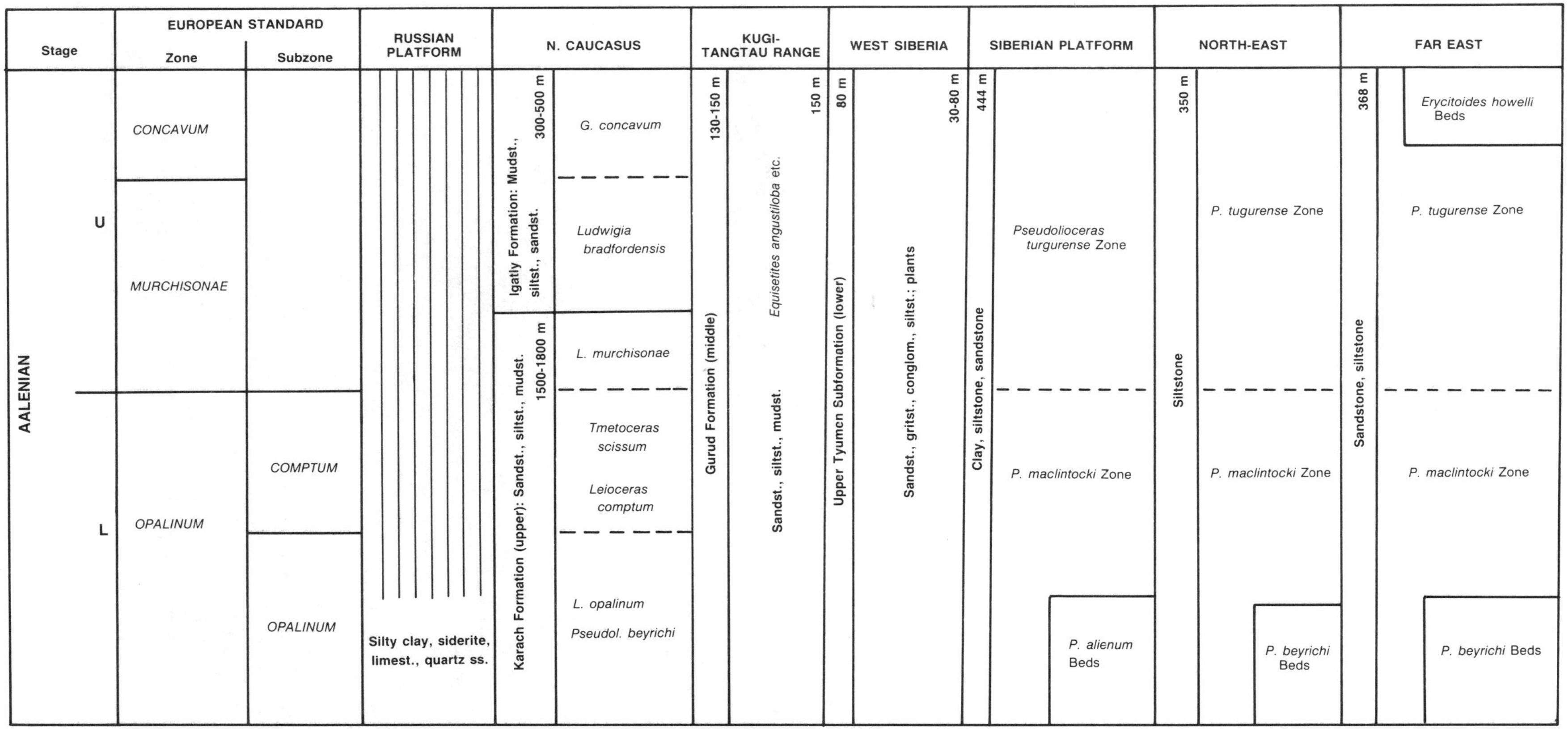

Figure 7. The Aalenian of the major regions of the U.S.S.R.

section is mainly siltstone, mudstone, and sandstone, and is characterized by *Pseudolioceras* (*P.*) *replicatum* Buckm., *P.* (*P.*) *beyrichi* (Schloenb.), and *P.* (*Tugurites*) *maclintocki* (Haugh), as well as by a bivalve assemblage.

The *P. tugurense* Zone is established by *Pseudolioceras* (*Tugurites*) *tugurense* Kalach. et Sey, *P.* (*T.*) *whiteavesi* (White) in sandstone and siltstone (as much as 250 m), and by the *Mytiloceramus* assemblage in the Alazeya Highland, Bolshoi Anyuj, Bolshoi Anadyr, Khatyrka Basin, and the Sugoi, Viliga, B. Aulandzha, M. Turomha, and Upper Olomon Rivers.

Far East

Here is the Aalenian reference section for the eastern USSR. The coast of Tugur Bay at the Sea of Okhotsk also includes the stratotypes of the regional zones. The *P. maclintocki* Zone (with *P.* (*P.*) *beyrichi* beds at the base) was distinguished here as the lower substage, and the *P. tugurense* Zone (with beds containing *Erycitoides howelli* in the upper part) in the upper substage (Sey and Kalacheva, 1972, 1980). The boundary between the zones is tentatively drawn at the appearance of *P.* (*Tugurites*) *tugurense* and *P.* (*T.*) *whiteavesi*.

Lower Aalenian deposits (*P. maclintocki* Zone) rest with erosion surfaces on the upper Lower Toarcian (*P. monestieri* Zone), and consist of 60 m of sandstone with abundant *Pseudolioceras beyrichi* (Schloenb.). These ammonites, characteristic of the basal Aalenian in Western Europe, date this part of the section as early Opalinum Standard Zone. Siltstones (as much as

100 m) higher up contain *P. maclintocki* (Haugh.) and "*Grammoceras*" sp. indet., and are conditionally upper Opalinum Zone.

The upper substage (*P. tugurense* Zone) consists mainly of siltstone (268 m) and yields abundant *Pseudolioceras* (*Tugurites*) *tugurense* Kalach. et Sey, *P.* (*T.*) *whiteavesi* (White), *Erycitoides* (*E.*) *howelli* (White), *E.* (*Kialagvikes*) *spinatus* West., and various species of *Mytiloceramus*. This peculiar ammonite assemblage can be dated as late Murchisonae-Concavum Chronozones. This is confirmed by a similar ammonite assemblage and succession in southern and northern Alaska and Canada, which at Wide Bay, southern Alaska, also contain European forms, i.e., the *Erycitoides howelli* Zone of Westermann (1964). The upper boundary of the Aalenian is drawn, very tentatively, at the disappearance of *P. whiteavesi* (White), *P. tugurensis* Kalach. et Sey, and *Erycitoides* spp. (Sey et al., 1986).

SUMMARY

The Aalenian is widespread in the USSR, but it is only in the Caucasus that the European Standard Zones can be established. In northern and eastern Asia, rare ammonite finds make it possible thus far to distinguish only extended regional zones corresponding to substages. The *Pseudolioceras maclintocki* Zone at the base, with beds containing *Pseudolioceras,* corresponds to the Lower Aalenian; the *P. tugurense* Zone to the Upper Aalenian. In continental facies (Kugitang, western Siberia), the Aalenian is distinguished only tentatively.

BAJOCIAN
G. Ya. Krymholts

HISTORY AND STANDARD ZONES

The Bajocian stage was distinguished by d'Orbigny in 1850 (d'Orbigny, 1842–1851, p. 606) and named after the town of Bayeux in Normandy (Bayeux, Calvados Department; in Latin transcription, Bajoce), around which "this stage is best developed and most characteristic in all respects" (d'Orbigny, 1852, p. 477). A number of sites were named, some of them stone quarries, now abandoned and overgrown. The best exposures are found on cliffs facing the English Channel, of which Rioult (1964) regarded the one at Les Hachettes as the type section. This author gave the following succession with local names (ascending order);

1. "La Malière." Clayey and sandy limestones with glauconite (exposed 2–3 m), with rare bivalves and Terebratulidae. From nearby exposures dated as Concava and basal "Sowerbyi" Zones. Upper surface eroded and bored.

2. "La Couche verte." Discontinuous conglomerate and accumulation of slightly angular fragments (30 cm), filling depressions in site 1 and composed of its fragments, including phosphoritized diverse fauna, e.g., ammonites of "Sowerbyi," and mainly, Sauzei Zone. Upper surface eroded and bored.

3. "Ferruginous Oolite Bayeux." (a) Basal conglomerate (25 cm), pebbles with ferruginous incrustation. (b) Upper part with abundant stromatolithic nodules. Redeposited fauna includes ammonites from site 2 and the Humphriesianum Zone. (c) Limestone (10–15 cm) with numerous ferruginous oolites, abundant, diverse fauna including ammonites, indicating condensed Subfurcatum/Niortense Garantiana, and lower Parkinsoni Zones. (d) Crowned by marly limestone (20 cm), with local accumulation of ferruginous oolites, with ammonites of Parkinsoni Zone.

4. "Spongy Limestone." Limestone (10–12 cm), more or less marly, with distinct boundary. In the lower part, abundant calcareous sponges, decreasing upward; also stylolites. Ammonites, rare and poorly preserved, of upper Parkinsoni Zone. Upward, grading into site 5.

5. "Transitional Beds." Three limestone beds, with clay interbeds (40–50 cm). Ammonite indicate lower Bathonian, Zigzag Zone.

6. "Port-en-Bessin Marl Bed." Alternating calcareous clay

and clayey limestone (35–40 m). Ammonites of lower 10 m are Lower Bathonian; of higher part, Progracilis Zone of Middle Bathonian.

In other sections of the type locality, the same succession is recorded; thickness changes slightly except for beds 2 and 3. As shown, the upper substage of the Bajocian is almost exclusively represented, but largely condensed in a 15-cm-thick layer; most of the Early Bajocian is a hiatus, and partly formed sediments were eroded.

Rioult (1964), in his discussion of d'Orbigny's evidence based on this section, concluded that d'Orbigny placed beds 3 (conglomerates of Humphriesianum Zone) through 5 (Transitional Beds) in the Bajocian and beds 1 and 2 (including Sauzei Zone) in the Toarcian.

Analysis of the ammonite lists in d'Orbigny (1842–1851, 1850) for the Toarcian and Bajocian shows that some species from overlying beds were erroneously assigned by him to underlying beds, and vice versa. Correcting this misunderstanding, Mayer-Eymar (1864) distinguished the Aalenian (see above), and assigned to it beds corresponding to the upper Toarcian and lower Bajocian in their original interpretation. Proceeding from the rules of priority, i.e., the absence of the Aalenian in d'Orbigny's scheme or the lack of any indication of a corresponding break, Arkell (1933, etc.) regarded the Bajocian as a stage directly following the Toarcian. He distinguished the units, corresponding to the Aalenian, as the lower substage of the Bajocian, which thus acquired a three-fold division. Most workers are against this viewpoint, and it was not adopted by the International Colloquium on the Jurassic System (Resolution, 1964).

Regarding the upper boundary of the Bajocian, d'Orbigny drew it 10 m above the base of "Port-en-Bessin Marl" (d'Orbigny, 1852), i.e., between the Lower and Middle Bathonian as presently understood (Rioult, 1964). This high position of the Bajocian/Bathonian boundary accepted by d'Orbigny is confirmed, for instance, by the fact that he placed *Zigzagiceras zigzag* (d'Orbigny, 1842–1851, p. 616) an index species of the Lower Bathonian, in the Bajocian. Later authors, beginning with Eudes-Deslongchamps (1864), commonly took the base of the Port-en-Bessin Marl as the base of the Bathonian, correlating it with the Fuller's Earth in England. There were also other differing opinions, such as those of Haug (1910, p. 998), who terminated the Bajocian in the Garantiana Zone and placed beds containing *Parkinsonia parkinsoni* in the Bathonian.

Such a viewpoint has now been abandoned. It is emphasized, however, that both boundaries of the Bajocian presently have a different position from that proposed by d'Orbigny. The stratotype is imperfect, but the study of other, more complete sections gives a rather distinct and objective general idea of this stage, its boundaries, and subdivisions. Presently, the range of the Bajocian is used as defined at the International Colloquium on the Jurassic System held in Luxembourg in 1962 (Resolution, 1963). In the Standard Scale, it begins with the Discites Zone following the Concavum Zone of the Aalenian, and is completed by the Parkinsoni Zone, followed by the Zigzag Zone of the Bathonian.

Oppel originally subdivided the Bajocian into two (Oppel, 1856–1858, p. 334), and later (p. 882), into three zones (in ascending order): *Ammonites [Otoites] sauzei, Am. [Stephanoceras] humphriesianum,* and *Am. [Parkinsonia] parkinsoni.* The Bajocian zones, as used by Arkell (1956), were traced by him through all areas of classical development of the Jurassic in Western Europe. The characterization of these zones in the type area of northern France by the French scientists (Mouterde and others, 1971) is mainly used below. Bajocian subzones have not yet been worked out adequately.

Lower Bajocian

The "*Sonninia sowerbyi* Zone" was distinguished earlier at the base of Bajocian, including the earlier, Russian, edition of this work. The invalidity of this index species and data from southern England led Parsons (1974) to propose two zones in this part of the section; these were later accepted in West Germany (Dietl, 1977). These zones have characteristic ammonite assemblages, and there are reasons to distinguish them also in the USSR.

1. *Hyperlioceras discites* Zone. Buckman, 1915. Index species—*H. discites* (Waagen). With *Hyperlioceras* spp., *Toxolioceras, Euhoploceras, Fontannesia,* and *Trilobiticeras.*

2. *Witchellia laeviuscula* Zone. Haugh, 1894. Index species—*W. laeviuscula* (Sow.). (a) *Sonninia ovalis* Subzone. Oechsle, 1858. Index species—*S. ovalis* (Qu.). Characteristic are large *Sonninia,* including *S. ovalis* and *S. rudis* (Qu.); also the *S. adicra* (Waagen) group, and *Shirbuirnia; Hyperlioceras* and *Euhoploceras* are absent. (b) *Witchellia laeviuscula* Subzone. Haug, 1894. With *Witchellia* spp., *Sonninia jugifer* (Waagen); *S. gingensis* (Waagen). The first *Bradfordia praeradiata* (Douv.), *Normannites,* and *Emileia,* rare *Skirroceras,* and *Otoites contractus* (Sow.) are recorded.

3. *Otoites sauzei* Zone. Oppel, 1856. Index species—*O. sauzei* (Orb.). *Witchellia* disappear; *Sonninia* ex gr. *patella* appear; common species include *Skirroceras, Emileia,* and *Otoites,* particularly *O. sauzei* (Orb.) and *O. pauper* (West.), *Emileia brocchii* (Sow.) and *E. polymera* (Waagen), *Sonninia propinquans* (Bayle) and *S. patella* (Waagen), and *Stephanoceras (Skirroceras) leptogyrale* (Buckm.) and *S. (S.) bayleanum* (Opp.). In West Germany, *Emileia* are also recorded below the Sauzei Zone.

4. *Stephanoceras humphriesianum* Zone. Oppel, 1856. Index species—*S. humphriesianum* (Sow.). Lower boundary at disappearance of *Emileia* and appearance of the first *Stephanoceras* ex gr. *humphriesianum.* (a) *Dorsetensia romani* Subzone. Haug, 1892. (*Humphriesianum* Subzone auct.). Index species—*D. romani* (Opp.). Dominating are *Stephanoceras* s.s., e.g., *S. umbilicum* (Qu.), and *Chondroceras* and *Dorsetensia.* (b) *Teloceras blagdeni* Subzone. Maske, 1907. Index species—*T. blagdeni* (Sow.). Also with *T. subblagdeni* (Schmidt. et Krumb.),

T. coronatum (Schloth.), *Normannites orbignyi* (Buckm.), *Stemmatoceras,* and *Intinsaites;* first rare *Cadomites.*

Upper Bajocian

5. *Strenoceras niortense* Zone. Dietl, 1981 (=*S. subfurcatum* Zone, Buckman, 1913). Index species—*S. niortense* (Orb.). Significant turnover of ammonite fauna: *Teloceras* disappear; the Perisphinctaceae, *Strenoceras* and *Garantiana (Orthogarantiana)* appear with some overlap. Three subzones can be distinguished (from below): (a) In southeastern France, *Caumontisphinctes aplous* Buckm.; (b) *C. polygyralis* Buckm.; (c) *Garantiana baculata* (Qu.).

In West Germany: (a) *Teloceras banksi;* (b) *C. polygyralis;* and (c) *G. baculata.*

Dietl (1981) demonstrated that it was necessary to replace the former index species "*Strenoceras*" *subfurcatum* (Ziet.); the holotype belongs to *Garantiana* and originated from the overlying zone.

6. *Garatiana garantiana* Zone. Buckman, 1893. Index species—*G. garantiana* (Orb.). Lower boundary at disappearance of *Strenoceras* and appearance of *Pseudogarantiana.* In France, three subzones are distinguished within the *garantiana* range zone (Pavia and Sturani, 1968; Mouterde and others, 1971) (from below): (a) *Garantiana (Pseudogarantiana) dichotoma* (Bentz); (b) *Garantiana subgaranti* (Wetzel); (c) *Bigotites* with *B. nicolescoi* (Gross.), etc. A similar subdivision into subzones was adopted in West Germany (Westermann, 1967).

7. *Parkinsonia parkinsoni* Zone. Oppel, 1856. Index species—*P. parkinsoni* (Sow.). Distinguished for range of *Parkinsonia.* (a) *Parkinsonia subaretis* Subzone. Mouterde and others, 1971. Index species—*P. subarietis* (Wetzel). Characterized by evolute *Parkinsonia,* large *Prorsisphinctes,* and last *Garantiana (Subgarantiana)*; in places *G. (Pseudogarantiana).* Also with *Parkinsonia acris* (Wetzel), *P. rarecostata* (Buckm.), *Prorsisphinctes pseudomartinsi* (Siem.), etc. (b) *Parkinsonia densicosta* Subzone. Pavia and Sturani, 1968. Index species—*P. (Durotrigensia) densicosta* (Qu.). Also present are *P. (D.) dorsetensis* (Wright), *P. (D.) pseudoferruginea* (Nicol.), *P. parkinsoni* (Sow.), and *P. rarecostata* (Buckm.). (c) *Parkinsonia bomfordi* Subzone. Pavia and Sturani, 1968. Index species—*P. bomfordi* (Ark.). Also common are *P. (Durotrigensia) subplanulata* (Wetzel) and *P. (D.) neuffensis* (Opp.); above, *Parkinsonia (Gonolkites)* appear, which are mainly characteristic of Lower Bathonian.

SOVIET UNION

The *Russian Platform* marine facies occurs only in the south (Fig. 8) in some depressions. At the northwestern margin of the Donets Folded Structure, the Bajocian begins with conglomatic coquina containing *Witchellia* spp., probably belonging to the Laeviuscula Zone and separated from the underlying deposits by a break. Resting above are sandstone, siltstone, and sandy clay with limestone interbeds, bearing above *Stephanoceras humphriesianum* (Sow.). The thickness of Lower Bajocian is 20 to 90 m.

The upper substage is transgressive and made up of sandstone, limestone, and clay. *Strenoceras niortense* (Orb.) and *Garantiana* spp. are found, and, in the upper part, *Parkinsonia rarecostata* Buckm. (=*P. doneziana* Boriss. auct.) and *P. subarietis* (Wetzel). Frequently found is *Meleagrinella doneziana* (Boriss.), which extends into the lower Bathonian. The ammonites allow the undivided Niortensis-Garantiana Zones and the Parkinsoni Zone to be distinguished. The Upper Bajocian is 50 to 140 m thick.

Upper Bajocian clastic rocks with rare fauna occur in the west, the Dnieper-Donets Depression; in the east, the Caspian Synclinorium; and in the north, the southern slope of the Voronezh Anticlinorium. Along the Volga, in the Ul'yanovsk-Saratov Trough, the Upper Bajocian can be traced up to Samarskaya Luka (river bend) in the vicinity of Kujbyshev by *Parkinsonia rarecostata* Buckm. (Sazonov, 1957, p. 37). On the southwestern Russian Platform, the Upper Bajocian occurs in the Dobruja Trough with *Garantiana garantiana* (Orb.).

Mediterranean Geosynclinal Belt

In the southern USSR, the marine Bajocian occurs in the Carpathians, in Crimea, on the northern and southern slopes of the Greater Caucasus, and the Minor Caucasus, the Great Balkhan, and the Pamirs. The sequence in the northern Caucasus can be used as a reference section, since deposits and fauna have been studied more thoroughly there than in other areas. Structure, composition, and thickness vary. In most cases, the Bajocian rests conformably on the Aalenian; in places, an erosion surface is present, or the Bajocian is transgressive on older deposits. The Lower Bajocian in central Daghestan is represented by the Kumukh Formation, which commonly rests with an erosion surface on the Iglatli Formation. The Kumukh consists of alternating mudstone, siltstone, and less frequently, sandstone and limestone in variable proportions; thickness ranges from 400 to more than 900 m. All four standard zones of the Lower Bajocian are present. The Discites Zones yields the guide species *Hyperlioceras mundum* Buckm.; the Laeviuscula Zone has the index species.

Detailed study of ammonite assemblages in continuous sections of the Igatli-Kumukh Formations in central Daghestan allowed Kazakova (1978) to establish a decreasing trend in the abundance of Aalenian ammonites and a simultaneous increase of genera and abundance of typically Bajocian taxa.

In the Sauzei Zone the index species, *Otoites golubevi* Krimh. and *Megalytoceras submetrerum* Besn. occur.

The Humphriesianum Zone contains the index species, *Stephanoceras scalare* Macke, *S. zieteni* (Qu.), *Dorsetensia liostraca* Buckm., *D. subtecta* Buckm., and *Thysanolytoceras cinctum*

Stage	EUROPEAN STANDARD Zones	EUROPEAN STANDARD Subzones	RUSSIAN PLATFORM	N. CAUCASUS ZONES	KUGITANG-TAU RANGE	WEST SIBERIA	SIBERIAN PLATFORM	NORTH-EAST	FAR EAST
BAJOCIAN U	PARKINSONI	BOMFORDI / DENSICOSTATA / SUBARIETIS	*Parkinsonia rarecostata*	PARKINSONI	Low. & Mid. Degibadam Mb.: sandst., mudst., siltst. with *Garantiana*, *Parkinsonia* — 175 m	Up. Tyumen Member (partly): Sandst., mudst., siltst. — 60-150 m	*Cranocephalites vulgaris* Zone — Siltstone 22-39 m	*C. vulgaris* Zone — Siltst., mudst., sandst. 525-570 m	*Umaltites era* Beds
	GARANTIANA		*Garantiana garantiana*	GARANTIANA					
	NIORTENSE		*Strenoceras niortense*	NIORTENSE			*Boreiocephalites borealis* Zone — Siltstone 30 m	*B. borealis* Zone — Siltst., sandst.	*Lyroxyites* cf. *kellumi*
			Sandst., siltst., clay, limest. interbeds — 50-140 m	Dzhangur Formation: Clay, siltst. — 500-600 m					Elgin Formation (low.): sandst., siltst. — 900 m
	HUMPHRIES.	BLAGDENI / ROMANI	*Stephanoceras humphriesianum* (upper part)	HUMPHRIES.	Upper Gurund Meniby Sandst., mudst. with bivalves — 30 m		*M. porrectus / M. clinatus* — Clay (upper part), siltst. 35 m	*Mytiloceramus clinatus* — Sandst., siltst. 200 m	Epikan Formation: siltst. — *Partischiceras grossicostatum / M. clinatus* 1300 m
			Sandst., siltst., clay, limest. interbeds — 20-90 m	Kumukh Formation: Mudst., siltst., limest. — 400-900 m			*Mytiloceramus lucifer* Beds — Clay 70 m	*Arkelloceras-Mytiloceramus lucifer* Beds — Mudst., siltst. 120 m	*Arkelloceras tozeri – M. lucifer* Beds 180 m
L	SAUZEI			SAUZEI					
	LAEVIUSCULA	LAEVIUSCULA / OVALIS	Limest.: *Witchellia* spp.	LAEVIUCULA			*Pseudolioceras fastigatum* Beds — Sandst., siltst. 25 m	*P. fastigatum, Mytiloceramus jurensis, M. menneri* — Siltst., sandst. 110 m	Up. Umalta Member: sandst., siltst. — *P. fastigatum – M. jurensis* Beds 220 m
	DISCITES			*Hyperlioc. mundum*					

Figure 8. The Bajocian of the major regions of the U.S.S.R.

Besn. In the upper portion, the Blagdeni Subzone is distinguished by *Teloceras coronatum* (Schloth.) and *Normannites caucasicus* Krimh.

The lower part of the Kumukh Formation is distinguished in southern Daghestan as the Pachalkent Member ("Subformation"); the upper Humphriesianum Zone is present in the Tsmur Member, which also includes the lower Upper Bajocian.

The Upper Bajocian is most complete in the western northern Caucasus, between the Kuban' and Belaya Rivers, where it consists of clay and siltstone (Dzhangur Formation, as much as 500 to 600 m). It appears that the Lower Bajocian is absent, and that these deposits rest unconformably on the Aalenian and older rocks. The Upper Bajocian is established in its entirety. The Niortensis Zone also contains *Leptosphinctes* str., including endemic species, *Cleistosphinctes* spp., *Orthogarantiana humilis* (Zatw.), and *Sphaeroceras brogniarti* (Sow.). The Garantiana Zone also yields *Garantiana platyrryma* Buckm. and *Pseudogarantiana* cf. *minima* (Wetzel). The Parkinsoni Zone is characterized by *Parkinsonia rarecostata* Buckm., *P. subplanulata* Wetzel, *P. depressa* (Qu.), and *P. crassa* Nicol.

In the eastern northern Caucasus, the Upper Bajocian is sometimes divisible into two parts on the basis of abundant *Garantiana* s.l. and *Parkinsonia* sp., respectively. The lower part can be approximately correlated with the two lower standard zones; the upper, with the upper standard zone.

The Bajocian in the northern Caucasus grades upward into the Bathonian without lithologic change. In other places, Bathonian deposits did not survive the pre–Late Jurassic erosion, which sometimes also destroyed parts of the Bajocian.

The *Turan Plage* and adjacent folded structures are predominantly continental Jurassic. Temporal subsidence took place in some areas and sea water penetrated from the south. The most complete Jurassic section is in the Kugitangtau Range, in the southwestern spurs of Gissar (Resolutions, 1984). Lower and lower Upper Bajocian are represented by alternating sandstone, siltstone, mudstone, and coal lenses. This is the upper member of the Gurud Formation. The bivalves *Pseudocardinia, Kija, Isognonom,* and *Bureiamya,* and numerous plant remains point to variable continental facies, including fresh-water and shallow marine. The thickness is less than 30 m. The Upper Bajocian also includes the lower and middle members of the Degibadam Formation: sandstone, siltstone, mudstone, and coal (as much as 180 m) with bivalves and ammonites, especially *Garantiana* cf. *bifurcata* (Ziet.), *Parkinsonia orbygniana* Wetzel, *P. doneziana* Boriss., and *P. parkinsoni* (Sow.). The limited data do not allow distinguishing of zones, although the Garantiana and Parkinsoni Zones appear to be present and the substage boundaries can be identified.

West Siberian Plate

The Bajocian cannot be clearly separated. It is part of the Upper Tyumen Member, consisting of sandstone, mudstone, and siltstone, with coalified plant debris only. These are deposits of an extensive lacustrine-alluvial plain. The spore-pollen assemblages studied do not permit identification of stages.

Siberian Platform

Jurassic continuous marine sedimentation took place only in the north. Considering the structural complication, relatively complete Bajocian sections are found.

On the Anabar Bay coast (Strat. Jurassic System, 1976), sandstone and siltstone (25 m) and the overlying clay (~70 m) appear to be Lower Bajocian. The bivalves *Arctotis, Mytiloceramus lucifer* (Eichw.), *M. jurensis* (Kosch.), etc., are found; "*Hyperlioceras* sp." (=?*Pseudolioceras (Tugerites)*) is reported from the lower part; above, *Normannites* and *Stephanoceras*(?) occur. This interval presumably corresponds to the lower three zones of the Bajocian; the Humphriesianum Zone probably comprises the upper 15 m of the clays and 20 m of clay and siltstone with *Paramegateuthis, Mytiloceramus porrectus* (Eichw.), and *M.* ex. gr. *kystatymensis.* On the left bank of the lower Lena River, *Pseudolioceras (Tugerites) fastigatum* West. and *P. (T.) constistriatum* West. were found, i.e., the beds with *P. fastigatum,* dated as Discites and Laeviuscula Zones (Westermann, 1969; Sey and others, 1986).

Beginning in the Upper Bajocian, the deposits on the eastern Siberian Platform contain boreal ammonite genera found only in northern seas. Thus, local stratigraphic units—zones distinguished on the basis of endemic ammonite genera and species—can be correlated only approximately with the standard stratigraphic scale. The most complete Jurassic (particularly Bathonian) section, used as reference for northern Siberia, is exposed at the western and eastern cliffs of Anabar Bay.

The lower Upper Bajocian siltstone (30 m), with globular nodules of calcareous siltstone and pyramidal calcite growths, contains the belemnites *Paramegateuthis parabajosicus* Naln. in the lower part, and also the ammonites *Boreiocephalites pseudoborealis* Meled. and *B.* cf. *warreni* (Freb.) in the upper part. The entire member is characterized by the bivalves *Mytiloceramus kystatymensis* (Kosch.), *Arctotis* ex gr. *sublaevis* Bodyl., *Tancredia subtilis* Lah., *Malletia* sp., etc., and the foraminifers *Recurvoides anabarensis* Bassov, *Ammobaculites lapidosus* Gerke et Scharov., *A. borealis* Gerke, *Verneuilina sibirica* Mjatal., etc. On the basis of *Boreiocephalites,* the *P. pseudoborealis* Zone (lona) was distinguished.

The highest part of the Bajocian, distinguished as the *Cranocephalites vulgaris* Zone, consists of siltstone with globular nodules of calcareous siltstone (22 to 39 m). The upper third contains numerous species of *Cranocephalites,* e.g., *C. vulgaris* Spath, *C. (C.) pompeckji* (Mads.), *C. (C.) nordvikensis* Vor., and *C. (Pachycephalites) maculatus* Spath. The entire zone is characterized by a rich belemnite assemblage, e.g., *Pachyteuthis (P.) optima* Sachs et Naln. and *Cylindroteuthis (C.) spathi* Sachs et Naln., and by such bivalves as *Mytiloceramus retrorsus* (Keys.) and *Arctotis sublaevis* Bodyl. The formanifers and bivalves are similar to those in the lower part of the Bajocian.

Northeast

In the northern Pacific Geosynclinal Belt, Jurassic sections are quite different; they developed in the composite structural pattern of the Verkhoyanye-Chukotka area. One of the most complete Bajocian sections with a good fossil record is in the Viliga Basin (Strat. Jurassic System, 1976) on the northwestern coast of the Sea of Okhotsk (Arman-Gizhiga Trough). At the base of the Bajocian, siltstone and sandstone occur (20 m), with *Pseudolioceras* (*Tugerites*) ex gr. *fastigatum* (West.) and accumulations of *Mytiloceramus menneri* (Kosch.) and *M. jurensis.* Resting above is sandstone, alternating with siltstone (90 m) and containing *Mytiloceramus menneri* (Kosch.), *M. jurensis* (Kosch.), and *Zetoceras* sp. (Phylloceratinae). This interval is placed in the Discites-Laeviuscula Zones. Mudstone and siltstone, with sandstone in the lower and upper parts (total, 120 m) are placed in the Sauzei Zone. *Mytiloceramus lucifer* (Eichw.) and other species are typical. *Arkelloceras elegans* Freb., *A.* cf. *maclearni* Freb., and *Bradfordia alaseica* Repin are known from coeval deposits of the Kolyma and Anabyr Basins.

The Upper Bajocian consists partly of sandstone alternating with mudstone and siltstone (200 m). Most characteristic among the diverse *Mytiloceramus* species is *M. elongatus* (Kosch.). The Lower/Upper Bajocian boundary is conditionally drawn at the base of clay and siltstone strata (400 to 460 m), which, according to the *Mytiloceramus* assemblage, correspond to the entire beds with *Mytiloceramus clinatus* (=beds with *M. porrectus* in the Strat. Jurassic System, 1976) and *M. kystatymensis.* At the base of these strata is a marked change in the *Mytiloceramus* assemblage, characterized by appearance of *M. porrectus* (Eichw.), *M. retrorsus* (Keys.), *M. tongusensis* (Lah.), and large (to giant) *M. ex gr. marinus* (Kosch.) dominating the upper part of the sequence. The latter, by analogy with northern Siberia, may be correlated with the *Boreiocephalites borealis* Zone, but the substage boundary is perhaps within these strata, i.e., between beds with *M. clinatus* and *M. kystatymensis.* In the Northeast, *B. borealis* (Spath) was collected in the Yana Basin.

The overlying strata of alternating (sometimes rhythmic) siltstone, sandstone, and mudstone (525–570 m) comprise the assemblage of *M. ex gr. marinus* (Kosch.), *M. polaris* (Kosch.), and *M. tuchkovi* Polub., indicating their correlation with the beds with *M. polaris.* In the Nyavlenga Basin, equivalents of these beds yield *Cranocephalites vulgaris* Spath, *C. nordivikensis* Vor., and *C. inconstans* Spath—characteristic representatives of the Upper Bajocian *Cranocephalites vulgaris* Zone.

Far East

In more southern parts of the Pacific Geosynclinal Belt, the section in the Bureya Basin is characteristic (Bureya Trough; Strat. Jurassic System, 1976). The Lower Bajocian is represented by the Upper Umalta Member, sandstone and siltstone (400 m). The lower 220 m yield *Pseudolioceras* (*Tugurites*) *fastigatum* Westermann and *Mytiloceramus jurensis* (Kosch.), after which "beds" were named, as well as other *Mytiloceramus* species, forming a characteristic assemblage. In the upper 180 m, the *Mytiloceramus* assemblage is different, and characterized by *M. gr. lucifer* (Eichw.), index species for "beds." The *M. lucifer* beds have also yielded ammonites, e.g., *Holcophylloceras* cf. *ussuriensis* Vor., *Arkelloceras tozeri* Freb., and *A. elegans* Freb.

The higher Lower Bajocian along the Soloni River comprises part (1300 m) of the Epikan Formation, mostly siltstone with rare interbedded sandstone. *Partschiceras grossicostatum* (Imlay), *Mytiloceramus porrectus* (Eichw.), and *M.* cf. *clinatus* (Kosch.) occur in the lower part; *Partschiceras, Lissoceras,* and *M. kystatymensis* (Kosch.) occur in the upper.

A characteristic Upper Bajocian section also occurs on the Soloni River. Sandstone and siltstone (as much as 900 m) of the Elga Formation rest on siltstones of the Epikan Formation with slight unconformity. The lower part contains *Lyroxyites* cf. *kellumi* Imlay; the upper contains *Umaltites era* (Krimh.), *Chinitnites* sp., *Epizigzagiceras* cf. *evolutum* Freb., and *Partschiceras grossicostatum* (Imlay), as well as a rich bivalve assemblage including *Mytiloceramus pseudolucifer* (Afitsky), *M.* cf. *bulunensis* (Kosch.), *Camptonectes* (*Boreionectes*) *broenlundi* (Ravn, *C.* (*B.*) *mimikirensis* Kurata et Kimura, *Meleagrinella ovalis* (Phill.), and *Musculus strajeskianus* (Orb.) (Sey and Kalcheva, 1979, 1980).

SUMMARY

On the Siberian Platform and in the Pacific Belt, Bajocian ammonites are comparatively rare. Nevertheless, it is now possible to correlate the ammonite succession of the northern and eastern areas of the USSR, and of eastern Greenland, Alaska, and Canada. This permits unambiguous placement of the Bajocian boundary (Sey and Kalacheva, 1987). Of great significance also is the inoceramid succession, which is consistent in the entire territory (Polubotko and Sey, 1981). The abundant *Mytiloceramus* is widely used for a detailed subdivision and correlation of the Middle Jurassic section, including the Bajocian.

BATHONIAN
S. V. Meledina

HISTORY AND STANDARD ZONES

The name Bathonian was introduced by d'Omalius d'Halloy (1843), for his second (of four) stages in the Jurassic System. He included the Lower Oolite, Fuller's Earth Rock, Great Oolite, Bradford Clay, Forest Marble, and Cornbrash—formations first recorded in the vicinity of Bath (southwest England) by Smith and subsequently used by Conybeare, Phillips, and Lyell.

D'Orbigny (1842–1851, p. 607) retained the stage name Bathonian, including the Cornbrash, but he placed the Lower Oolite and the Fuller's Earth Rock into the simultaneously established Bajocian stage. D'Orbigny did not characterize the Bathonian, but pointed out that it corresponded to Bathonian beds in the scheme by d'Omalius, and he listed 17 ammonite species as characteristic of the Bathonian.

The Bathonian stage was named after the town of Bath in England, in the vicinity of which it was first established, and where it crops out in a number of exposures and quarries, but no stratotype was designated. Torrens (1967), in his studies of the Bathonian in England, emphasized the unsuitability of exposures around Bath for a stratotype due to incompleteness and inadequate characterization by ammonites. But he did designate and describe stratotypes for the Bathonian zones. The boundaries of the Bathonian, i.e., the stage range as presently understood (Arkell, 1956), have changed considerably since the inception of the stage.

The Bathonian was subdivided by Oppel (1856–1858) into two parts, the *Terebratula lagenalis* and the *T. digona* Zones. Oppel and most of his successors began the Callovian stage with the *Macrocephalites macrocephalus* Zone; the Bathonian/Callovian boundary is still defined in this way. The lower boundary of the Bathonian is now drawn at the basis of the Zigzag Standard Zone. Haug (1910) subdivided the Bathonian into two zones based on ammonites, the *Oppelia fusca* Zone (below) and *O. aspidoides* Zone.

The modern zonal scheme in Europe is based on studies in England, France, and West Germany. In England, the type area, the present zonation was proposed by Arkell, based on his monographic ammonite study (Arkell, 1951–1958). It was later detailed by Torrens (1965, 1974), who also gave data on zonal stratotypes used below.

Lower Bathonian

1. *Zigzagiceras zigzag* Zone. Oppel, 1865. Index species—*Z. zigzag* (Orb.). Lower boundary at appearance of *Parkinsonia* (*Gonolkites*) *convergens* (Buckm.), *P.* (*P.*) *pachypleura* Buckm., and *Morphoceras parvum* Wetz., a characteristic assemblage. Classically developed in southeastern France, lower Alps area (Sturani, 1967). (a) *Parkinsonia convergens* Subzone. Arkell, 1951. Index species—*P.* (*Gonolkites*) *convergens* Buckm. Also *P.*

(*G.*) *subgaleata* Buckm., *P.* (*P.*) *pachypleura* Buckm., *Procerites subprocerus* Buckm., and rare Morphoceratidae. (b) *Morphoceras macrescens* Subzone. Sturani, 1967. Index species—*M. macrenscens* (Buckm.). Also *M. multiforme* Ark., *Ebrayiceras pseudoanceps* Ebray, *E. jactatum* (Buckm.), *Parkinsonia* (*Oraniceras*) *wurttembergica* (Opp.), and *P. pachypleura* (Buckm.). (c) *Oxycerites yeovilensis* Subzone. Neumayr, 1871.* Index species—*O. yeovilensis* Roll. Oppeliidae dominate, i.e., *O. limosus* (Buckm.) and *O. nivernensis* Gross.; *Oecotraustes* (*Paraoeceotraustes*) *bomfordi* (Ark.); *Procerites fullonicus* (Buckm.) and *Siemiradzkia aurigera* (Opp.); and last Parkinsonia, *P.* (*Oraniceras*) *wurttembergica* (Opp.). (d) *Asphinctites tenuiplicatus* Subzone. Rehbinder, 1913. Index species—*A. tenuiplicatus* (Brauns). Last Morphoceratidae: *Asphinctites bathonicus* West. and *A. recinctus* Buckm.; also *Procerites fullonicus* (Buckm.); most Oppeliidae have disappeared.

In England, the first three subzones are distinguished; the first also contains *Asphinctites*. In West Germany, Swabia (Hahn, 1968) and Franconia (Zeiss, 1977b), and France (Mouterde and others, 1971), the Tenuiplicatus Subzone marks the upper Lower Bathonian.

Middle Bathonian

2. *Procentes progracilis* Zone. Buckman, 1909–1930. Index species—*P. progracilis* (Cox et Ark.).† Large Perisphinctidae, especially index species, and *P. mirabilis* (Ark.); also *Micromphalites micromphalus* (Phill.), *Clydoniceras tegularum* Ark., and some *Tulites* spp.

3. *Tulites subcontractus* Zone. Woodward, 1894. Index species—*T. subcontractus* Mor. et Lyc. Typically *Tulites* spp., including *T. modiolaris* (Smith) and *T.* (*Rugiferites*); *Krumbeckia reuteri* Ark.; less frequent, *Oecotraustes* (*Paraoecotraustes*) *splendens* Ark. and *O.* (*P.*) *formosus* Ark.

The upper part of this zone in England has been distinguished as *Morrisiceras morrisi* Zone (Torrens, 1965, 1974), characterized by *M. morrisi* (Opp.) and other species, as well as by *Lycetticeras comma* Buckm. and *Oxycerites waterhousei* Buckm. However, this zone is not ubiquitous in West Germany (Hahn, 1968; Zeiss, 1977b); it is regarded as a subzone in France (Mouterde and others, 1971), which seems reasonable.

In zonal schemes of France (Mouterde and othes, 1971) and Franconia (Zeiss, 1977), the Middle Bathonian is considered as

---

*Neumayr named the zone after *Oppelia fusca*. However, representatives of this species, confined to this level, were subsequently renamed *Oxycerites yeovilensis* (see Rioult, 1964).

---

†First as *Ammonites gracilis* J. Buckm., subsequently renamed *Procerites progracilis* (Cox, Arkell, 1949).

being equal to the Subcontractus Zone. However, in the type area, central England, as well as in some other areas with classical Bathonian deposits, e.g., Swabia (Westermann, 1958; Hahn, 1968), the subdivision of the Middle Bathonian into two zones is well justified, and this should be retained in the standard scale.

Upper Bathonian

4. *Prohecticoceras retrocostatum* Zone. Lissajous, 1923. Index species—*P. retrocostatum* (Gross.). Characteristic also are *Epistrenoceras histricoides* (Roll.), *Oecotraustes** (*Paraoecotraustes*) *maubeugei* Stephanov, *O.* (*P.*) *waageni* Stephanov, *O.* (*Alcidellus*) *densecostatus* Liss., *O.* (*P.*) *Paradoxus* (Roem.), *Clydoniceras* (*Delecticeras*) *delectum* (Ark.), and *Wagnericeras fortecostatum* (Gross.).

The ammonite assemblage changes in certain regions, particularly in the lower part of the zone. As a consequence, different schemes use different indices for the lower part of the Upper Bathonian: *Oxycerites aspidoides* Zone (England: Arkell, 1956; West Germany: Westermann, 1958); *Prohecticoceras retrocostatum* Zone (France: Mouterde and others, 1971; West Germany, Franconia: Zeiss, 1977b; Hungary: Galacz, 1980); or it is divided into two zones (England: Torrens, 1965, 1974; Swabia: Hahn, 1968; Austria: Krystyn, 1972). Significantly, the Retrocostatum and Aspidoides Zones have different ranges in the different schemes, which is impermissible.

In the Russian edition of this volume, we called this unit *Oxycerites aspidoides* Zone, indicating that the Late Bathonian age of the species (the holotype) is questionable (Elmi and Mangold, 1966). Dietl (1982), in a reexamination of the distribution of ammonites in Würtemberg, showed that the Upper Bathonian *O. aspidoides* may be called *O. orbis* (Giebel), whereas true *O. aspidoides* is basal Bathonian or top Bajocian. Retaining the range of the Aspidoides Zone, we now call it the Retrocostatum Zone, probably including two subzones. Regionally, two (Mouterde and others, 1971), three (Westermann, 1958), and even four (Zeiss, 1977b) subzones are distinguished, depending on the local features.

5. *Clydoniceras discus* Zone. Buckmann, 1913. Index species—*C. discus* (Sow.). Lower boundary at appearance of *C. discus* and *C. hollandi* Buckm. The best section was in a quarry near the town of Hildesheim in northern West Germany, where this zone consists of clay with a rich ammonite assemblage, described by G. Westermann (1958). In England, the Discus Zone was subdivided by Arkell into two subzones. (a) *C. hollandi* Subzone. Buckmann, 1924. Represented by the Bradford Clay where only two specimens of *C. hollandi* Buckm. were found, together with a single *Siemiradzkia*. (b) *C. discus* Subzone, represented by the lower Cornbrash, Hinton Sand, and Forest Marble. Characteristic also are *Clydoniceras thrapstonense* Ark., *C. douglasi* Ark., *Delecticeras evolutum* West., and *Choffatia* (*Homeolplanulites*) *acuticostata* (Roem.).

**Or *Oxycerites* (G. Westermann, ed.).

In northwestern and eastern France, the Discus Zone has similar ammonite fauna as in England, and is also divided into two parts (Mouterde and others, 1971). In West Germany, this zone was recognized by G. Westermann (1958) and W. Hahn (1968) without subdivision. We believe that the distinction of the subzones is based on insufficient evidence.

SOVIET UNION

Until recently, the Bathonian of the USSR (Fig. 9) was divided into two substages, because of the impossibility of distinguishing three Bathonian substages in many regions of the USSR.

Russian Platform

Fossiliferous marine Bathonian deposits are known only from the western Baltic Depression, and the south. At the northwestern margin of the Donets Folded Structure, the Lower Bathonian rests conformably on the Bajocian and is represented by layered clay with siderite interbeds, similar to those of the Upper Bajocian. They are characterized by *Pseudocosmoceras michalskii* (Boriss.), *P. masarovici* Mourach., *Meleagrinella doneziana* (Boriss.), *Lenticulina dainae* Kos., and *Darbyella kutsevi* Dain. The thickness of the Lower Bathonian is 40 to 50 m, increasing westward to 60 to 70 m. The Lower Bathonian is overlain by tufogenic sandstone, locally calcareous and cross-grained, with interbeds of bog-iron ore, clay, and limestone (Lower Kamenka Member, 50–60 m). The sandstones abound in the bivalve *Meleagrinella doneziana* (Boriss.); also found are rare *Geocoma carinata* (Goldf.), *Ferganoconcha schabarovi* Tschern., *F. sibirica* Tschern., *Tancredia* sp., the brachiopods *Lingula sterlini* Makrid., and ophiuran remains. Bog-iron ore contains numerous plant impressions, the most important of which are *Equisetum* and smooth-margined *Nilssonia*, indicative of the Middle Jurassic. An occurrence of the member conformable on the Lower Bathonian suggests the Middle to Upper Bathonian. Above follows the Upper Kamenka Member (lacustrine clays), dated as possibly Late Bathonian–Early Callovian.

In the Dnieper-Donets Depression, the Lower Bathonian is made up of layered gray clay with siderite interbeds (110 m). It contains the ammonites *Pseudocosmoceras michalskii* (Boriss.) and *Ps. masarovici* Mourach., and foraminifers including *Lenticulina colganica* Dain and *L. dainae* Kos. (*Pseudolosmoceras michalskii* Zone). Resting conformably above is the Nezhin Formation, gray microlayered clay and siltstone (40–50 m) with siderite interbeds, with rare *Ammodiscus baticus* Dain, *Thurammina* sp., *Glomospira* sp., and shark teeth. Stratigraphic position and *A. baticus* suggest Middle to Upper Bathonian.

Shallow-marine Bathonian with rare ammonites, bivalves, and foraminifers occurs in the Caspian Synclinorium, southern Ul'yanovsk-Saratov Trough, and on the southwestern Russian Platform, Dobruja Trough. Indicative of the Bathonian are the ammonites *Pseudocosmoceras michalskii* (Boriss.), the bivalves

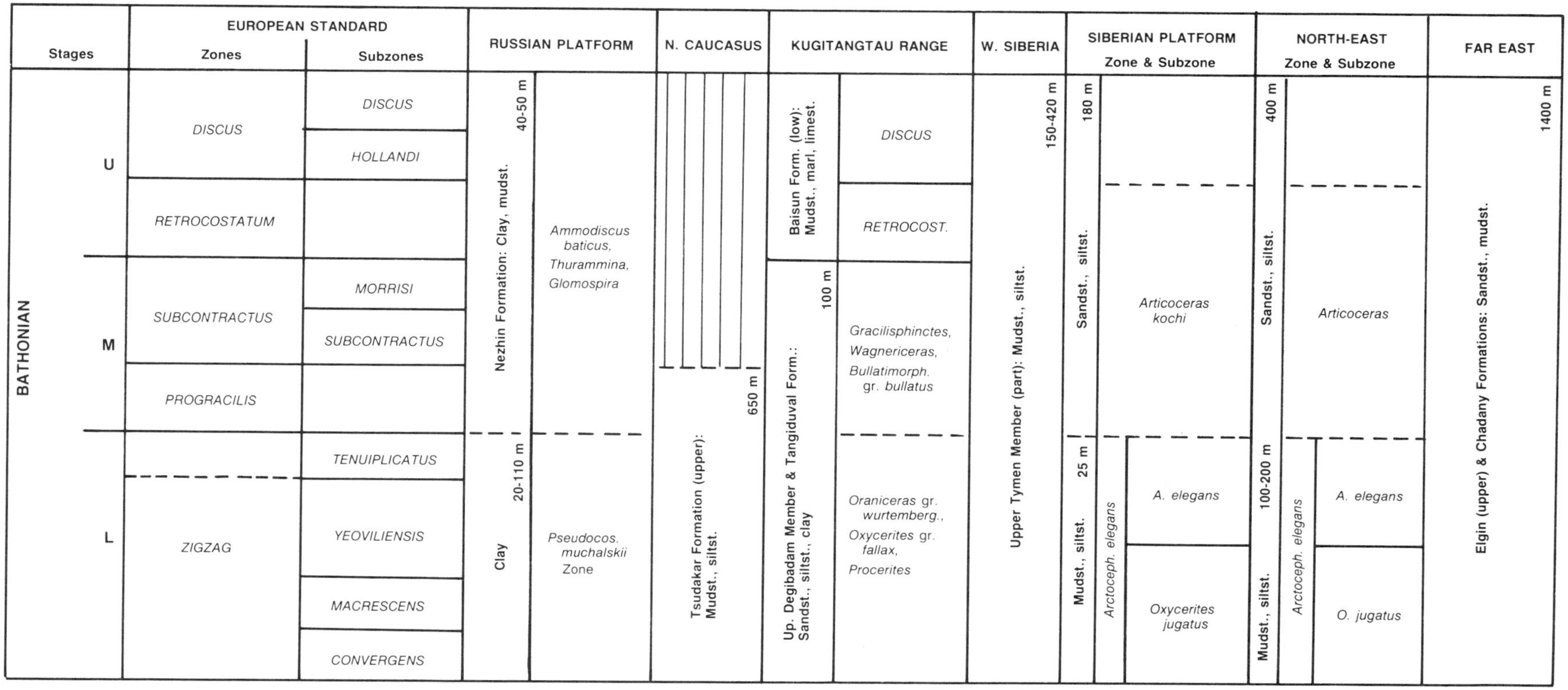

Figure 9. The Bathonian of the major regions of the U.S.S.R.

Meleagrinella doneziana (Boriss.) and *Nucula sana* Boriss. and foraminifers including *Ammodiscus baticus* Dain and *Lenticulina dainae* Kos.

The Middle Jurassic, including the Bathonian, on the Russian Platform is not always easily subdivided, and the age is not always clearly established.

Mediterranean Geosynclinal Belt

The marine Bathonian occurs in Crimea, on the southern slope of the Greater Caucasus, and in Minor Caucasus, Great Balkhan, and the Pamirs. In the northern Caucasus, the Bathonian is practically unrecorded. The Lower Bathonian is preserved, where it forms a single sequence with the Bajocian; the Upper Bathonian is recorded from a number of sites (Beznosov, 1973; Resolution, 1984).

In central Daghestan, the Lower Bathonian comprises the upper part of the Tsudakhar Formation; it is composed of mudstone and siltstone (650 m) with a sandstone in the lower part. *Parkinsonia valida* Wetzel, *P. (Oraniceras) wurttembergica* (Opp.), *Pseudocosmoceras michalskii* (Borris.), *Procerites* cf. *schloenbachi* Gross., *Lissoceras psilodiscus* (Schloenb.), and *Morphoceras* ex gr. *macrescens* Buckm. were found evidence for most of the Zigzag Zone.

The Lower Bathonian is also present in the northwestern Caucasus and the Malaya Laba Basin, and is represented by clay equivalent to the Upper Bajocian clay, but slightly more arenaceous (≤300 m). The clay contains *Oxycerites* aff. *fallax* (Guer.) (=*fusca* Qu.), *Lissoceras psilodiscus* (Schloenb.), and *Nannolytoceras* cf. *azerbojdzanensis* Besn.

The Bathonian is traced throughout the *Turan Plate* and the southwestern Gissar Range. It is made up exclusively of terrigenous rocks, i.e., different sandstones, siltstones, and clays. The most complete (with rich ammonite fauna) and recently well studied section is in the Kugitangtau Range (Krymholts and Zahkarov, 1971; Jurassic System, 1971; Resolutions, 1977). This Bathonian section can be accepted as reference not only for the Turan Plate and southwestern Gissar, but also for the entire southern USSR. The Bathonian in Kugitangtau is divisible into two parts, the lower corresponding to the Lower and Middle Bathonian of the standard scale, the upper one to the Upper Bathonian.

The lower part of the Bathonian is represented by the upper member of the Degibadam Formation and the Tangiduval Formation, alternating sandstone, siltstone, and mudstone with interbeds of detrital limestone (~150 m). According to Beznosov and Kutuzova (1972), the lower part of the Tangiduval contains *Parkinsonia (Oraniceras)* ex gr. *wurttembergica* (Opp.) and *Procerites* sp.; upward, they are replaced by *Oxycerite* ex gr. *fallax* (Guer.) and *Procerites* sp.; and finally, by an abundant assemblage of ammonites, including *Siemiradzkia* spp., *Procerites* spp., "*Gracilisphinctes*" sp., *Wagnericeras* sp., and *Bullatimorphites* ex gr. *bullatus* (Orb.), plus oysters and worms. The Tangiduval Formation is placed into the Lower and Middle Bathonian. The lower ammonite assemblage belongs to the Zigzag Zone and the

Macrescens and Yeovilensis Subzones; the upper indicates the Middle Bathonian.

The Upper Bathonian makes up the lower part (75–100 m) of the Baisun Formation, with alternating layers of mudstone, siltstone, marl, and limestone. The lower part, with *Oxycerites fuscoides* West., *Prohecticoceras haugi* Pop.-Hatz., *Bulltimorphites bullatus* (Orb.), is the Retrocostatum Zone; the upper part, with *Clydoniceras discus* (Sow.), *Delecticeras delectum* Ark., *Choffatia acuticostata* Roem., and *Ch. homoeomorpha* Buckm., is the Discus Zone.

Directly (10–15 m) above the Upper Bathonian are the Early Callovian ammonites, *Macrocephalites* spp., marking the Bathonian/Callovian boundary.

West Siberian Plate

The Bathonian cannot be identified. The Bathonian–lowermost Callovian of western Siberia may include the upper part of the Upper Tyumen Member, siltstone and mudstone, and coal lenses and partings (150–420 m). In the eastern part of the area, in the Upper Tyumen Member, the foraminifer *Ammodiscus* sp. appears; the formation is characterized by abundant leiotrilete spores (of *Hausmannia* type), Gleicheniaceae, and Eboracia spores, as well as *Scyadopitus* spp., *S. affluens* (Bolch.), and *Classopollis*, and markedly depauperated in spores and pollen of "old" plants.

Siberian Platform

Bathonian marine deposits are known from the Arctic coast and the Lena River. The Lower Bathonian abounds in ammonites of the *Arctocephalites elegans* Zone, with the *Oxycerites jugatus* Subzone in the lower part. In the Anabar area, mudstones (12 m) below yield *A. elegans* Spath, *A. callomoni* Freb., and *Oxycerites jugatus* Ersch. et Meled.; above is sandy siltstone (5 m) including *A. elegans* Spath and *A. nudus* Spath. In the Lower Bathonian of this and other areas of Siberia, the belemnites *Pachyteuthis*, *Cylindroteuthis*, and *Paramegateuthis* are widespread; characteristic bivalves include *Mytiloceramus bulunensis* (Kosch.), *M. sobopolensis* (Kosch.), *M. tuchkovi* (Polub.), *Isognomon isognomonoides* (Stahl), *Entolium demissum* (Phill.), *Protocardia striatula* (Phill.) and *Tancredia subtilis* Lah.

The Middle and Upper Bathonian stratigraphy remain inadequately known. Presumably, the *Arcticoceras kochi* Zone corresponds to the Middle and lower Upper Bathonian. Throughout Siberia, this zone is lithologically similar to the Lower Bathonian, i.e., sandstone and siltstones, and is crowned by a clay unit (30–85 m). The ammonite assemblage consists of *Arcticoceras* spp. and *Pseudocadoceras* ex gr. *mundum* Sason.; in the cis-Verkhoyanye Trough, there are also single *Cadoceras* (*Oligocadoceras*). Belemnites are represented by *Pachyteuthis (P.) optima* Sachs et Naln., *P. (P.) parens* Sachs et Naln, *Paramegateuthis timanensis* Gust., and *P. nescia* Naln.; bivalves, by species including *Mytiloceramus vatgt* (Kosch.), *M. tschubukulachensis*

(Kosch.), *Tancredia donaciformis* Lyc., and *Meleagrinella ovalis* (Phill.).

Northeast

Bathonian deposits are mainly terrigenous with abundant inoceramid remains; less frequent are other bivalves and cephalopods.

Lower Bathonian deposits, similar to those of the Bajocian, are best exposed in the Viliga Basin, where they comprise a siltstone member (100–129 m) containing *Mytilocermus bulunensis* (Kosch.), *Arctocephalites elegans* Spath, and *A.*(?) *stepankovi* Tuchk. This unit can be correlated with the *Arctocephalites elegans* Zone and the beds with *Mytilocermus bulunensis*.

Middle and Upper Bathonian deposits have a poor fossil record. In many areas of the North-East, the equivalents of the *Arcticoceras kochi* Zone are distinguished on the basis of finds of *Arcticoceras* sp. indet. This zone may comprise the upper part of the sandstones, siltstones, and tuffs (300–340 m) in the Anyuj Basin, as indicated by finds of *Arcticoceras* sp. and *Pseudocadoceras* ex gr. *mundum* Sason.

Far East

A thick sandstone and siltstone sequence (1,400 m) is conditionally dated as Bathonian. It comprises the upper Elga and Chaganyj Formations, containing a diverse bivalve assemblage, including *Camptonectes* (*C.*) *laminatus* (Sow.), *Modiolus strajeskianus* Orb., *M. bolodekensis* Vor., and *Meleagrinella ovalis* (Phill.), as well as the rare ammonoid *Partschiceras subobtusiforme* (Pomp.).

SUMMARY

Bathonian deposits, although widespread in our country, are, in the different regions, subdivided into units of varying age ranges. Correlations of regional zonal subdivisions with the standard stratigraphic scale therefore differ in reliability, for various reasons. In central and northern areas of the Russian Platform, the Bathonian is regressive, with an extremely scarce fauna. In northeastern Asia, in spite of the extensive development of marine facies, difficulties of correlation with the standard scale are due to the endemism of the marine faunas.

CALLOVIAN
S. V. Meledina

HISTORY AND STANDARD ZONES

The Callovian was distinguished by d'Orbigny in 1850 (d'Orbigny, 1842–1851, p. 608) and named after Kelloway in Wiltshire, 3 km northeast of Chippenham, England. W. Smith (1815) had described from here the "Kelloways Stone," with abundant cephalopods, among them *Ammonites* [*Sigaloceras*] *calloviensis* Sow. D'Orbigny wrote that "this is a derivative of the English Kelloway (Calloviensis), where this stage was first defined," but he did define the stage. He pointed out that these were the "Callovian rocks of Phillips' scheme," which that author (Phillips, 1829) distinguished at the Yorkshire cliffs in northeastern England. D'Orbigny made use of Phillips's data in his paleontological characterization of the Callovian.

Subsequently, the stratotype of the Callovian was slightly changed. Arkell (1933) initially proceeded from the stage name and regarded Wiltshire as the type area. However, after later considering d'Orbigny's interpretation in detail, Arkell (1946, 1956) designated the Yorkshire coast as the stratotype, based on the stratigraphic description and paleontological characterization by Phillips (1829). D'Orbigny (1842–1851) described 37 ammonite species as characteristic for the Callovian, and many of them have remained indices or guides of the Callovian zones.

Presently, the lower boundary of the Callovian is drawn at the base of the Macrocephalus Standard Zone; the upper, at the top of the Lamberti Zone. In the type locality in Yorkshire, the lower boundary is placed at the base of the Upper Cornbrash Formation. The upper boundary was discussed by Arkell (1939, 1946), who studied the vertical ammonite ranges in the Callovian-Oxfordian in the Woodham brick pit and other classic sections of England. He recognized that *Vertumniceras mariae* (Orb.) occurs above *Quenstedtoceras lamberti,* and he placed the boundary between the range zones of these species. At the type locality, the Callovian/Oxfordian boundary is drawn above the Hackness Rock Member at the base of the Oxford Clay Formation.

Lower Callovian

1. *Macrocephalites macrocephalus* Zone. Oppel, 1856–1858. Index species—*M. macrocephalus* (Schloth.). The assemblage also comprises *Macrocephalites* spp., *Choffatia funata* (Opp.), *C. comptoni* (Pratt) Corroy, *Bullatimorphites bullatus* (Orb.), *B. calloviense* Maub., and *Kepplerites* (*Kepplerites*) *cerealis* (Buckm.); very rarely, *Bomburites bombur* (Opp.) and *B. devauxi* (Gross.). (a) *Macrocephalites macrocephalus* Subzone. Characterized by large, compressed, smooth or fine-ribbed *Macrocephalites,* including *M. verus* Buckm. (b) *Macrocephalites kamptus* Subzone. Callomon, 1955. Index species—*M. kamptus* (Buckm.). Characteristic are the evolute inflated microconches of "*Kamptokephalites.*"

2. *Signaloceras calloviense* Zone. Oppel, 1856–1858. Index species—*S. calloviense* (Sow.). With *Kepplerites* s.s. and *K.* (*Gowericeras*), *Sigaloceras* s.s., *S.* (*Gulielmina*), *Cadoceras* s.s., *Pseudocadoceras, Chamoussetia;* and a few Macrocephalitidae, i.e., "*Indocephalites*" and "*Pleurocephalites*"; and Peris-

phinctidae, i.e., *Proplanulites;* and *Reineckeia.* (a) *Proplanulites koenigi* Subzone. Buckman, 1913. Index species—*P. koenigi* (Sow.). Characteristic are some *Macrocephalites* and abundant *Proplanulites,* including *P. koenigi* (Sow.), *P. teisseyrei* Tornq., *P. subcuneatus* Teiss., and *P. subbackeriae* (Orb.); *Cadoceras sublaevis* (Sow.), *C. durum* Buckm., and *C. modiolaris* (Orb.); *Pseudocadoceras* cf. *grewingki* (Pomp.); *Choffatia difficilis* (Buckm.); and *Chamoussetia chamousseti* (Orb.). (b) *Sigaloceras calloviense* Subzone. Type species—*S. calloviense* (Sow.). Also with first *S. (Gulielmina) quinqueplicata* Buckm. (c) *Kosmoceras enodatum* Subzone. Callomon, 1955. Index species—*K. (Gulielmites) enodatum* (Nik.) (=*Sigaloceras (Catasigaloceras) enodatum,* according to J. Callomon). Also with *K. (G.) planicerclus* (Buckm.); *Cadoceras* s.s., *Pseudocadoceras,* and *Proplanulites;* very rare *Kepplerites (Gowericeras) gowerianus* (Sow.); Macrocephalitinae absent.

Middle Callovian

3. *Kosmoceras jason* Zone, 1852. Index species—*K. (Gulielmites) jason* (Rein.). Also *Rondiceras* ["*Cadoceras*"] ex gr. *milaschevici* (Nik.), *Pseudocadoceras boreale* Buckm., *Hecticoceras regulare* (Pill), *H. pavlovi* (Tsytovitch); *H. hecticum* (Rein.) and *H. glyptum* Buckm., etc.; *Reineckeia anceps* (Rein.) and *R. rehmanni* (Opp.); Pseudoperisphinctidae. (a) *Kosmoceras medea* Subzone. Callomon, 1955. Index species—*K. (Gulielmites) medea* Callomon. (b) *Kosmoceras jason* Subzone. Also *K. (G.) gulielmi* (Sow.).

4. *Erymnoceras coronatum* Zone. D'Orbigny, 1852. Index species—*E. coronatum* (Brug.). Also other *Erymnoceras* spp., *Rondiceras milaschevici* (Nik.), *Pseudocadoceras* ex gr. *boreale* Buckm., and *Kosmoceras (Zugokosmoceras) obductum* (Buckm.), *K. (Z.) grossouvrei* (Douv.), and *K. (Spinikosmoceras) castor* (Rein.), etc.; and *Reineckeia anceps* (Rein.), *R. greppini* (Opp.), and *R. stuebeli* Stein. (a) *Kosmoceras obductum* Subzone. Callomon, 1955. Index species—*K. (Zugokosmoceras) obductum* (Buckm.). Also including *K. (Spinikosmoceras) castor* (Rein.), *Erymnoceras coronatum* (Brug.), *E. doliforme* Rom., and *E. schloenbachi* Rom. (b) *Kosmoceras grossouvrei* Subzone. Callomon, 1955. Index species—*K. (Zugokosmoceras) grossouvrei* (Douv.). Characterized by Pseudoperisphinctidae, transitional to *Peltoceras,* e.g., "*Perisphinctes*" *mosquensis, comptoni,* and *scopinensis; Kosmoceras (Spinikosmoceras) castor* (Rein.); rare *Erymnoceras.*

Upper Callovian

5. *Peltoceras athleta* Zone. Oppel, 1856–1858. Index species—*P. athleta* (Phill.). Also including *Peltoceras subtense* Bean, *P. (Rursiceras) reversum* (Leck.), *P.(R.) pseudotorosum* (Prieser), *Kosmoceras tidomoorense* Ark., *K. (K.) annulatum* (Qu.), *K. (K.) duncani* (Sow.), *K. (Lobokosmoceras) proniae* Teiss., *Reineckeia (Collotia) odyssea* (Mayer), *R. (C.) angustilobata* Brasil, *R. (Reineckites) stuebeli* (Steinm.), *Longaeviceras*

longaevum Buckm., *Distichoceras, Horioceras, Aspidoceras* (*Euaspidoceras*) *clynelishense* Ark., *Hecticoceras puteale* (Leck.), and *H. pseudopunctatum* (Lah.).

Some authors used different index species for this zone, i.e., *Kosmoceras ornatum, K. duncani, K. proniae,* or *K. castor.* (a) *Kosmoceras phanium* Subzone. Sykes, 1975. Index species—*K. (Lobokosmoceras) phanium* (Buckm.). Also *K. (Spinikosmoceras) acutistriatum* Buckm., *K. (S.) aculeatum* Eichw., *K. (S.) ornatum* (Rein.), *K. (Gulielmiceras) rimosum* (Quenst.), *K. (G.) gemmatum* (Phill.), and *Binatisphinctes* ["*Perisphinctes*"] *comptoni* (Pratt). (b) *Kosmoceras proniae* Subzone. Cope and others, 1980. Index species—*K. (Lolokosmoceras) proniae* (Teiss.). Also *K. (L.) rowlstonense* (J. et B.), *K. (Kosmoceras) bigoti* (Douv.), *K. (K.) duncani* Sow., large *Peltoceras,* e.g., *P. athleta* (Phill.) and *Longaeviceras placenta* (Leck.). (c) *Kosmoceras spinosum* Subzone. Cope and others, 1980. Index species—*K. spinosum* (Sow.). Also dominant are *K. (K.) tidmoorense* (Arkell) and *K. (Lobokosmoceras) kuklicum* Buckm.; *Distichoceras, Horioceras, Hecticoceras,* and *Grossouvria* are common.

6. *Quenstedtoceras lamberti* Zone. Hebert, 1857. Index species—*Q. lamberti* (Sow.). Also *Q. (Q.) leachi* (Sow.), *Q. (Q.) intermissum* Buckm., *Eboraciceras ordinarium* (Leck.), *E. cadiformae* Buckm., *E. grande* Ark., *E. sutherlandae* (Sow.), *Prorsiceras gregarium* (Leck.), *Kosmoceras compressum* (Qu.), *Grossouvria poculum* (Leck.), *G. auriculare* Buckm., *G. trina* Buckm., *Peltoceras (Peltoceratoides) subtense* (Leck.), *P. (Parapeltoceras) arduennense* (Orb.), and *Hecticoceras nodosulcatum* (Lah.). (a) *Quenstedtoceras henrici* Subzone. Cope and others, 1980. Index species—*Q. henrici* (R. Douv.). *Quenstedtoceras* with rounded venter dominant, also *Eboraciceras, Kosmoceras (K.) compressum* (Quenst.), *K. (K.) spinosum* (Sow.), and *K. (K.) tidmoorense* Arkell. (b) *Quenstedtoceras lamberti* Subzone. Cope and others, 1980. With predominance of index species and *Eboraciceras* spp., i.e., *E. sutherlandiae* (Sow.); also including *Kosmoceras (K.) compressum* (Quenst.), *Aspidoceras clynelishense* Arkell, *Hecticoceras* spp., and *Distichoceras.*

SOVIET UNION

Marine Callovian deposits are widespread (Fig. 10). The presence of many common ammonite genera, subgenera, and species in various regions allow correlations between regional biostratigraphic units, and with the standard zonation.

Russian Platform

Callovian deposits on the central and southern Russian Platform are most complete in the Moscow Synclinorium (the right bank of the Oka River, Ryazan' area). The Lower Callovian commonly consists of clays with pyrite, marl, phosphorite nodules, and ferruginous sandstones and sands. Its thickness in the Moscow Synclinorium attains 10 to 15 m; in the Ul'yanovsk-Saratov Trough it is more than 30 m thick. Distinguished in the Lower Callovian are *Macrocephalites macrocephalus* beds and the *Cadoceras elatmae* and *Kepplerites gowerianus* Zones.

Stage	EUROPEAN STANDARD		RUSSIAN PLATFORM	N. CAUCASUS	KUGITANGTAU RANGE		WEST SIBERIA		SIBERIAN PLATFORM		NORTH-EAST	FAR EAST
	Zones	Subzones	Zone & Subzone	Zone & Subzone		Zone			Zone			
CALLOVIAN — U	LAMBERTI	LAMBERTI	30 m — Clay, cool. marl — LAMBERTI	7,5 m — Iron form. (lower part): Limest., dolom. — LAMBERTI	150-200 m — Clay, organ. limest.	LAMBERTI	20-60 m — Mudst., siltst.	*Eboracic. subordin.*	20 m — Siltst.	*E. subordin.*		60 m — Sandst. — *Longaeviceras*
		HENRICI										
	ATHLETA	SPINOSUM	ATHLETA	ATHLETA		ATHLETA		*Longaevic. keyserlingi*	20 m — Clay mudst.	*L. keyserl.*		
		PRONIAE										
		PHANIUM										
CALLOVIAN — M	CORONATUM	GROSSOUVREI	18 m — Clay, cool. marl — CORONATUM	50-60 m — Armkhin Form.: Limest., sandst., siltst., conglom. — CORONATUM: *Kosmoc. pollux*	Kugitang Form. (lower part) — Clay, organ.-detri. limest.	CORONATUM			5 m — Clay	*Rondic. milaschevici, Erymnoceras*		
		OBDUCTUM		*Coronatum*								
	JASON	JASON	JASON	JASON		JASON						
		MEDEA										
CALLOVIAN — L	CALLOVIENSE	ENODATUM	30 m — Clay, ferrug. sandst. — CALLOVIENSE: CALLOV.	45-60 m — Baisun Form. (upper part) — Clay, marl, siltst. — CALLOV. TO MACROCEPH.		CALLOVIENSE	5-13 m — Mudst., siltst.	*Kepplerites*	30 m — Clay		300-600 m — Sandst., siltst.	Talyndzhan Form.: Sandst., siltst., coal — 600 m
		CALLOVIENSE						*Cadoceratinae*		*Cadoceras emelianzevi*		
		KOENIGI	KOENIGI									
	MACROCEPHALUS	CAMPTUS	*Cadoceras elatmae*			MACROCEPH.			30 m — Siltst.	*C. elatmae*	*Cadoceras anabaren.*	
		MACROCEPHALUS	MACROCEPHALUS									

Figure 10. The Callovian of the major regions of the U.S.S.R.

The middle part of the Lower Callovian, the *Cadoceras elatmae* Zone, is most distinctly characterized by ammonites. Due to the abundance of *C. elatmae* (Orb.) and other *Cadoceras* species, this part of the Callovian can be traced on the entire Russian Platform, including northern areas. In the best section in the Malinovy Gorge (Saratov area), the *C. elatmae* Zone is represented by a 25-m-thick clay with marl nodules. *Macrocephalites* occur below and in the upper part of the *C. elatmae* range zone, i.e., the *Macrocephalites* range zone is greater than the *C. elatmae* range zone.

Nikitin (1885) found *Macrocephalites* on the Oka River, near the town of Elat'ma, and distinguished the Lower Callovian as "a level with *Cadoceras elatmae* or beds with *Macrocephalites.*" Sokolov (1901) indicated *Macrocephalites krylowi* Milasch. on the Kzhma and Adz'va Rivers in the Pechora Basin in the *Arcticoceras ishmae* Zone, below the *C. elatmae* Zone. Examination of Sokolov's specimen shows, however, that it belongs to *Arcticoceras.*

The upper part of Lower Callovian on the Russian Platform poses difficulties because of contradictory data on the stratigraphic ranges of certain ammonite genera and species. Beds with *Kepplerites gowerianus* were distinguished in the Ul'yanovsk-Saratov Trough; a zone bears the same name in the Moscow Synclinorium (Krymholts, 1972b), and in the *Chamoussetia chamousseti* Zone in the Ul'yanovsk-Saratov Trough (Kamysheva-Elpatievskaya and others, 1974).

The author has recently distinguished a fourth biostratigraphic unit above *C. elatmae* Zone and equivalent to the *Proplanulites koenigi* Subzone. It contains *Cadoceras simulans* Spath, *C. elatmae* Nik., *Pseudocadoceras mundum* (Sas.), *Chamoussetia chamousseti* (Orb.), *Kepplerites (Gowericeras) gowerianus* (Sow.), *K. (K.) galilaei* (Opp.), *K. (Toricellites) approximatum* Buckm., *Proplanulites* cf. *majesticus* Buckm., *Macrocephalites* cf. *formosus* (Sow.), and *Choffatia* sp.; and above, in the Calloviense Subzone, *S. (S.) calloviense* (Sow.), *S. (S.) trichophorum* Buckm., *Chamoussetia* sp., *Macrocephalites* cf. *uetzinguensis* Greif, *Pseudocadoceras* cf. *grewingki* (Pomp.), and *Cadoceras* sp. The similarity in generic and species composition of ammonites in the upper Lower Callovian of the Russian Platform to that of the stratotype makes unnecessary any special biostratigraphy of this part of the section. The Calloviense Standard Zone is identified with Koenigi and Calloviense Subzones, in the Pechora and Moscow synclinoria, the Ul'yanovsk-Saratov Trough, and the Dnieper-Donets Depression. Equivalents of the Enodatum Standard Subzone, distinguished by Callomon in the stratotype, are unknown from the Russian Platform, where *Kosmoceras enodatum* Nik. occurs in the Jason Zone (Meledina, 1977).

The Middle Callovian is widespread on the Russian Platform. As in the stratotype, it is divisible into Jason and Coronatum Zones (Resolutions, 1962). The Callovian is particularly widespread in the southern Moscow Synclinorium, in the Moscow, Ryazan, Tula, Ivanovo, Vladimir, Kostroma, Yaroslavl, and Kalinin areas. According to Gerasimov (Krymholts, 1972b), the Middle Callovian varies in composition and is usually only a few meters thick. It increases to 65 m in the Kaluga and Smolensk areas. Zonation in the Middle Callovian is not always possible.

Zonal assemblages of ammonites on the Russian Platform, similar to those in the stratotype, are characterized by genera and species of Kosmoceratidae, Perisphinctidae, Cardioceratidae, and to a lesser degree, Pachyceratidae and Oppeliidae. Reinekeiidae are absent. In the Jason Standard Zone of the Oka Basin, all subzonal index species of *Kosmoceras* occur, i.e., *K. (Gulielmites) enodatum* Nik., *K. (G.) medea* Call., and *K. (G.) jason* (Rein.); and in the Coronatum Zone, found together with the index species is *K. (Zugokosmoceras) grossouvrei* (Douv.), a subzonal index species. However, the stratigraphic position of these species has not been determined, so that subzones cannot be identified.

The Upper Callovian is recorded from the same area as the Middle Callovian, and is everywhere thin (20–30 m). Zones were recognized only in the Pechora, Polish-Lithuanian Synclinorium, Ul'yanovsk-Saratov Trough, and Dnieper-Donets Depression.

On the Russian Platform, the Athleta and Lamberti Standard Zones have been identified, based on ammonite assemblages largely similar to those in the stratotypes. Often standard subzones can also be determined, i.e., in the Athleta Zone by characteristic *Kosmoceras* species, and in the Lamberti Zone by *Quenstedtoceras* species.

In the Pechora Synclinorium, the *Longaeviceras keyserlingi* Zone, also recorded in Siberia, is coeval to the Athleta Zone. The uppermost Callovian standard zone has not been distinguished here, but its former presence is established by characteristic Lamberti Zone fossils in condensed beds at the base of the Oxfordian, together with typical Lower Oxfordian species. Arctic Cardioceratidae are predominant, e.g., *Eboraciceras subordinarium* Buckm., *E. ordinarium* Buckm., and *Vertumniceras* sp.

Mediterranean Geosynclinal Belt

The marine Callovian occurs in the Crimea, on the northern slope of the greater Caucasus, the Minor Caucasus, Great Balkhan, and the Pamirs. Deposits are also widespread in the northern Caucasus. Fossils, particularly ammonites, frequently occur in condensed deposits or are redeposited, making a zonation difficult in certain areas.

The most complete and detailed Callovian is in the eastern northern Caucasus, in the Fiagdon-Assa area, and in Daghestan (Beznosov, 1973). The Lower and Middle Callovian are developed in the Armkha Formation. Its basal member, conglomerate and conglomeratic sandstone, biodetrital and clayey limestone (2 to 6 m), yields *Macrocephalites macrocephalus* (Schloth.), *M. tumidus* (Rein.), *Sigaloceras calloviense* (Sow.), and *Kepplerites gowerianus* (Sow.), indicating Macrocephalus and Calloviense Standard Zones. Early Callovian faunas are also known from the Kamennomostskaya Formation, at the Belaya-Urup interfluve. The Middle Callovian of the upper Armkha Formation is divisible into zones and subzones.

The lower part (32 m) of the limestone and calcareous siltstone member (48 m) is the Jason Zone, including *Kosmoce-*

ras jason (Rein.), *K. baylei* Tint., *K. gulielmii* (Sow.), *Hecticoceras metomphalum* Bon., *Okaites mosquensis* (Fisch.), and *Reineckeia anceps* (Rein.). The upper 16 m of the calcareous silt member is the Coronatum Zone, with characteristic species in its lower part: *Erymnoceras coronatum* (Brug.), *E. doliforme* Rom., *E. baylei* Jean., *Rollierites minuendum* Roll., *Kosmoceras castor* (Rein.), etc.; and in the upper part, with species typical for the Pollux Subzone, e.g., *Erymnoceras renardi* Nik., *Rollierites dimidiatum* Roll., *Kosmoceras pollux* (Rein.), *K. ornatum* (Schloth.), *K. crassum* (Tint.), and *Reineckeia falcata* Till.

The Upper Callovian is present in Daghestan (Irganai-Gergi area) in the lower Iron Formation, Athleta and Lamberti Zones; it is made up of limestone and dolomite (7.5 m). The lower zone yields *Peltoceras athleta* (Phill.), *P. borissjaki* Amann., *P. baylei* Pries., and *Kosmoceras ornatum* (Schloth.); the upper, *Quenstedtoceras lamberti* (Sow.), *Q. pavlovi* R. Douv., *Q. leachi* (Sow.), *Q. flexicostatum* (Phill.), and *Kosmoceras gemmatum* (Phill.). In most areas of the northern Caucasus, however, Late Callovian ammonites are redeposited and occur in a condensed layer 0.2 to 0.3 m thick, together with Lower and Middle Callovian ammonites.

On the *Turan Plate,* the complete Callovian occurs in the Kugitangtau Range, Gissar, and has been finely subdivided (Resolutions, 1977). The Lower Callovian consists of marl, clayey limestone, and below, mudstone, of the upper Baisun (45–60 m), and, (?)lower Kugitang Formations. Macrocephalus and Calloviense Zones have been identified on the basis of ammonites. The Middle Callovian of the Kugitang Formation (lower part) is composed of clayey and bioclastic limestones (90–150 m) of the Jason and Coronatum Zones. The Jason Zone contains the index species and *Kosmoceras castor* (Rein.), *K. enodatum* (Nik.), *Reineckeia anceps* (Rein.), diverse Perisphinctidae; the Coronatum Zone yields the index species, *Erymnoceras banksi* (Sow.), *E. renardi* (Nik.), *E. turkmenensis* Amann., and *E. chikhackevi* Amann. The Upper Callovian (45 m) resembles the Middle Callovian in its lithology. The Athleta Zone has *Peltoceras* spp., *Kosmoceras duncani* (Sow.), *K. ogulbibiae* Amann., *Reineckeia stuebeli* Steinm.; the Lamberti Zone contains diverse *Quenstedtoceras, Kosmoceras, Peltoceras, Euaspidoceras, Hecticoceras,* and *Choffatia.*

Western Siberian Plate

The Callovian is present in a number of formations, replacing each other laterally. Lower, Middle(?), and Upper Callovian ammonites are recorded in western Siberia; but only the Upper Callovian is known well enough to judge its extent and zonation (Mesezhnikov and others, 1984). The recognition of the Lower Callovian is rather vague. Its lower boundary may be within the Tyumen Formation (southern sections), but it is conventionally drawn at its top (northwestern sections). In most cases, the Upper Jurassic part of the Tyumen Formation has not been determined. The maximum thickness of the Callovian in the upper Tyumen reaches 13 m in the Surgut area. In certain sections in the north-

west part of the Plate, the lowermost 5 to 8 m of marine mudstone of the Abalak Formation is placed into the Lower Callovian on the basis of unidentified Cadoceratinae. Of major significance is a find of *Kepplerites (Sigaloceras)* sp. indet. (Pal'yanovo 96 borehole, interval 2,494 to 2,509 m), indicating the upper Lower Callovian.

The Middle and Upper Callovian from the extreme northwest (Lyapin Depression) to the southeast (Ket'River, Bely Yar Village) of the Western Siberian Plate consists mainly of marine gray and dark gray mudstone, in places bituminous. The lower parts have strong lateral facies changes. In the Frolovo, Tobo-Tanapcha and part of the Berezovo areas, this is the Lower Abalak Member (8–20 m) (Callovian-Lower Oxfordian); in the Shaim area, the lower part of the Lower Shaim Member (4–11 m) (Callovian); in the Lyapin area, the Lower Mar'yanovka Member; and in the Omsk and Eremino-Pikhtovo areas, the lower Mar'yanovka Formation (15–27 m) (Middle Callovian-Kimmeridgian). In the Vasyugan area, it is the Lower Vasyugan Member (18–47 m) (Middle Callovian–Lower Oxfordian), in the South Yamal area, the lower Yarrota Formation (40–145 m) (Callovian), and in the Yenisei it is the Tochino Formation (10–55 m) (Callovian) (Strat. Jurassic System, 1976).

No reliable Middle Callovian faunas are yet known. Upper Callovian is distinguished by *Longaeviceras, Quenstedtoceras* s.s., *Qu. (Soaniceras),* and *Eboraciceras.* Zonation of the Upper Callovian is rather difficult to discern in Siberia, since *Longaeviceras* is found in both Upper Callovian zones. Nevertheless, in some cases, occurrence of *Longaeviceras* without *Quenstedtoceras* indicates the *Longaeviceras keyserlingi* Zone; relatively abundant *Eboraciceras* and, mainly, *Quenstedtoceras,* indicate the *Eboraciceras subordinarium* Zone.

Siberian Platform

In the north, the Callovian is almost complete. Abundant ammonites, both endemic and in common with Western Europe, make it possible to distinguish all substages and the zones of the lower and upper substages. The sections in the eastern Yenisei–Khatanga, and Lena-Anabar Troughs serve as reference for the Siberian Platform (Meledina, 1977).

The Lower Callovian is divisible into the *Cadoceras elatmae* and *C. emelianzevi* Zones. They are conditionally placed in this substage, except its lowermost part, since on the Russian Platform *Cadoceras elatmae* occurs in the upper part of the Macrocephalus Zone.

The *Cadoceras elatmae* Zone consists of clay or mudstone (30 m), with large (0.5 m) siltstone and small (2 cm) pyrite nodules. Clays, and more frequently, siltstone nodules, yield the ammonites *C. (Paracadoceras) elatmae* Nik., *C. (P.) anabarense* Bodyl., *C. (Bryocadoceras) falsum* Vor.; the belemnites: *Pachyteuthis (P.) subrediviva* (Lem.); and diverse bivalves including *Limea borealis* (G. Pcel.), *Homomya obscondita* Kosch., and *Gresslya lunulata* Ag.

2. The *Cadoceras emelianzevi* Zone is ubiquitous and commonly only a few meters thick. It consists of siltstone and sandy siltstone, containing *C. (C.) emelianzevi* Vor., *C. (C.)* aff. *bathomphalum* Imlay, *Meleagrinella ovalis* (Phill.), *Camptonectes (Boreionectes)* ex gr. *broenlundi* (Ravn), and *Entolium demissum* (Phill.).

The Middle Callovian is locally represented by beds with *Rondiceras milaschevici* and *Erymnoceras* sp., but in Siberia it is commonly, entirely, or partly missing. At the base there is always an erosional surface. Clay with abundant small (pea-size) pyrite nodules and rare siltstone nodules (5.4 m, B. Begichev Island) yields species including *Rondiceras milaschevici* (Nik.), *R. tschefkini* (Orb.), *Pseudocadoceras grewingki* (Pomp.), *P. insolitum* Meled., *Erymnoceras* sp., and *Meleagrinella.*

The Upper Callovian is divisible into two zones, correlated with the Athleta and Lamberti Standard Zones, respectively. Due to numerous erosions and breaks, the total thickness ranges from 0 to 40 m.

1. The *Longaviceras keyserlingi* Zone consists of clay and mudstone with siltstone interbeds, with *Longaeviceras* being characteristic; also the belemnite *Cylindroteuthis (C.) optima* Sachs et Naln., and bivalves including *Isognonom taimyrensis* Zakh. et Schur., *Gresslya sibirica* Bodyl., *Thracia scythica* Eichw., and *Comptonectes (Boreionectes) boernlundi* (Ravn.).

2. The *Eboraciceras subordinarium* Zone, consisting of arenaceous siltstone with globular siltstone nodules (0.4 m), yields numerous ammonites, including *Eboraciceras subordinarium* Buckm., *E. nikolaevi* (Bodyl.), *E. taimyrense* Meled., *Longaeviceras filarum* Meded., *Quenstedtoceras (Soaniceras)* spp., *Vertumniceras nikitinianum* (Lah.); and bivalves including *Artica syssolae* (Keys.), *Camptonectes* cf. *lens* (Sow.), and *Gresslya sibirica* Bodyl.

Northeast

In the northern Pacific Geosynclinal Belt, Callovian deposits vary greatly in facies and thickness, and due to the scarcity of fossils, cannot be subdivided in most areas; for example, in the Oldzhoi-Polousny and In'yali-Debin Troughs, and in the Omolon Massif (Strat. Jurassic System, 1976). In the Omolon Massif, Bulun Basin, the upper 300 m of sandstone, siltstone, and gritstone yield *Cadoceras (Paracadoceras)* cf. *anabarense* Bodyl., indicating the *E. subordiarium* Zone.

Far East

In the more southern part of the Pacific Geosynclinal Belt, it is difficult to distinguish the Callovian deposits due to scarcity of fossils. In some areas, including the Bureya Trough, the Callovian also comprises continental coal-bearing sediments (e.g., Talyndzhan Formation in the Bureya Basin).

Upper Callovian deposits are recorded from the Torom Trough. North of Mamga Bay, on cliffs of Tugur Bay, sandstones and siltstones rest with erosional surface, and in places with distinct unconformity, on various earlier Middle Jurassic horizons. *Longaeviceras*(?) cf. *keyserlingi* (Sok.) suggests that the lower 60 m belong to the *keyserlingi* Zone (Sey and Kalacheva, 1977).

SUMMARY

Callovian deposits are ubiquitous in all major regions of USSR. In many regions (the Russian Plain, Caucasus, Crimea, central Asia), Callovian Standard Zones are distinguished. For the extensive territory of Siberia (central Siberia; northeast and far east areas of the USSR), a regional zonal scale has been compiled. Ammonite genera and species in common between regions permit correlation of the zonal scales among themselves and with the stratotype.

OXFORDIAN
M. S. Mesezhnikov

HISTORY AND STANDARD ZONES

The Oxfordian was distinguished by d'Orbigny in 1850 (d'Orbigny, 1842–1851), who placed it between the Callovian and Corallian stages and named it after the town of Oxford, England. However, the term Oxfordian was used before, in 1829, by Brogniart, who included practically the entire Middle Jurassic. Therefore, on the suggestion by Arkell (1946), all interpretations of Oxfordian and other "stage" names before the work of d'Orbigny (1842–1851) are now regarded as invalid.

The position of the Oxfordian stratotype has also long been debated. Referring to the name of the stage, and also to the rather complete sections in Oxfordshire, Dorsetshire, and Wiltshire, with characteristic fauna, English geologists have requested that the stage stratotype should be in southern or central England. However, in this case, drawing the lower stage boundary becomes practically impossible. Thus, we support Arkell's (1933) suggestion that the stratotype should be in Yorkshire, following d'Orbigny, who pointed to these sections known to him by the work of Phillips (1829).

According to Arkell's (1933, 1956) data, amplified by K. Wright, on the Callovian/Oxfordian boundary in Yorkshire, the sea cliffs between Scarborough and Greeshorpe Bay expose the succession given below:

1. Oxford Clay*, gray sandy clay (30–45 m) with ammonites of the Mariae Zone.

2. Lower Calcareous Grit, yellow calcareous sandstone, fauna of the Cordatum Zone, Bukowskii and Percaelatum (=*costicardia*) Subzones (15–45 m).

3. Hambelton Oolite Series, calcareous, often oolite and cross-grained sandstone (25–30 m), fauna of the Cordatum Zone.

4. Berkshire Oolite Series, calcareous in places, oolite sandstone (3–5 m; locally, 30 m), and fauna of the Plicatilis Zone.

5. Osmington Oolite Series, limestone, oolitic sandstone with corals, and calcareous sandstone (~15 m), fauna of the Plicatilis Zone.

6. Glos Oolite Series, limestone, coral sandstone, and calcareous siltstone (15 m). Lower part with ammonites of the Plicatilis Zone; upper part with *Prionodoceras, Perisphinctes,* and *Decipia.*

7. Upper Calcareous Grit, gray clayey limestone, and locally, ferruginous calcareous sandstone (5–15 m; locally, 20 m), with *Amoeboceras.*

The faunal characterization by d'Orbigny was imprecise. Thus, because of his inclusion of *Quenstedtoceras mariae,* the lower boundary of the Oxfordian has long remained unclear. The

Mariae Zone was placed in the Callovian, although rather abundant *Cardioceras* were found there. At the same time, his distinction of the Corallian stage made the upper boundary vague. Although Oppel soon showed the identity of part of the Corallian with the lower Kimmeridgian, for a long time the widespread coral facies in the Upper Oxfordian of England prevented identification of an unambiguous Oxfordian/Kimmeridgian boundary.

The lower stage boundary was defined by Arkell (1933, 1946) after examination of the original stratotype in Yorkshire. In contrast to southern and central England, where uniform clay persists from the upper Lower Callovian to the middle Lower Oxfordian, the Oxford Clay of Yorkshire rests on limestone and clayey limestone (Hackness Rock) containing the fauna of the Athleta Zone in the lower part, and fauna of the Lamberti Zone in the upper part. The Oxford Clay in Yorkshire contains ammonites of the Mariae Zone; thus, the Callovian/Oxfordian boundary was drawn between the Lamberti and Mariae Zones.

The upper stage boundary was defined by Salfeld (1914) after the revision of Perisphinctidae from the Oxfordian/Kimmeridgian boundary beds. He proposed the new zone of *Ringsteadia anglica* (=*R. pseudocordata*) in the upper Oxfordian, and also noted the appearance of *Pictonia* at the base of the Kimmeridgian. In spite of some uncertainties in the distribution of the Upper Oxfordian ammonites in south and central England (Arkell, 1956; Callomon, 1964), the Oxfordian/Kimmeridgian boundary between Pseudocordata and Baylei Zones is now universally acepted.

Sections in England were used for compiling the standard zonal scale. However, when the sections of England and France were correlated, the zonal succession of the British Isles was found to be incomplete. This circumstance and related paleogeographic reconstructions in Western Europe for the middle Oxfordian (which begins with a major transgression from Tethys and the consequent shrinking of the Boreal Basin) resulted in the omission of certain horizons from the middle part of the English Oxfordian. Arkell (1956) assumed that the Plicatilis Zone in England generally corresponded to the Transversarium Zone of continental Europe; Callomon (1964), however, introduced the notion of Oxfordian Tilt, and suggested that only the upper part of the Plicatilis Zone (Parandieri Subzone) corresponds to the Transversarium Zone, and that the upper part of this zone is not recorded in England. Recently, however, beds corresponding to the upper Transversarium Zone were found in Scotland (*Amoeboceras nunningtonense* Subzone; Sykes and Callomon, 1979), although the upper boundaries of Transversarium Zone and Nunningtonense Subzone may not coincide. Thus, the standard scale of the English Oxfordian should be supplemented by the French Transversarium Zone (Mouterde and others, 1971) between the Plicatilis and Cautisnigrae Zones.

---

*Sometimes, by analogy with central and south England where only the Upper Oxford Clay is assigned to the Oxfordian, the clay resting on the Hackness Rock in Yorkshire is called Upper Oxford Clay (Arkell, 1933) or Yorkshire Oxford Clay (Wright, 1968).

Stage		EUROPE		SUBMEDITERRANEAN PROVINCE (Mouterde et al., 1971)		BOREAL PROVINCE (Sykes & Surlyk, 1976)
		Zones	Subzones	Zones	Subzones	Zones
OXFORDIAN	U	PSEUDOCORDATA		PLANULA		ROSENKRANTZI
				BIMAMMATUM	HAUFFIANUM	REGULARE
					BIMAMMATUM	
		DECIPIENS			HYPSELUM	SERRATUM
		CAUTISNIGRAE		BIFURCATUS		GLOSENSE
	M	TRANSVERSARIUM	SCHILLI	TRANSVERSARIUM	SCHILLI	TENUISERRATUM
			PARANDIERI		PARANDIERI	
		PLICATILIS	ANTECEDENS	PLICATILIS	ANTECEDENS	DENSIPLICATUM
			VERTEBRALE		VERTEBRALE	
	L	CORDATUM	CORDATUM	CORDATUM	CORDATUM	CORDATUM

Figure 11. Correlation of the Middle-Upper Oxfordian of the Boreal, Subboreal, and Submediterranean Provinces.

The substage division in England has long remained binary. The Lower Oxfordian comprised Mariae and Cordatum Zones, the Upper Oxfordian, Plicatilis, and Bimammatum (sensu Arkell)* Zones (Arkell, 1956). Spath (1933) proposed the term Neooxfordian for the Cautisnigrae, Decipiens, and Pseudocordata Zones as presently interpreted, corresponding to the Argovian stage. He was followed by Zeiss (1957), who distinguished the Middle Oxfordian between the Cordatum and Transversarium Zones. Thus, the Middle Oxfordian of Zeiss initially corresponded to the Plicatilis Zone; the Upper Oxfordian to the Neooxfordian of Spath. However, French geologists showed that the Plicatilis Zone in England also includes the lower part of the Transversarium Zone (Enay and others, 1974), and that the fauna of these zones is rather similar. Therefore, they included in the Middle Oxfordian both the Plicatilis and Transversarium Zones (Mouterde and others, 1971). The present division of the Oxfordian is seen in Figure 11.

For the upper part of the Oxfordian in the Mediterranean and Submediterranean Provinces, the terms Lusitanian (Choffat, 1885), Sequanian (Marcou, 1848), Rorackian (Gressly, 1867), and Argovian (Marcou, 1848) were often used. All were introduced for different carbonate facies, and their time ranges differ geographically with the respective facies. For instance, the Sequeanian of Marcou corresponds to the Upper Oxfordian–Lower Kimmeridgian, whereas the Sequanian of Haug is only uppermost Oxfordian. Most frequently the term Lusitanian is used, which, following Haug, was regarded as synonymous with Upper Oxfordian. However, the upper Lusitanian boundary was not well defined and may be in the lower Kimmeridgian, whereas the lower boundary is clearly in the Middle Oxfordian. A resolution at the Luxembourg Colloquium on the Upper Jurassic (Resolution, 1964) concerned the objective use of facies stage names, e.g., Lusitanian, Rorackian, Argovian, and Sequanian.

Lower Oxfordian

1. *Vertumniceras mariae* Zone. H. Douville, 1881. Index species—*V. mariae* (Orb.). Characterized by coarse-ribbed *Vertumniceras* and *Pavloviceras;* first *Cardioceras* (=*Scarburgiceras*); and Oppeliidae, *Creniceras,* and *Taramelliceras.* (a) *Cardioceras scarburgense* Subzone. Buckman, 1913. Index species—*C. (Scarburgiceras) scarburgense* (Y. et B.). Characterized also by *Vertumniceras mariae* (Orb.), *Quenstedtoceras (Pavloviceras) roberti* Buckm., *Q. (P.) omphaloides* (Sow.). (b) *Cardioceras praecordatum* Subzone. Davies, 1916. Index species—*C. (Scarburgiceras) praecordatum* H. Douville, 1881. Also characteristic are *C. (S.) alfacordatum* Spath, *C. (S.) gloriosum* Ark., and diverse *Peltoceras, Quenstedtoceras (Pavloviceras)* and *Vertumniceras mariae* (Orb.).

---

*Arkell (1956) assumed that some poorly correlated ammonite-bearing beds in the Upper Oxfordian of England corresponded to the Bimammatum Zone of southern Europe. He also included the *Idoceras planula* Zone in the latter.

2. *Cardioceras cordatum* Zone.* D'Orbigny, 1852. Index species—*C. (C.) cordatum* (Sowerby). Characteristic fauna with diverse Cardioceratidae and Aspidoceratidae. (a) *Cardioceras Bukowskii* Subzone. Arkell, 1941. Index species—*C. (Scarburgiceras) bukowskii* Maire. Also characteristic are *C. (S.) gloriosum* Ark. and *Goliathiceras (Korythoceras) korys* Buckm. (b) *Cardioceras cordatum* Subzone. Characteristic are *Cardioceras* s.s., *Goliathiceras,* and *Scoticardioceras.*

Middle Oxfordian

3. *Perisphinctes plicatilis* Zone. Hudleston, 1878. Index species—*P. (Arisphinctes) plicatilis* (Sowerby). Characteristic are diverse *Perisphinctes, Cardioceras (Scoticardioceras, Vertebriceras, Plasmatoceras),* and Aspidoceratinae. (a) *Cardioceras vertebrale* Subzone. Arkell, 1947. Index species—*C. (Vertebriceras) vertebrale* (Sow.). Characteristic are *Scoticardioceras, Vertebriceras,* and *Perisphinctes.* (b) *Perisphinctes antecedens* Subzone. Arkell, 1947. Index species—*P. (Dichotomosphinctes) antecedens* Salf. Characteristic are comparatively rare Cardioceratidae, *Dichotomosphinctes,* and the first *Perisphinctes* s.s., most recently elevated to a zone at the base of the Middle Oxfordian by Spanish and Polish authors.

4. *Gregoryceras transversarium* Zone. Oppel, 1863. Index species—*G. transversarium* (Qu.). Characteristic are diverse Perisphinctidae and Oppeliidae (France and West Germany). (a) *Perisphinctes parandieri* Subzone. Callomon, 1960. Index species—*P. parandieri* Loriol. Characteristic are *Perisphinctes,* Oppeliidae, and *Glochiceras.* (b) *Larcheria schilli* Subzone. Boone, 1922. Index species—*L. schilli* Opp. Characteristic are diverse *Perisphinctes* and the first rare *Amoeboceras.*

Upper Oxfordian

5. *Perisphinctes cautisnigrae* Zone. Arkell, 1945. Index species—*P. (P.) cautisnigrae* Ark. Characteristic are diverse *Perisphinctes,* first *Decipia lintonensis* Ark., and *Amoeboceras (Prionodoceras) glosense* (Bigot et Brasil).

6. *Decipia decipiens* Zone. Salfeld, 1914. Index species—*D. decipiens* (Sow.). Characteristic are also *Decipia lintonensis* Ark., *Perisphinctes,* and comparatively diverse *Amoeboceras,* including *A. pseudocaelatum* Spath.

7. *Ringsteadia pseudocordata* Zone. Salfeld, 1914. Index species—*R. pseudocordata* (Blake et Hudl.). Characteristic also include *Ringsteadia, R. anglica* Salf., *R. frequens* Salf., and *Microbiplices;* late *Prionodoceras, P. marstonense* Spath, and *P. serratum* (Sow.).

Except for the Transversarium Zone, the above zonal standard was based on sections of England and Normandy. The relatively stable Early Oxfordian basins permitted application of this zonation to practically all of Europe, northern Asia, and

North America. Beginning with the Middle Oxfordian, faunal differentiation in separate basins becomes ever more pronounced. This resulted in the compilation of a parallel zonal scheme for the Middle and Upper Oxfordian in the Submediterranean Province, which was initiated by Oppel (1863). The present version of this scheme is presented in Figure 11. A parallel zonal scheme was also required for boreal and, partly, subboreal basins (including Scotland), since Perisphinctidae are practically absent in these basins. A scale for the western Arctic was worked out by P. Sykes (Sykes and Surlyk, 1976), and subsequently presented in greater detail by R. Sykes and Callomon (1979) (Figure 11). This scale is applicable mainly to basins of the northern USSR, western Siberia, the Volga and Oka Basins, the Caspian area, and Mangyshlak. Some changes, however, had to be introduced in the lower zone of the Upper Oxfordian and in the uppermost Oxfordian.

SOVIET UNION

The Oxfordian is rather widespread and mainly marine (Fig. 12). The most extensive marine facies is on the Russian Platform.

Russian Platform

On the central parts of the platform, the Oxfordian consists of clay; in the west and northwest (Byelorussia, Lithuania), marl and limestone are also common; in the north (Pechora Synclinorium) are silt and oolitic carbonate sandstone; in the south (northwestern margin of Donets Basin), the Upper Oxfordian is dominated by Nerinean limestone.

The central Russian Platform, primarily the Moscow area, and the Oka and Upper Volga Basins are of major stratigraphic significance (Nitikin, 1881, 1885; Lahusen, 1883; Ilovaisky, 1903; Smorodina, 1926; Sasonov, 1957). The Oxfordian is rather clearly divisible into two parts (Krymholts, 1972b). The lower part (3–20 m) is made up of gray to dark gray clay, is sometimes marly, and was traditionally assigned to the Lower Oxfordian (*Cordatum* Beds). It has become obvious that the stratigraphic range of this member is much greater and covers both the Lower and Middle Oxfordian. The base of the Oxford Clay in the Oka River yields abundant *Cardioceras (Scarburgiceras)* spp., among them *C. (Sc.) praecordatum* Douv., as well as *Quenstedtoceras (Pavloviceras) pavlovi* (Douv.). This part of the section is clearly coeval with the entire Mariae Zone. In the extreme northeast (Pechora Basin, Adz'va River) and in the southeast (Caspian Depression, Berdyanka River, and Mangyshlak), the base of the Oxfordian is dominated by *Quenstedtoceras mariae* and related forms, as well as by *Q. (Pavloviceras).*

Higher Lower Oxfordian is characterized by diverse *Cardioceras.* Possibly, all standard subzones of the Cordatum Standard Zone can be distinguished. At any rate, the associations of *Cardioceras* s.s., including *C. cordatum* (Sow.) (Lahusen, 1883, Pl. 5, Fig. 34; Borisyak, 1908, Pl. 1, Figs. 8–9), together with *Pachycardioceras,* and of *Cardioceras* s.s. with *Scoticardioceras* higher

---

*Some authors (e.g., Arkell, 1956; Zeiss, 1957; Knyazev, 1975) consider the subzones of the Cordatum Zone as independent zones.

Stage	EUROPEAN STANDARD		RUSSIAN PLATFORM	N. CAUCASUS	KIGITANGTAU RANGE	WEST SIBERIA	SIBERIAN PLATFORM	NORTH-EAST	FAR EAST
	Zones	Subzones	Zone & Subzone	Beds	Beds				
U	PSEUDO-CORDATA		Amoeboceras ravni (2-14 m)	(700 m) (300-500 m)	(350-400 m)	(60-150 m) R. pseudo-cordata Zone / A. ravni Zone	(6-10 - 140 m) A. ravni Zone	(800-1300 m)	(200-400 m)
	DECIPIENS		A. serratum (Black clay)	Limestones, dolomites	P. cautisnigrae	Amoeboceras Beds	Amoeboceras Beds	Amoeboceras & Buchia kirghisensis Beds	Dichotomosphinctes & Buchia concentrica Beds
	CAUTISNIGRAE		A. alternoides — alternoides / ilovaiskii		P. bifurcatus		A. alternoide Zone		
M	TRANSVERSARIUM	SCHILLI	C. tenuiserratum — tenuiserratum (3-20 m)	Iron Formation (upper) P. plicatilis	P. plicatilis & transversarium	Cardioceras tenuiserratum Zone		Siltstones, sandstones, argillites	Argillites, sandstones
		PARANDIERI	— zenaidae						
	PLICATILIS	ANTECEDENS	C. densiplicatum — densiplicatum (350-400 m)	Limestones, dolomites	Euaspid. perarmatum	C. densiplicatum Zone	Plasmatoceras Beds		
		VERTEBRALE	— popilaniense (Grey clay)						
	CORDATUM	CORDATUM	CORDATUM	Limstones, marls, clays C. cordatum	Kugitang Formation (upper): Limestones, dolomites C. cordatum	Cardioceras s.s. Beds	C. cordatum Zone / C. percaelatum Zone	Cardioceras Scarburgiceras Beds	Praebuchia lata
		PERCAELATUM					C. gloriosum Z. gloriosum Beds / praecordatum Beds		Scarburgiceras-Praebuchia impressae Bed
		BUKOWSKII				Scurburgiceras Beds	C. obliteratum Zone		
L	MARIAE	PRAECORDATUM	MARIAE						
		SCARBURGENSE							

Figure 12. The Oxfordian of the major regions of the U.S.S.R.

up in the section, indicate the Percaelatum (=*costidardia*) and Cordatum Subzones. However, species ranges and some subzonal boundaries have to be determined more precisely.

Much more definite is the subdivision of the Middle Oxfordian. In excellent sections on the Unzha River near the town of Makarjev, described by Nikitin (1884), the following biostratigraphic units are distinguished. (1) *Cardioceras densiplicatum* Zone: (a) lower part with *C.* (*Subvertebriceras*) *densiplicatum* Boden, *C.* (*Vertebriceras*), and abundant *C.* (*Plasmatoceras*) *popilanense* Boden (*popilanense* Subzone); (b) upper part dominated by *C. densiplicatum* Boden, *C.* (*Plasmatoceras*) *tenuicostatum* (Nik.), the first *Cawtoniceras*, and *Maltoniceras* appear (*densiplicatum* Subzone). (2) *Cardioceras tenuiserratum* Zone: (a) lower part characteristically with *C.* (*Subvertebriceras*) *zenaidae* Ilov. and *C.* (*Plasmatoceras*) *tenuicostatum* (Nik.) (*zenaidae* Subzone); (b) upper part dominated by *C.* (*Miticardioceras*) spp., including *C.* (*M.*) *tenuiserratum* (Opp.) (*tenuisseratum* Subzone).

Despite the small thickness of these beds (3.5 m), they are traced over extensive areas and easily distinguished in sections along the Oka River, vicinity of Ryazan', in Pechora Basin (Pizhma River), Caspian area (Berdyanka River), and in Mangyshlak. In all these areas, the faunal assemblages of certain zones and subzones of the Middle Oxfordian remain unchanged.

The Upper Oxfordian on the central Russian Platform consists of black and dark gray clay (2 to 7 m; rarely, 14 m) increasing in the Pechora Basin to as much as 25 to 30 m. At the Unzha River, the base of this member has a characteristic horizon of bituminous shale (0.2 m).

In the lower part of the section, *Amoeboceras alternoides* Nik. predominates (neotype: Nitikin, 1916, Pl. 1, Fig. 1). The *A. alternoides* Zone is strictly coeval to the Glosense Zone in the Boreal Standard scale of R. Sykes and Callomon. It is clearly divisible into two units: *A. ilovaiskii* Subzone below, dominated by *Amoeboceras ilovaiskii* (M. Sok.) known, for example, from the oil shale on the Unzha River; and the *A. alternoides* Subzone, above. Resting on top are beds dominated by the *Amoeboceras* (*Prionodoceras*) of the *serratum* (Sow.) group. *Amoeboceras alternans* (Buch) occurs in the upper subzone of the *A. alternoides* Zone, and in the lower part of the *A. serratum* Zone.

The subdivision of the higher Oxfordian is less definite, yielding *Amoeboceras leucum* Spath (=*C.* cf. *bauhini* Opp. of Ilovaisky, 1903, Pl. 11, Fig. 2), *A. freboldi* Spath, *A. tuberculatoalternans* (Nik.), and *Ringsteadian cuneata* (Trd). The species ranges in general correspond to the Regulare and Rosenkrantzi Standard Zones. However, the ammonite ranges in this section need to be worked out more precisely. Significantly, Gerasimov has noted that uppermost Oxfordian gray and dark gray clays, in places glauconitic, rest with erosional surfaces on older Upper Oxfordian in the Moscow, Kostroma, and Yaroslavl areas (Krymholts, 1972b). Mesezhnikov established similar relations in the Ryazan area. The available data indicate that this member in some cases rests directly on the Serratum Zone (Kuz'minskoe near Ryazan), and in other cases overlies somewhat higher beds with *Amoeboceras* cf. *freboldi* Spath. Although Upper Oxfordian

is complete on the central Russian Platform, its uppermost part needs more precise zonation.

The Alternoides and Serratum Standard Zones are extremely widespread in the European part of the USSR and in western Kazakhstan. In the extreme northeast of the Russian Platform, Pechora Basin, as well as in Novaya Zemlya, and in northern western and eastern Siberia, the Serratum Zone is followed by the *Amoeboceras ravni* Zone (Mesezhnikov, 1967).

Mediterranean Geosynclinal Belt

Oxfordian occurs in the Carpathians, Crimea, Caucasus, Turkmenia, Uzbekistan, and Tadzhikistan (the Pamirs). In the northern Caucasus (Daghestan-Baksan), the Oxfordian (700 m) makes up most of the upper Iron Formation. Below, it consists of limestone, sometimes alternating with clay and marl; above, of dolomite, locally dominating. The lower boundary of the Oxfordian is unknown or dubious here because *Vertumniceras mariae* (Orb.) and *Quenstedtoceras* (*Pavloviceras*) *pavlovi* (Douv.) are recorded (Beznosov, 1973) from the underlying, allegedly Upper Callovian, beds.

Rare ammonite finds indicate three local biostratigraphic units in the Oxfordian:

1. Below, Beds with *Cardioceras cordatum*, dated as Lower and lower Middle (Vertebrale Subzone) Oxfordian, also yield *Cardioceras* (*Scoticardioceras*) *excavatum* (Sow.), *C.* (*Vertebriceras*) *vertebrale* (Sow.), *C.* (*Plasmatoceras*) *tenuicostatum* (Nik.), *Vertumniceras nikitinianum* (Lah.), *Peltoceras eugenii* (Rasp.), *Parapeltoceras arduenense* (Orb.), and *Campilytes delmontanum* (Opp.). The remainder of the Middle Oxfordian is represented by:

2. Beds with *Arisphinctes plicatilis*, which also yield *A. lucingensis* (Favre), *Perisphinctes warthae* Buk., *Dichotomosphinctes antecedens* Salf., *Karanaosphinctes cothillensis* Ark., and *Amoeboceras ilovaiskii* M. Sok.

The Upper Oxfordian may be named beds with *Perisphinctes cautisnigrae*, which, besides this index species, also yield *P. falcula* Rouch., *Divisosphinctes bifurcatus* (Qu.), and *Euaspidoceras perarmatum* (Sow.). Ammonites of the upper two Oxfordian Standard Zones have not been found, but these levels contain in places numerous corals and brachiopods.

On the *Turan Plate*, southwestern Gissar, the Oxfordian is represented most completely at Kugitang; it consists of limestone and dolomite of the upper Kugitang and lower Guardak Formations (350–400 m). The presence of *Cardioceras* (*Scarburgiceras*) *praecordatum* (Douv.), *C.* (*S.*) *lahuseni* Maire, and *C.* (*C.*) *cordatum* (Sow.) indicates the Mariae and Cordatum Standard Zones; whereas finds of *Euaspidoceras perarmatum*, *Perisphinctes bifurcatus* (Qu.), and *P. wartae* Buk. are evidence for the presence of Middle and lower Upper Oxfordian. The Tyubetan section, 30 km northwest of Kugitang, has yielded *Gregoryceras* ex gr. *transversarium* (Qu.), *Perisphinctes plicatilis* (Sow.), and other Middle Oxfordian forms (Krymholts, 1972b; Resolutions, 1977).

Western Siberia Plate

The Oxfordian of Siberia (60–150 m) is relatively complete, despite numerous erosional intervals in the Late Oxfordian. In western Siberia (Mesezhnikov, 1978), Oxfordian deposits consist of marine mudstone, less frequently siltstone and sandstone, assigned to the Abalak, Mary'yanovka, and Vasyugan Formations. In the southeast, marine deposits are successively replaced by coastal continental deposits of the Naunak Formation and continental variegated siltstone of the Tyazhin Formation. The Oxfordian ammonite assemblages of western Siberia are zoned as in northern Middle Siberia (Knyazev, 1975; Mesezhnikov, *in* Strat. Jur Syst., 1976) and have been worked out recently (Mesezhnikov and others, 1984).

LOWER OXFORDIAN

1. Beds with Scarburgiceras. With *Cardioceras* (*Scarburgiceras*) cf. and ex gr. *alphacordatum* Spath, *C.* (*S.*) cf. *praecordatum* R. Douv., and *C.* (*S.*) ex gr. *scarburgense* (Young et Bird); corresponding to the *obliteratum* and *gloriosum* zones of Knyazev (1975).

2. Beds with *Cardioceras* s.s. With *C.* (*C.*) cf. and ex gr. *cordatum* (Sow.), and *C.* (*C.*) *percaelatum* Pavl., *C.* (*C.*) spp.

MIDDLE OXFORDIAN

3. *Cardoiceras densiplicatum* Zone. Characterized by *C.* (*Subvertebriceras*) *zenaidae* Ilov., *C.* (*Plasmatoceras*) cf. *tenuicostatum* (Nik.), *C.* (*P.*) *salymense* Popl., and *C.* (*Vertebriceras*) sp.

4. *Cardioceras tenuiserratum* Zone. With *C.* (*iticardioceras*) cf. *tenuiserratum* (Oppel) and *C.* (*M.*) sp.

The Upper Oxfordian contains abundant small, unidentified *Amoeboceras* below; in the uppermost beds, it has *Amoeboceras freboldi* Spath and *A.* cf. *leucum* Spath, which indicate the *Amoeboceras ravni* Zone. In the Subpolar Urals, the *Ringsteadia pseudocordata* Zone corresponds to these beds and contains *Ringsteadia marstonensis* Salf., *R. frequens* Salf., and *R.* aff. *frequens* Salf., whereas Cardioceratidae are absent.

Siberian Platform

In the north, the fossiliferous Oxfordian is known from eastern Taimyr (Basov and others, 1963; Kaplan and others, 1974; Knyazev, 1975) and the Anabar River (Knyazev, 1975); it consists mainly of sand and sandstone (ranging from 6 to 10 m at Anabar to 140 m at Chernokhrebetnaya River, eastern Taimyr).

Knyazev (1975) worked out a detailed local zonation for the Lower Oxfordian:

1. *Cardioceras obliteratum* Zone. *Vertumniceras nikitiniatum* (Lah.), *Quenstedtoceras* (*Pavloviceras*) aff. *roberti* (Buckm.), *Cardioceras* (*Scarburgiceras*) *obliteratum* Knyaseve. Mariae Standard Zone, Scarburgense Subzone.

2. *Cardioceras gloriosum* Zone. Below, the beds with

C. praecordatum, yielding the *C.* (*Scarburgiceras*) *martini* Reeside and *C.* (*S.*) *gloriosum* Ark.; and above, beds with *C. gloriosum,* also with *Goliathiceras* (*Korythoceras*). Mariae Standard Zone, Praecordatum Subzone, and Cordatum Zone, Bukowskii Subzone.

3. *Cardioceras percaelatum* Zone. Diverse *Cardioceras* s.s. (*percaelatum* Pavl., *mountjoyi* Freb., etc.), first *C.* (*Vertebriceras*), and *Goliathiceras* (*Pachycardioceras*) spp.

4. *Cardioceras cordatum* Zone. *Cardioceras* s.s., *C.* (*Scoticardioceras*) *excatum* (Sow.), and *C.* (*Vertebriceras*) *vertebrale* (Sow.). Note that local zones (3) and (4) correspond to the standard subzones, Cordatum Standard Zone.

The Middle Oxfordian in northern Siberia is characterized by abundant *Cardioceras* (*Plasmatoceras*) *tenuicostatum* (Nik.), found together with *C.* (*Vertebriceras*) spp., *C.* (*Scoticardioceras*) *excavatum* (Sow.), and *C.* (*Subvertebriceras*) *densiplicatum* Boden (Knyazev, 1975). These beds correspond to the *Cardioceras densiplicatum* Zone. Higher horizons may be eroded here, but in northeastern Taimyr, at the Chernokhrebetnaya River, is a 4-m-thick sandstone member lacking ammonites, which could be upper Middle Oxfordian (Kaplan and others, 1974).

At the base of the Upper Oxfordian is the *Amoeboceras alternoides* Zone. Above are thick (75 m) strata, with only small *Amoeboceras,* earlier determined as *A. alternans* (Buch). The Oxfordian section in northern Siberia is crowned by the *Amoeboceras ravni* Zone, which contains also *A. leucum* Spath, *A. schulginae* Mesezhn., *A. pectinatum* Mesezhn., *A. regulare* Spath, and *A. freboldi* Spath (Mesezhnikov, 1967), as well as *A. marstonense* Spath. Considering that the *Amoeboceras ravni* and *Pictonia involuta* Zones are conformably superposed in southern Taimyr, the *A. ravni* Zone presumably corresponds to the Regulare and Rosenkrantzi Standard Zones of the Boreal Oxfordian.

Northeast

The Oxfordian is rather widespread (Paraketsev and Polubotko, 1970). The lower boundary may be placed conventionally at the appearance of rare *Praebuchia kirghisensis* (Sok.), and in places at accumulations of *Meleagrinella* ex gr. *ovalis* (Phill.), which are highly characteristic for the northern Okhotsk area. The upper half of the stage is characterized by the first true *Buchia, B. concentrica* (Sow.). The upper stage boundary is drawn at the base of the beds with *Buchia concentrica* (Sow.) and *Amoeboceras kitchini* (Salf.).

The most complete marine Oxfordian is known from the In'yali-Debin and Polousny structural facies areas, where they consist of sandy siltstone and mudstone (800–1,300 m). The lower part of this sequence yields single *Quenstedtoceras* sp. indet. in the Nera, Moma, and Omslovka Basins; the middle part, *Cardioceras* (*C.*) *percaelatum* Pavl., *C.* (*C.*) *cordatum* (Sow.), and *C.* (*Scoticardioceras*) *excavatum* (Sow.) in the Charky Basin and on the Yana River; and the upper part, *Amoeboceras* aff. *alternans* (Buch) in the Charky Basin and Polousny Range and *A.* aff. *alternoides* (Nik.) in the Lyglykhtakh Basin. All Oxfordian substages are therefore developed. Southward, in the northern Okhotsk areas, Oxfordian facies shallows, with sandstones, in places with littoral brachiopods and bivalves without ammonites. In most of the Omulev and Alazeya-Oloi structural facies areas, the Oxfordian facies is shallow volcanogenic-terrigenous, and less commonly, volcanogenic.

Far East

The fossiliferous Oxfordian is known from only a few sites. Sandstones (400 m), with *Cardioceras (Scarburgiceras) praecordatum* Douv. and *C. (S.)* cf. *gloriosum* Ark. from the west coast of Tugur Bay (Sey and Kalacheva, 1977), are of the Mariae Zone and lower Cordatum Standard Zone. Higher horizons contain (Sey and Kalacheva, 1985) *Perisphinctes (Dichotomosphinctes)* cf. *muhlbachi* Hyatt and *Cardioceras (Maltoniceras) aff. schellwieni* Boden, and are placed in the Middle Oxfordian. The beds with *Praebuchia lata* contain ammonites apparently mainly of the Middle Oxfordian. Upper Oxfordian (beds with *Buchia concen-trica*) are also characterized by *Perisphinctes (Dichotomosphinctes) kiritaniensis* Sato.

SUMMARY

Over most of the USSR, although the lower and upper boundaries of the Oxfordian are rather well known and the zonation is outlined, in most areas some zonal boundaries and correlations with the standard scale need more study. In northern Siberia and the northern European part of USSR, these detailed studies should at present be directed mainly at the Middle and part of the Upper Oxfordian, as well as at the more precise definition of zonal units. On the central Russian Platform, the exact stratigraphic ranges of certain species need to be determined and biostratigraphic boundaries defined. In the northern Caucasus and Turkmenia, the lower boundary of the Oxfordian must be identified, and the Middle and Upper Oxfordian zonation needs to be made more precise.

KIMMERIDGIAN
M. S. Mesezhnikov

HISTORY AND STANDARD ZONES

The Kimmeridgian was established by d'Orbigny in 1850 (d'Orbigny, 1842–1851), between the Coral and Portlandian Stages, and named after the village of Kimmeridge in Dorset, England.

The Kimmeridge Clay in Dorset was named by d'Orbigny as the type section so that the position of the Kimmeridgian stratotype is quite reliably determined, e.g., the cliffs of Kimmeridge Bay, between Brandy and Chapman Pool Bays (Arkell, 1947; Cox, 1979). The stage boundaries remained undefined. The lower boundary was rendered more precise by Oppel (1856–1858) after eliminating the Coral Stage, part of which was included by him into the Kimmeridgian (see Oxfordian). Salfeld (1913, 1914) finally determined the boundary at the base of his *Pictonia baylei* Zone.

Much more difficult is the upper stage boundary. D'Orbigny, when establishing the Portlandian stage, included among its characteristic ammonites *Ammonites [Gravesia] gravesiana* Orb. and *Am. [Pavlovia] rotundus* Sow., which in Bologne, France, occur above clays assigned to the Kimmeridgian, and in England, in the middle and upper Kimmeridge Clay. Since the latter was indicated by d'Orbigny as the Kimmeridgian type formation, English geologists placed the upper Kimmeridgian boundary at the top of the Kimmeridge Clay, whereas all other European stratigraphers, particularly the French and Russians, were drawing this boundary at the base of the beds with *Gravesia*. This problem is discussed in more detail below, in the section on the Tithonian (Volgian). Here it is only emphasized that the solution of this problem cannot be found by deciding whether d'Orbigny used a "faunal" or "formational" stage definition. It is much more promising to determine where certain boundaries should be drawn. For example, the top of the Kimmeridge Clay creates a paradoxical situation, where throughout Eurasia (except England) and North Africa, the following succession should be established: Lower Kimmeridgian–Lower Tithonian–Middle Tithonian, etc., or Lower Kimmeridgian–Lower Volgian substage–Middle Volgian substage, etc. In that case, the Middle and Upper Kimmeridgian would occur only in England, but elsewhere be represented by the Lower Volgian/Tithonian. Of course, it is highly inadvisable to draw such a boundary in the first place, and an official confirmation of the "continental" interpretation of the upper Kimmeridgian boundary is obviously needed. The Second Colloquium on the Jurassic System, held in Luxembourg in 1967, recommended that this boundary be drawn at the base of the Gravesia Zone (Resolution, 1970).

In addition to historical difficulties involved in drawing the upper Kimmeridgian boundary, there are difficulties due to the lack of evidence and resulting from the indistinct zonation of the middle Kimmeridge Clay. It is noteworthy that the thick section of the Kimmeridge Clay is, at least for the Boreal Realm, a unique example of a complete Kimmeridgian-Volgian transition. The uppermost Kimmeridgian has now also been identified in Aquitain, by an association of *Aulacostephenus* ex gr. *autissiodorensis* with *Gravesia* (Hantzpergue and Lafairie, 1983). In other sections, some beds are probably missing, so that the Kimmeridgian and Volgian ammonite faunas become clearly distinct. In England, Ziegler (1964), and, particularly, Cox (1979) and Cox and Gallois (1977), found typical Kimmeridgian (*Aulacostephanus volgensis*) and Volgian (*Gravesia*) ammonites together. On the other hand, the revised zonation for the middle Kimmeridge Clay by Cope (1967) eliminated the *gravesiana* and *gigas* Zones of Salfeld. Thus, until recently, the Kimmeridgian/Volgian boundary was drawn between the Autissiodorensis and Elegans Standard Zones. Lately, Cox again distinguished a zone based on *Gravesia* spp., but at the expense of the upper Autissiodorensis Zone, characterized by co-occurrence of *Gravesia* and *Aulacostephanus.** If this suggestion is followed, the stage boundary in the stratotype is lowered by 27 m. However, two other facts are more important. First, the *Gravesia* spp. Zone of Cox does not correspond to the *gravesiana* and *gigas* zones of Salfeld, but to a lower level. Therefore, there is no isochronous marker horizon with *Gravesia,* traceable throughout Europe and even in western Siberia (Subpolar Urals). Second, *Aulacostephanus* and *Gravesia* are not found together except in Dorset and Aquitain, so that the newly proposed upper boundary of the Kimmeridgian cannot be traced. The position of the upper stage boundary should therefore probably remain as previously defined, and confirmed by the International Colloquium in 1967 (Resolution, 1970). But in detailed correlations, it should be noted that outside England and the southwestern Paris Basin, the uppermost, Autissiodorensis, Zone is often missing.

The type section of the Kimmeridgian within the mentioned boundaries consists of gray and black clay, bituminous in the upper part and in places carbonate with nodular interbeds, and marl and clayey limestone partings. Ziegler (1964) distinguished the following units within this monotonous sequence at Ringstead.

1. Black, soft, fragmented clay (2.5 m) with a marl interbed in the central part, yielding *Pictonia* spp., *Prorasenia.*

2. Black, thin-bedded, and fragmented clay with pyrite nodules (12 m), *Rasenia* spp., and *Amoeboceras* (*Amoebites*) spp.

3. Black, commonly thin-bedded, sometimes hard calcareous clay (40 m); *Aulacostephanus* (*Aulacostephanoides*) *mutabilis* (Sow.) et spp. and *Aspidoceras.*

4. Dark gray, soft, and fragementary clay (40 m) with shale interbeds and several nodule horizons; *Aulacostephanus* s.s., *A.* (*Aulacostephanoceras*), *Amoeboceras* (*Nannocardioceras*), *Sutneria,* and *Aspidoceras.* Some 15 km east of Ringstead on the Kimmeridge Bay coast, higher beds occur.

5. Shale (15 m) with limestone interbeds; *Aulacostephanus* (*Aulacostephanoceras*), *Amoeboceras,* and *Aspidoceras.*

6. Shale (65 m) with limestone interbeds; *Aulacostephanus* (*Aulacostephanoceras*) *autissiodorensis* (Cotteau), *A.* spp., *Amoeboceras,* and *Propectinatites.*

Note that, for English geologists, the Kimmeridgian with the above-mentioned boundaries means only the Lower Kimmeridgian (Arkell, 1956), whereas for other European and also Soviet geologists, the sequence is as given below:

Lower Kimmeridgian (s. gallico)

1. *Pictonia baylei* Zone. Salfeld, 1913. Index species—*P.* (*Pictonia*) *baylei* Salf. Characteristic also are *Pictonia normandiana* (Tornq.), *Prorasenia quenstedti* Schind., and *Triozites.*

2. *Rasenia cymodoce* Zone. Douville, 1881. Index species— *R. cymodoce* (Orb.). Characteristic also are *Rasenia involuta* Spath, *E. evoluta* Spath, *Zonovia uralensis* (Orb.), *Prorasenia triplicata* Spath, and *Amoeboceras* (*Amoebites*) spp. Birkelund (1978) distinguished four faunal horizons: (a) horizon with *Rasenia* cf. *cymodoce* (Orb.) and *Prorasenia* cf. *triplicata* Spath; (b) horizon with *Rasenia involuta* Spath and *R.* (*Eurasenia*) spp.; (c) horizon with *Rasenia evoluta* Spath and *Zonovia uralensis* (Orb.); and (d) horizon with *Rasenia* (*Semirasenia*) *askepta* Ziegler and *R.* (*Rasenioides*) *lepudula* (Opp.).

Upper Kimmeridgian

3. *Aulacostephanus mutabilis* Zone. Salfeld, 1913. Index species—*A. mutabilis* (Sow.). Characteristic also are *Aulacostephanus linealis* (Qu.), *A.* (*Aulacostephanites*) *eulepidus* Schneid., *A.* (*A.*) cf. *sosvaensis* (Sason.), and *Aspidoceras* (*Orthaspidoceras*) spp.

4. *Aulacostephanus eudoxus* Zone. Oppel, 1885. Index species—*A.* (*Aulocostephanoceras*) *eudoxus* (Orb.). Characteristic also are *A.* (*A.*) *pseudomutabilis* (Lor.), *A.* (*A.*) *volgensis* (Vischn.), *Amoeboceras* (*Nannocardioceras*) *krauzei* (Salf.), *Aspidoceras,* and *Sutneria eumela* (Qu.).

5. *Aulacostephanus autissiodorensis* Zone. Ziegler, 1961.† Index species—*A.* (*Aulacostephanoceras*) *autissiodorensis* (Cotteau). Characteristic also are *A.* (*Aulocostephanoceras*) *volgensis* (Vischn.), *A.* (*A.*) *undorae* (Pavl.), *A.* (*A.*) *jasonoides* Pavl., *Amoeboceras* (*Nannocardioceras*), and *Propectinatites websteri* Cope.

Faunal differentiation since the Middle Oxfordian continued through the Kimmeridgian, when Boreal and Tethyan ammonites formed quite different associations, leading to a separate zonal scale for southern Europe (and southern USSR) (Fig. 13). The top of the Kimmeridgian is clearly traced along the base of beds with *Gravesia* (with the above reserves). The base of the Autissiodorensis Zone is coeval with that of the Beckeri Zone; both are underlain by the Eudoxus Zone. The occurrence of *Aulacostephanoides* and *Aulacostephanites* in the Acanthicum Zone, and *Orthaspidoceras* in the Mutabilis Zone also allows a reliable

---

*In Hantzpergue and Laufaurie's scheme (1983), proposed for Aquitain, the *Gravesia irius* Subzone of the Autissiodorensis Zone probably corresponds to this zone. Thus the position of the upper Kimmeridgian boundary remains unchanged.

---

†*Autissiodorensis* and *eudoxus* zones were distinguished by Ziegler (1961) instead of *pseudomutabilis* Zone by Salfeld.

STAGE		SUBBOREAL	SUBMEDITERR. PROVINCE
KIMMERIDGIAN	U	AUTISSIODORENSIS	BECKERI
		EUDOXUS	EUDOXUS
		MUTABILIS	ACANTHICUM
	L	CYMODOCE	DIVISUM
			HYPSELOCYCLUM
		BAYLEI	PLATYNOTA

Figure 13. The Kimmeridgian of the Subboreal and Submediterranian Provinces.

correlation of these zones. Correlation of the Lower Kimmeridgian zone in northern and southern Europe is more arbitrary.

In northernmost areas of the Boreal Realm, only Cardioceratidae are found in Kimmeridgian deposits. The *Amoeboceras kitchini* Zone (Mesezhnikov, 1968) is Lower Kimmeridgian, whereas beds with *Euprinoceras* and *Haplocardioceras* (Mesezhnikov, 1976) correspond to two upper zones of the Upper Kimmeridgian. The stratigraphic position of the Mutabilis Zone in the *Cardioceras* facies of the Arctic Kimmeridgian is not yet resolved.

SOVIET UNION

Kimmeridgian deposits are less widespread than Oxfordian ones and commonly with smaller thickness (Fig. 14). But, except for central Asia and some areas of the Caucasus, they are normally marine. The Kimmeridgian is a part of the thick Upper Jurassic coal measures only in the east of the Siberian Platform. Limited occurrence of the Kimmeridgian can, to a large extent, be accounted for by Early Volgian erosion; in areas with complete Lower Volgian (Volga area at Ul'yanovsk, eastern slope of the Subpolar Urals, Lower Yenisei), the Kimmeridgian is also present with rather thick, continuous strata.

Russian Platform

The Kimmeridgian is mostly made up of clay and carbonaceous clay, but sometimes, especially its upper substage, it is represented only by a thin interbed of phosphorite nodules (Gerasimov, 1978). Only in the west of the platform (Dobruja Trough, L'vov Depression) is the stage relatively thick and mostly in

carbonate facies. The Lower Kimmeridgian on the central Russian Platform consists of gray glauconitic strata, in places calcareous clay (20–25 m), but commonly it does not exceed 5 to 7 m. These beds are characterized by *Amoeboceras (Amoebites) kitchini* (Salf.), *A. (A.) cricki* (Salf.), *Prorasenia stephanoides* (Opp.), *Desmosphinctes praelarei* (Favre), and *Rasenia (Eurasenia) trimera* (Opp.). Subdivision and detailed correlation within the zonal standard are, as yet, impossible (Fig. 14). The Upper Kimmeridgian is most fully developed on the eastern Russian Platform, where it consists of gray calcareous clay and clayey marls. Three biostratigraphic units are distinguished:

1. *Aspidoceras acanthicum* Zone. Pavlow (1886). With diverse *Aspidoceras*. Presently, exposures are below the water table of the Ul'yanovsk Reservoir.

2. *Aulacostephanus eudoxus* Zone. With *Aspidoceras* spp., *Physodoceras liparum* (Opp.), *Aulacostephanus (Aulacostephanoceras) eudoxus* (Orb.), *A. (A.) volgensis* (Vischn.), *A. (A.) jasonoides* (Pavl.), *Amoeboceras (Nannocardioceras) subtilicostatum* (Pavl.), and *Sutneia* sp.

3. *Aulacostephanus autissiodorensis* Zone. (a) Below, with *A. (Aulacostephanoceras) autissiodorensis* (Cotteau), *A. (A.) volgensis* (Vischn.), *A. (A.) kirghisensis* (Orb.), *Amoeboceras (Nannocardioceras) subtilicostatum* (Pavl.), and *Sutneria* cf. *subeumela* (Schneid.)–*Sutneria subeumela* Subzone (Geyer, 1969). (b) Above, with *A. (A.) autissiodorensis* (Cotteau), *A. (A.) kirghisensis* (Orb.), *A. (A.) undorae* (Pavl.), *Virgataxioceras fallax* (Ilov.), *Sutneria* sp., and *Glochiceras* spp.–*Virgataxioceras fallax* Subzone (Mikhailov, 1962b).

Recently, equivalents of the Mutabilis and Eudoxus Standard Zones were found in southwestern Lithuania and the south Kaliningrad area (Rotkite, 1978).

Mediterranean Geosynclinal Belt

In the Central northern Caucasus (Fiagdon-Assa), the Kimmeridgian is represented by the lower Balta Formation, limestones with sandstone interbeds (~110 m). Probably most widespread is the Lower Kimmeridgian with *Ataxioceras* and *Lithacoceras*. Abundant ammonites in the Gizel'don River section (Sakharov, Khimshiashvili, 1967) indicate Lower and lower Upper Kimmeridgian. A 3-m-thick unit within limestones yields abundant ammonites, including *Idoceras planula* (Hehl), *I. balderum* (Opp.), *I. malletianus* (Font.), *Rasenia* aff. *thermarum* (Opp.), *R.* cf. *striolaris* Opp., *Glochiceras fialar*, *Aulacostephanus (Xenostephanoides) ebrayoides* Ark. et Ca., *Aspidoceras longispinum* (Gem.), and *A. acanthicum* (Opp.). Since the early Tithonian *Lithacoceras ulmense* (Opp.) was recorded from the thick overlying dolomites, we believe higher Kimmeridgian beds are presumably also present in the Gizel'don River section.

On the Turan Plate, the lower, larger part of the Gaurdak Formation (~1,000 m) is conventionally dated as Kimmeridgian. It consists mainly of anhydrite with limestone and dolomite interbeds, and of rocksalt layers.

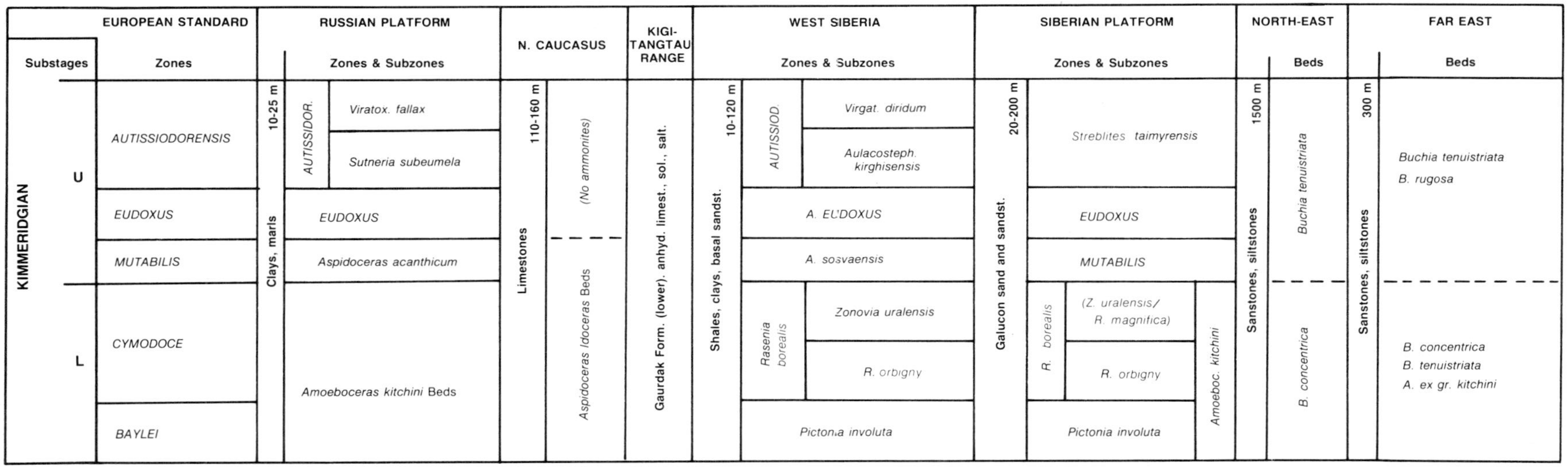

48

Figure 14. The Kimmeridgian in the major regions of the U.S.S.R.

Western Siberia Plate

Marine Kimmeridgian is ubiquitously present, mainly with clay and mudstone, locally with silt and siltstone. The coastal facies is calcareous, with glauconitic siltstone and sandstone. Within the closed part of western Siberia, the Kimmeridgian comprises the Georgievsky, and, in the west, the upper Abalak Formations (10–40 m); on the eastern slope of the Subpolar Urals, it comprises the Lopsiya Formation. Along the periphery of western Siberia, the thickness of the Kimmeridgian attains 80 to 120 m on the eastern slope of the Subpolar Urals, and 210 m at the Lower Yenisei. The most detailed zonation (five zones) was accomplished on the eastern slope of the Subpolar Urals.

LOWER KIMMERIDGIAN

1. *Pictonia involuta* Zone. *P. involuta* Mesezhn., *P.* spp., *Prorasenia hardyi* Spath, *P. bowerbankii* Spath, *Rasenia orbignyi* (Tornq.), *R. suburalensis* Spath, *Amoeboceras* (*Amoebites*) *kitchini* (Salf.), and *A.* (*A.*) *pinguiforme* Mesezhn.

2. *Reasenia borealis* Zone. *R. borealis* Spath, *R. coronata* Mesezhn., *Zonovia uralensis* (Orb.), *Z. subelshamensis* Mesezhn, and *Amoeboceras* (*Amoebitis*) *kitchini* (Salf.). Below, beds with *Rasenia orbigny* (Tornqu.); above, beds with *Zonovia uralensis* (Orb.), are indicated within the zone.

UPPER KIMMERIDGIAN

3. *Aulacostephanus sosvaensis* Zone. *A.* (*Aulacostephanoides*) *sosvaensis* (Sason.), *A.* (*A.*) *attenuatus* Ziegler, *A.* (*Pararasensis*) aff. *quenstedti* (Durand), *A.* (*P.*) *biplicatus* Mesezhn., *A.* (*P.*) spp., *Zononvia* sp., and *Amoeboceras* (*Amoebites*) spp.

4. Eudoxus standard zone. *Aulacostephanus pseudomutabilis* (Lor.), *A.* (*A.*) *yo* (Orb.), *A.* (*Aulacostephanoceras*) *volgensis* (Vischn.), *A.* (*A.*) *kirghisensis* (Orb.), *Amoeboceras* (*Nannocardioceras*) sp., and *A.* (*Euprionoceras*) sp.

5. *Virgataxioceras dividuum* Zone. *V. dividuum* Mesezhn., *Aulacostephanus* (*Aulocostephanoceras*) *volgensis* (Vischn.), and *S.* (*A.*) *undorae* (Pavl.).

East of the Severnaya Sos'va Basin, in the closed part of western Siberia, Lower Kimmeridgian beds are distinguished on the basis of single ammonite finds and widespread foraminiferal assemblages, resembling the Subpolar Urals. The Upper Kimmeridgian *Aulacostephanoides* is extremely rare and confined only to the western part. However, Upper Kimmeridgian foraminiferal assemblages are traced over an extensive area, mostly in the southern half of the region. These data, and those from Volgian deposits, show that Upper Kimmeridgian is eroded over most of western Siberia, and Upper Volgian is discordant on various Upper Kimmeridgian levels.

In northeastern western Siberia and on the Lower Yenisei, where Kimmeridgian attains its maximum thickness, the Upper Kimmeridgian is characterized by the Arctic Cardioceratidae *Hoplocardioceras* and *Euprionoceras*.

Eastern Siberia

The most representative Kimmeridgian sections, at the Yenisei-Anabar interfluve, consist of sand and sandstone, locally siltstone (25–200 m). In the central Khatanga Depression (Pakhsa Peninsula) only, the reduced (11 m) Kimmeridgian is made up of clay and clayey siltstone.

In the Kheta Basin (Saks and others, 1969), the Kimmeridgian is divisible into five zones.

LOWER KIMMERIDGIAN

1. *Pictonia involuta* Zone. *P. involuta* Mesezhn., *P. ronkinae* Mesezhn., *Amoeboceras* (*Amoebites*) *spathi* Schulg., *A.* (*A.*) *pingueforme* Mesezhn., and *A.* (*A.*) *kitchini* (Salf.).

2. *Rasenia borealis* Zone. Also with *R. repentina* Mesezhn., *R. orbigny* (Tornq.), *R. coronata* Mesezhn., *R. magnifica* Mesezhn., *Zonovia* spp., *Amoeboceras* (*Amoebites*) *kitchini* (Salf.), *A.* (*A.*) *subkitchini* Spath, and *A.* (*A.*) *pulchrum* Mesezhn. et Romm. This zone (Iona) is clearly divisible into a lower level, with *Rasenia orbigny* (Tornq.), and an upper level, with *R. magnifica* Mesezhn., *R. repentina* Mesezhn., and *Zonovia* spp.

UPPER KIMMERIDGIAN

3. Mutabilis Standard Zone. *Aulacostephanus* (*Aulacostephanoides*) *mutabilis* (Sow.), *Zonovia* spp., *Amoeboceras* (*Amoebites*) *kitchini* (Salf.), and the first *Nannocardioceras* sp.

4. Eudoxus Standard Zone. Also with *Aulacostephanus* (*Aulacostephanoceras*) cf. *eudoxus* Orb., *A.* (*A.*) *pseudolinealis* Mesezhn., *Amoeboceras* (*Euprionoceras*) *kochi* Spath, *A.* (*E.*) *sokolovi* (Bodyl.), and *A.* (*Nannocardioceras*) sp.

5. *Streblites taimyrensis* Zone. With *S. taimyrensis* Mesezhn., *Amoeboceras* (*Euprionoceras*) *sokolovi* (Bodyl.), and *A.* (*Nannocardioceras*) sp.

In Taimyr and the Pakhsa Peninsula, Lower Kimmeridgian deposits lack Perisphinctidae. The entire sequence of 130 to 150 m contains only *Amoebites*, i.e., the *Amoeboceras kitchini* Zone (Mesezhnikov, 1968).

Within the Anabar-Lena confluence, the Kimmeridgian has not been found, but its former presence is attested by finds of *Amoeboceras* (*Amoebites*) in the Volgian basal conglomerate along the Molodo River (Lower Lena Basin; Bidzhiev and Mikhailov, 1965). To the south, the Kimmeridgian is part of the Chechuma coal measures.

Northeast

The Kimmeridgian is extremely widespread, thick (600–1,500 m), and is mainly composed of clay shales and siltstones with intercalated polymictic and tufogenic sandstone and tuff. Ammonites are rare and subdivision is by *Buchia* (Paraketsov and Polubotko, 1970; Zakharov, 1969). The Lower Kimmeridgian is distinguished as beds with *Buchia concentrica* (Sow.). In the Kolyma Massif and the Ol'dzhoi-Polousny Trough, *Amoeboceras* (*Amoebites*) cf. *kitchini* (Salf.) is confined to these beds. The Upper Kimmeridgian is characterized by *Buchia tenuistriata* (Lah.).

Far East

Data on Kimmeridgian are scarce. In the Torom and Uda Troughs (Sey and Kalacheva, 1977), Lower Kimmeridgian beds with *Amoeboceras* (*Amoebites*) ex gr. *kitchini* (Salf.), *Ochetoceras* sp., *Buchia concentrica* (Sow.), and *B. tenuistriata* (Lah.) can be distinguished.

SUMMARY

A refined zonation of the Lower Kimmeridgian is available only for western and eastern Siberia. The Upper Kimmeridgian zonation is applicable for a much larger area: the Volga Basin and Trans-Volga area, Pechora Basin, western and eastern Siberia, and the Baltic area. It is emphasized that Kimmeridgian zonal units in the USSR, in spite of differences in the ammonoid assemblages, can be closely correlated with the corresponding units of the European standard scale.

TITHONIAN (VOLGIAN)
M. S. Mesezhnikov

HISTORY AND STANDARD ZONES

D'Orbigny (1842–1851) distinguished the Portlandian as the uppermost stage of the Jurassic System. Differences between the indicated type section (Portland Island) and the fossil assemblage (outcrops at Bologna), graduation of marine Portlandian into fresh-water Purbeck below the Jurassic/Cretaceous boundary, and the occurrence of a markedly distinct ammonite assemblage in coeval beds of southern and eastern Europe caused doubt as to whether the Portlandian should be retained as a stage in the standard scale. Thus, for over a century, the problem of the uppermost Jurassic stage has remained the focus of attention of stratigraphers. Supra-Kimmeridgian beds in different parts of Eurasia are characterized by ammonoid associations so different that parallel stage names are still used. Even in the Oxfordian, and particularly, the Kimmeridgian, Mediterranean and Boreal faunal realms are rather distinct; yet it was possible to use single stage names, since most (if not all) zones, stages, and substage boundaries could be correlated rather reliably. Above the Kimmeridgian, detailed zonal correlation is possible only with the Tethys, or within the Boreal Basin. Detailed correlation between Tethyan and Boreal sections can be made only for the lower Tithonian and lower Volgian. Thus, it is not surprising that the stage terminology of the uppermost Jurassic is confusing and controversial. More than 20 stage names were proposed for this interval, but only the Portlandian, Tithonian, and Volgian (Nikitin, 1881) are known. Each was proposed as a standard stage. In our opinion, the requirements of a standard stage are best met by the Tithonian (Fig. 15), i.e., definition by zones; faunal characteristics of lower and upper boundaries, and—if at a system boundary—their relatively continuous traceability; more or less uniform; and within a single paleogeographic province. The Portlandian has a controversial lower boundary (see Kimmeridgian), and its upper boundary in the type locality (southern England) is well below the system boundary which lies there in the middle of the nonmarine Purbeck Beds.

The upper boundary of the Volgian is also not clearly understood, because the precise zonal correlation of the Ryazanian

Beds with the Berriassian remains unresolved. Finally, both Portlandian and Volgian are developed in the Boreal Realm, whereas the stratotype of the lower stage of the Cretaceous System, Berriassian, is in the Mediterranean area.

Compared to the Portlandian and Volgian, the Tithonian has a number of significant advantages. It is represented entirely by marine deposits, has a quite well-defined lower boundary, and despite some controversy, the upper boundary is usually drawn within a single carbonate sequence of a single faunal province. The precise zonal and substage division of the Tithonian, however, still meets significant obstacles, beginning with the stage name.

Oppel (1865) chose a mythological, not geographical, name for his Tithonian stage, defining it as the beds resting on Kimmeridgian and being overlain by lower Neocomian. Thus, the name of the stage contained no indication of its type section or type formation, and its stratigraphic range was indicated in accordance with the limited knowledge of this time. Later investigations drew the Tithonian boundaries more precisely and changed them to a certain extent.

Oppel (1856–1858) ended the Kimmeridgian with the *Am.* [*Aulacostephanus*] *eudoxus* Zone. However, some years later, Neumayr established the *Am.* [*Hybonoticeras*] *beckeri* Zone in Franconia (Neumayr, 1873), above the *eudoxus* Zone, and placed it into the uppermost Kimmeridgian.[*] That meant beds included by Oppel in the Tithonian were then placed in the Kimmeridgian. Neumayr's viewpoint became widespread among Western European geologists, and after Haug's work (1898) became universally accepted. Thus, the lower Tithonian boundary is presently drawn at the top, not the base, of the Beckeri Standard Zone (Fig. 13).

Much more complicated is the problem of the upper Tithon-

---

[*]Subsequently, Ziegler (Hölder and Ziegler, 1958; Ziegler, 1962) showed that the Beckeri Zone corresponds to the upper part of the English *Aulacostephanus pseudomutabilis* Zone (=*A. autissiodorensis* Zone of B. Ziegler), confirming Neumayr's contention that the Beckeri Zone belongs to the Kimmeridgian.

		SOUTH SPAIN (Enay & Geyssant, 1975)	SOUTH-EAST FRANCE (Enay, 1971)	FRANKONIA (Zeiss, 1966, 1975, 1977; Barthel, 1962, 1975)			NORTH CARPATIANS (Zeiss, 1977a, Kutek Wierzbowsky, 1979)
TITHONIAN	U	"Durangites", Micracanthoc. micracanthum	Berriasella chaperi, B. delphinesis	Pseudolissoceras bavaricum			Paraulacosph. transitorius
	M	Micracanthoc. ponti	Subplanitoides concorsi, Sublithac. penicillatum				Pseudovirg. scruposus
		Semiformiceras fallauxi					Semiform. fallauxi
		S. semiforme					S. semiforme
	L	Neochetoceras darwini	Franconites vimineus s.l.	Danubisphinctes palatinum			Neochetoceras darwini
				Franconites vimineus			
			Dorsoplanitoides triplicatus s.l.	Neochetoc. mucronatum	Usseliceras parvinodosum		
					D. triplicatus		
					U. tagmerheimense		
		Hybonoticeras hybonotum	H. hyobonotum, (Glochi. lithographicum)	H. hybonotum	Subplanites moernheimensis		H. hybonotum
					S. rueppellianum		
					Lithacoceras riedense		

Figure 15. The Tithonian zonations for southern and central Europe.

ian boundary. When the Tithonian was distinguished, the Valanginian was the lowermost Cretaceous stage. However, by this time, Pictet (1867) had already distinguished the Berrias Limestone with characteristic ammonoid assemblages in southeastern France; Coquand (1868) had proposed the Berriassian substage, and Renevier (1864) had raised it to stage level. Despite the fact that the Berriassian was not immediately accepted as full stage, extensive studies—primarily by French biostratigraphers (e.g., Mazenot, 1939; Le Hegarat, 1973)—finally resulted in its inclusion into the Cretaceous standard scale. However, when the Berrias Limestone was distinguished, the problem arose regarding to what system it should be assigned. In his belief that the Tithonian was crowned by the Stramberg Limestone, Pictet (1867) placed the Berriassian beds into the Neocomian, and he was followed by Coquand (1871). Toucas (1890), however, included the Berriassian in the Tithonian—a controversy that still continues. The problem of the Jurassic/Cretaceous boundary is intertwined with any discussion of the relations between the Tithonian and Volgian. It is only noted here that most specialists at the International Colloquium on the Jurassic/Cretaceous Boundary held in Lyon-Neuchatel (Resultats. . ., 1975) favored drawing the system boundary at the base of the Grandis/Jacobi Zone (Grandis s.l. Zone), which is accepted here.

The absence of a Tithonian stratotype made its subdivision rather difficult. Oppel only included characteristic Tithonian sections, i.e., Stramberk* (Czechoslovakia), Rogoznik (Poland), South Tirol (Austria), and Solenhofen (West Germany). Arkell (1956) proposed three substages and listed typical formations for each of them: Stramberk Limestone for the Upper Tithonian, Rogoznik Beds for the Middle Tithonian, and Klentnize Beds (eastern Austria and Czechoslovakia) for the Lower Tithonian. However, such widely spaced sections did not clarify the complete faunal succession and relations.† Besides, no faunal evidence could be provided in Stramberk for drawing the Tithonian/Berriassian boundary. Finally, it appeared that the sections of the Pennines (northern Carpathians) comprise different fauna from that in southeastern France, Spain, and, partly, the Franconian and Swabian Alb. Thus there are as yet no universally accepted type sections of Tithonian substages, nor is there any clear consensus about their number. The Lower and Middle Tithonian are sometimes joined into a single Danubian substage, and the Upper Tithonian distinguished as the Ardechian substage (Ardechian

---

*Stramberg, in the German transcription.

†For instance, Donze and Enay (1961), assuming the Stramberk fauna to be mixed, proposed a new biostratigraphic subdivision of Stramberk Limestone, and therefore placed the Klentnize Beds above the Rogoznik Beds. Enay and Geyssart (1975) later rejected this correlation.

stage by A. Toucat). Some scientists, however, favor joining the Berriassian as the fourth substage to three Tithonian substages. Still others distinguish only two substages.

Most common nowadays is a triple subdivision of the Tithonian. The Franconian Alb (Zeiss, 1968, 1975) should probably also be regarded as a type area for the Lower Tithonian, along with the Klentnize Beds. Similarly, the sections of Rogoznik (Kutek and Wierzbowski, 1979), the Franconian Alb (Barthel, 1975), and southern Spain (Enay and Geyssant, 1975) can be regarded as reference sections for the Middle Tithonian. Finally, of great significance for the Upper Tithonian are, besides Stramberk, also sections of southeastern France (Aisy, Chomerac). The zonal correlations between these areas are of paramount significance for Tithonian stratigraphy and are shown in Figure 15.

Volgian

Compared with the Tithonian, the Volgian zonation seems more refined. The Volgian Stage (or formation) was distinguished by Nikitin* in 1881. In 1884, he distinguished two parts, and based on their stratigraphic position, called them the Lower and Upper Volgian stages. After Bogoslovsky (1897) established the Ryazanian Horizon, which most workers correlated with the Berriassian, it became clear that the Lower and Upper Volgian covered the interval between the Kimmeridgian and Berriassian, which corresponded to the Tithonian. Uncertainties regarding the equivalents of the lowermost Tithonian were overcome after Sokolov (1901), at Orenburg, distinguished the Vetlyanian Horizon, corresponding to the lower Tithonian, and Ilovaisky and Florensky (1941) described the Vetlyanian ammonites.

In 1953, the Vetlyanian was included in the Lower Volgian as its lower substage (Resolutions, 1955). Mikhailov (1957, 1962a, 1964, 1966) and Gerasimov (Gerasimov and Mikhailov, 1966; Gerasimov, 1969) made the Volgian zonation more precise. In 1964, it was decided to distinguish three Volgian substages: Lower (the Vetlyanian Horizon of Sokolov), Middle (the Lower Volgian stage of Nikitin), and Upper (the Upper Volgian stage of Nikitin). Mikhailov and Gerasimov (1966) proposed the section near Gorodishche village, 25 km north of the town of Ul'yanovsk, as the Volgian lectostratotype. An additional section for the upper substage is the Lopatino phosphorite quarry near Moscow. The second additional section is undoubtedly at Kashpir on the Volga River, directly south of Syzran'. An additional section of the lower substage is along the Berdyanka River (the Ural-Ilek interfluve).

In the type section, the Lower and lower Middle Volgian are represented mainly by clay and marl (19 m) with oilshale interbeds in the upper part, and, beginning with Virgatus Zone, mainly by sandstone and sand (6–10 m) with interbeds of phosphorite nodules (Gerasimov and Mikhailov, 1966; Gerasimov,

1969). With the latest specifications on the upper Middle Volgian substage (Casey and Mesezhnikov, 1985), the Volgian has the following zonal subdivision (standard zones).

Lower Volgian

1. *Ilowaiskya klimovi* Zone. Mikhailov, 1962a. Index species—*I. klimovi* (Ilov. et Flor.). Also with *Gravesia* cf. *gigas* (Ziet.), *Neochetoceras* cf. *steraspis* (Opp.), *Glochiceras* sp., and *Sutneria* cf. *subeumela* (Schneid.).

2. *Ilowaiskya sokolovi* Zone. Ilowvaisky and Florensky, 1941. Index species—*I. sokolovi* (Ilov. et Flor.). Also with *I. pavida* (Ilov. et Flor.), *Sutneria* sp., *Haploceras* cf. *elimatum* (Opp.), *Glochiceras* (*Paralingulaticeras*) cf. *lithographicum* (Opp.), and *G.* (*P.*) cf. *parcevali* (Font.).

3. *Ilowaiskya pseudoscythica* Zone. Ilovaisky and Florensky, 1941. Index species—*I. pseudoscythica* (Ilov. et Flor.). Also characteristic are *I. schaschkovae* (Ilov. et Flor.), *Pectinatites ianschini* (Ilov. et Flor.), *P.*(?) *tenuicostatus* Michlv, *Glochiceras* sp., *Sutneria* sp., and *Haploceras* sp.

Zeiss (1979; Kutek and Zeiss, 1975) separated a level with *P.*(?) *tenuicostatus* Michlv from the Pseudoscythica Zone as the uppermost horizon of the Lower Volgian. However, in none of the sections of the Pseudoscythica Zone studied, including the most complete section near Lake Inder (20 m), is *P.*(?) *tenuicostatus* Michlv. isolated from the rest of the zonal assemblage.

Middle Volgian

4. *Dorsoplanites panderi* Zone. Rozanov, 1906. Index species—*D. panderi* (Orb.). Below, with *Zaraiskites scythicus* (Vichchn.), *Z. quenstedti* (Rouill. et Vos.), *Pavlovia pavlovi* (Mich.), rare *Glochiceras* sp., *Sutneria* sp., and *Haploceras* sp.–Pavloviapavlovi Subzone; above, with *Zaraiskites scythicus* (Vishchn.), *Z. quenstedti* (Rouill. et Vos.), *Z. zarajskensis* (Mich.), *Dorsoplanites dorsoplanus* (Vischn.), *Pavlovia pavlovi* (Mich.), *P. menneri* Michlv, *Acuticostites acuticostatus* (Mich.), *Glochiceras* sp., *Haploceras* sp., and *Sutneria* sp.–Zaraiskites zarajskensis Subzone.

5. *Virgatites virgatus* Zone. Roullier, 1845. Index species—*V. virgatus* (Buch). Below, with *Virgatites virgatus* (Buch), *V. sosia* (Vischn.), *V. pusillis* (Mich.), *V. pallasi* (Orb.), and *Acuticostites acuticostatus* (Mich.)–*V. virgatus* Subzone; and above, *V. virgatus* (Buch), *V. rosanovi* Michlv, *Crendonites kuncevi* Michlv, *Lomonossovella lomonossovi* (Vischn.), and *Laugeites stchurovskii*–*V. rosanovi* Subzone. Together with Virgatitinae, the zone yields diverse, mostly undescribed, *Dorsoplanites,* including *D. serus* Geras. and *D. rosanovi* Geras (Gerasimov, 1978).

6. *Epivirgatites nikitini* Zone. Lahusen, 1883. Index species—*E. nikitini* (Mich.). Also characterized by *Epivirgatites lahuseni* (Nik.), *E.*(?) *bipliciformis* (Nik.), *Lomonossovella* spp., *Laugeites* spp. with two subzones (Casey and Mesezhnikov, 1985). Below, the *Lomonossovella blakei* Subzone (Pavlov, 1895) is rather widespread in the Moscow, Volga (Yaroslavl),

and Ul'yanovsk-Syzran areas, and yields, besides rare *E. nikitini* (Mich.), *E.*(?) *bipliciformis* (Nik.), *E. lahuseni* (Nik.), *Lomonossovella sergeii* Mesezhn., *Lomonossovella blakei* (Pavl.), *L. lomonossovi* (Mich.), *Laugeites stschurovskii* (Mich.), *L. lambecki glebovensis* Ivan., and *Credonites kuncevi* Michlv. The upper, *Epivirgatites nikitini,* subzone is developed in the Mid-Volga area and characterized by the index species with a few *E.*(?) *bipliciformis* (Nik.) and *E. lahuseni* (Nik.). The two horizons in the *E. nikitini* Zone had been noted by Mesezhnikov (1982), but only detailed studies of sections in the Kashpir area established their stratigraphic relations. The *nikitini* Subzone appears to rest directly on the *blakei* subzone.

7. *Paracraspedites oppresus* Zone. Casey, 1973. Distinguished in Lincolnshire, Yorkshire, and Dorset, England. In the lectostratotype of the Volgian near Gorodishche village, the zone yields *Paracraspedites* cf. *oppressus* Casey, *P.* sp., *E.*(?) *bipliciformis* (Nik.), rare *E. nikitini* (Mich.), and *Credonites (Neopavlovia) felix* Casey et Mesezhn.

Upper Volgian

7. *Kachpurites fulgens* Zone. Nikitin, 1888. Index species—*K. fulgens* (Traut.). Also including *Craspedites fragilis* (Traut.) and *C. okensis* (Orb.).

8. *Craspedites subditus* Zone. Nikitin, 1888. Index species—*C. subditus* (Traut.). Also *C. okensis* (Orb.), *Garniericeras catenulatum* (Fisch.), and *G. interjectum* (Nik.).

9. *Craspedites nodiger* Zone. Nikitin, 1888. Index species—*C. nodiger* (Eichw.). Also characteristic are *C. kaschpuricus* (Traut.), *C. mosquensis* Gerass., and *Garniericeras subclypeiforme* (Milasch.). Gerasimov (1969) distinguished two subzones. The lower, the *Craspedites mosquensis* Subzone, includes *C. mosquensis* Gerass., *G. nodiger* (Eichw.), *C. milkovensis* (Strem.), *C. kaschpuricus* (Traut.), *C. parakaschpuricus* Gerass., and *Garniericeras subclypeiforme* (Milasch.); and the upper subzone, the *Craspedites nodiger* Subzone, yields similar ammonoid assemblages, with *Craspedites mosquensis* Gerass.

The Volgian stage is zoned by continuous faunal assemblages; these assemblages are extensively distributed in the Boreal Belt. It is characterized by Virgatitinae, *Pavlovia, Dorsoplanites, Laugeites,* and *Craspedites.* Thus, it is not surprising that it is the Volgian that is also widely used in the Boreal Jurassic, outside the USSR, not the Portlandian. However, in recent years, new data on the uppermost Jurassic horizons have been obtained in England, which have significantly changed our views on the succession and nomenclature of its zonal units since 1956, the date of Arkell's monograph. Cope (1967) presented in great detail the zonal units of the lower Upper Kimmeridgian Clay in Dorset (the Middle Kimmeridge of Arkell) and changed their index species. Casey (1967) reversed the sequence of the Rotunda and Pallasioides Zones, distinguished the uppermost Portlandian *Paracraspedites oppressus* Zone, and established the presence of marine Upper Volgian in eastern England (Casey, 1973). Finally, Cope (1978) proposed a more precise zonation of the uppermost

Arkell, 1956	Cope, 1967, 1978; Wimbledon & Cope, 1978; Casey, 1967, 1973; Caset et al., 1977
	Subcraspedites lamplughi
	S. preplicomphalus
	S. primitivus
	Paracraspedites oppressus
Titanites giganteus	Titanites anguiformis
	Galbanites kerberus
Glaucolithites gorei	G. okusensis
	Glaucolithites glaucolithus
Progalbanites albani	Progalbanites albani
Pavlovia pallasioides	Virgatopavlovia fittoni
	Pavlovia rotunda
P. rotunda	P. pallasioides
Pectinatites pectinatus	Pectinatites pectinatus
Subplanites wheatleyensis	P. hudlestoni
S. grandis	
S. spp.	P. wheatleyensis
Gravesia gigas	P. scitulus
G. gravesiana	P. elegans

Figure 16. Zones of the uppermost Jurassic of England.

Kimmeridge Clay, and, together with Wimbeldon (Wimbeldon and Cope, 1978), proposed a detailed zonation of the Portlandian (Fig. 16). The present accepted correlations between the Volgian and the uppermost marine Jurassic in England were worked out by Arkell (1956), who correlated the Vetlyanian horizon (Lower Volgian) with the lower and middle parts of the Upper Kimmeridge Clay (Gravesianus and Pectinatus Zones), and the Middle Volgian with the upper part of the Upper Kimmeridge Clay (Rotunda and Pallasioides Zones) and the Portlandian. This correlation was accepted both by Soviet (Mikhailov, 1962a, 1964, 1966; Saks and others, 1963, 1969) and Western European investigators (Cope and Zeiss, 1964; Zeiss, 1968; Hölder, 1964). The most problematic correlation in Arkell's scheme was between the Panderi and Albani Zones. It was based on Arkell's transfer of the index species of the latter zone to *Zaraiskites.* However, N.P. Mikhailov (oral communication, late 1960s) found that, based on the similarity of the inner whorls, *Progalbanites* is related to *Virgatites,* rather than to *Zaraiskites.* Since 1974, this relation was accepted in the Soviet literature (e.g., Zakahrov and Mesezhnikov, 1974; Strat. Jurassic System, 1976).

In 1967, Casey assumed the presence of a regional erosional

disconformity in the Middle Volgian. He correlated the Albani and Nikitini Zones and concluded that there is a long break between the Nikitini and Fulgens Zones that corresponds to almost the entire Portlandian. Casey alleged that these correlations were based on finds of the Middle Volgian *Epivirgatites* in the Albani Zone of England. Although Casey later rejected this view, it was supported by Cope (1978) and served as the basis for a new correlation scheme, proposed by them, for the Middle Volgian and Portlandian.

We therefore must consider the occurrences of *Epivirgatites* Spath in Western Europe. In the Nikitini Zone of the Gorodishche section, Casey collected *Paracraspedites,* similar to those of the Oppressus Zone (Casey, 1973, Pl. 1, Fig. 4). The same bed also yielded *E. nikitini* (Mich.) (Mikhalsky, 1890, Pl. 12, Fig. 1). But we cannot believe in the existence of a long break between this bed and a lower bed of the same zone, which is filled with *E. nikitini* south of Gorodishche, in Kashpir. Casey and Mesezhnikov (1985) stated finally that, "Though each section taken separately (Russian Platform, M.M.) contains breaks, we presume that all major chronostratigraphic units of England might also be diagnosed on the Russian Platform." We therefore must consider the occurrences of *Epivirgatites* in Western Europe.

The generic characteristic is based only on the type species, *E. nikitini* (Mich.) (Pl. 15, Fig. 1); the two other species commonly assigned to the genus, *E. lahuseni* and *E. bipliciformis* (Nik., 1881), have not been adequately studied: shell flattened with subrectangular whorls; a low, steep umbilical wall, possibly flattened on the last whorl, separated from the sides by a sharp margin; sharp, relatively narrow ribs; projected and biplicate to virgatotomous. As examples of *Epivirgatites* in the Albani Zone of England and Normandy, Casey (1973) cited *Pavlovia worthensis* Spath (1936, Pl. 18, Fig. 6), "*Epivirgatites nikitini* Michalsky" (Sauvage, 1911, Pl. 9, Fig. 1) and *Lydistratites biformis* Buck. (Buckman, 1909–1930, Pl. 505a,b). Spath (1936, pp. 30–31) had quite definitely assigned the first two to *Lydistratites* Buckman, 1922; they do not display any of the mentioned *Epivirgatites* features. *Lydistratites biformis* (Buckman, 1909–1930, Pl. 505a) resembles *E. nikitini,* but differs considerably by the more inflated and involute shell, with radial and more widely spaced ribs (*ibid.,* Plate 505b). J. Cope (1978, Pl. 55) illustrates *E. nikitini* (Mich.) and *E.* cf. *nikitini* from the Albani Zone of Portland. The first is also a more involute and more distantly ribbed than *E. nikitini,* the second has to be closer to *L. biformis* (Buckm., Pl. 505b). Thus, the forms from the Albani Zone probably belong to new species of the poorly known *Lydistratites* (Cowie, 1984). Correlation of the Volgian with the uppermost marine Jurassic of England therefore poses no difficulties (Fig. 17). Only the position of the *Virgatopavlovia fittoni* Zone needs to be commented on. The range of the *fittoni* Zone can be established indirectly from the following evidence: (1) Evolution of *Pavlovia* in the Pallasioides and Rotunda Standard Zones of England and in the *iatriensis* (regional) zone on the eastern slope of the Subpolar Urals (*iatriensis* and *strajevskyi* subzones) follows a single pattern, from dense to coarse-ribbed forms, and indicates

that the Pallasioides and Rotunda Zones are coeval with the *iatriensis* Zone. (2) A few *Dorsoplanites* appear only in the upper *iatriensis* Zone, suggesting correlation with the lower part of the Panderi Zone (Pavlovi Subzone). Similarly, the next zone, *Dorsoplanites ilovaiskii,* is correlated with the *Zarajskensis* Subzone of the Panderi Zone (see Fig. 15); the *maximus* zone, as established in the Pechora Basin (Strat. Jurassic System, 1976) directly overlies the Panderi Zone, and thus corresponds to the lower Virgatus Zone. The Fittoni Standard Zone would therefore be correlated with the *zarajskensis* Subzone, since the Albani Standard Zone overying it also corresponds to the lower part of the Virgatus Zone.

Cope and Zeiss (1984) and Wimbledon and Cope (1984), as one of their basic arguments against the use of the Volgian in the Boreal Jurassic, quote the abruptly reduced thicknesses of several zones in the Gorodishche section. In some well-studied fossiliferous sections of the Russian Platform, however, the *Sokolovi* Zone exceeds 22 m; the *Pseudoscythicus* Zone, 4 m; the *Panderi* Zone, 30 m; and the *Virgatus* Zone, 18 m (Mesezhnikov and others, 1985). Within the Ural-Volga interfluve, the Volgian is even thicker, i.e., *Dorsoplanites* Zone, 65 m; and *Virgatites virgatus* Zone, 125 m (Bashlykova and others, 1971). The Volgian in the northwestern Caspian area (Novouzensk test hole) exceeds 350 m, similar to coeval beds in South England.

Zonal correlation between Volgian and Tithonian still poses much greater difficulty. There are only three levels for which detailed correlation may be discussed. The lowest is the Hybonotum Zone. Finds of *Gravesia, Neochetoceras* cf. *steraspis* (Opp.) and *Glochiceras* cf. *lithographicum* (Opp.) at Gorodishche on the Volga River (Gerasimov and Mikhailov, 1966; Strat. Jur. Syst., 1976) allow a reliable correlation, which is presently accepted universally.

The second level contains eastern forms, similar to *Zaraiskites* in the Neuburg beds of Franconia (Barthel, 1969, 1975), and, conversely, Tithonian *Isterites* and *Pseudovirgatites,* in the *Pseudoscythicus* and *Scythicus* Zones of central Poland (Brzostowka near Tomoszowa Masovetzka; Kutek and Zeiss, 1974, 1975). But difficulty of correlation persists because the occurrence of *Zaraiskites* ends near Neuburg, and the eastern boundary of *Isterites* occurrence is near Brzostowka. In distribution, the range zones of these ammonites may be restricted in marginal areas, compared to core areas. Kutek and Zeiss proposed one possible correlation of the Rennertshofen and Brzostowka Beds (Fig. 18), but another is equally possible, based on the range zones of certain ammonites in the Neuberg beds.

Barthel (1962, 1969, 1975) showed that the Neuburg Formation is divisible into an upper Unterhausen Member (beds 22 through 116), containing a diverse ammonite assemblage and regarded as the Bavaricum Zone (Zeiss, 1977a); and the lower Oberhausen Member below, with only *Isterites* (beds 117 through 190), and above with *Calpionella* and *Carssicolenia* (A Zone; bed 238, etc.). The base of the *Calpionella* A Zone coincides with that of the *P. transitorius* Zone, i.e., the Middle/Upper

SOUTHERN EUROPE		EASTERN EUROPE		NORTH-WESTERN EUROPE
BOISSIERI	CALLISTO	*Peregrinoceras albidum*		*Peregrinoeras albidum*
	PICTETI	*Surites tzikwinianus*		*Bojarkia stnomphala*
	PARAMIMOUNUM	*R. rjasanensis & S. spasskensis*		*Lynnia icenii*
OCCITANICA	DALMASI	*Hectoroceras kochi*		*Hectoroceras kochi*
	PRIVASENSIS			
	SUBALPINA	*Garniericeras & Riasanites*		*Praetollia runctoni*
GRANDIS/JACOBI		*Craspedites nodiger*	*C. kaschpuricus*	*Subcraspedites lamplughi*
			C. mosquensis	
DURANGITES		*Craspedites subditus*		*S. preplicomphalus*
TRANSITORIUS		*Kachpurites fulgens*		*S. primitivus*
		Paracraspedites oppressus		*Paracr. oppressus*
PONTI		*Epivirgat. nikitini*	*E. nikitini*	*Titanites anguiformis*
			Lomon. bakei	*Kerberites kerberus*
FALLAUXI		*Virgatites virgatus*	*V. rosanovi*	*Galbanites okusensis*
				Glauc. glaucolithus
			C. virgatus	*Progalbanites albani*
SEMIFORME	BAVARICUM	*Dorsoplanites panderi*	*Z. zarajskensis*	*Virgatopavl. fittoni*
			Pavl. pavlovi	*Pavlova rotunda*
				P. pallasioides
PALATINUS		*Ilowaiskya pseudoscythica*		*Pectinatites pectinatus*
VIMINEUS				
PARVINODOSUM		*I. sokolovi*		*P. hudlestoni*
TRIPLICATUS				
TAGMERSHEIMENSE				*P. wheatleyensis*
HYBONOTUM		*I. klimovi*		*P. scitulus*
				P. elegans

Figure 17. Correlation of the uppermost Jurassic and lowermost Cretaceous of Europe.

CENTRAL POLAND				SOUTH FRANCONIA		
Stage	Zones	Lithol.		Lithol.	Zones	Stage
VOLGIAN — M	*Z.zarajskensis*	Limestones, marls	**Neuberg Beds** — Oberhausen Member	U	*Paraulacosph. transitorius*	**TITHONIAN** — U
	Z.scythicus	b-1, 6-2, a-3, a-4		L	*Pseudovirgatites*	
	Psydovirgatites puschi	a-1, a-2				
VOLGIAN — L	*Ilowaikya pseudoscythica*	Marls, clays	Unterhausen Member		*Pseudolissoceras, Isterites*	**TITHONIAN** — M
			Rennertshofen Beds, Usseltal Beds		*Danubisphinc. palatinum*	**TITHONIAN** — L
					Neochetoc. mucronatum	
	I.klimovi		Altmultal Beds		*Hybonoticeras hybonotum*	

Figure 18. Correlation of the Volgian and Tithonian of Poland and Franconia (southern Germany).

Tithonian boundary (Barthel, 1975). Thus, the beds with *Isterites* in the lower part of the Oberhausen Member are a biostratigraphic unit of the Middle Tithonian, above the *P. bavaricum* Zone.

Correlation of ammonites from the Unterhausen Member with the Middle Tithonian of Rogozhik (Kutek and Wierzbowski, 1979) and southeastern Spain (Enay and Geyssant, 1975) suggests that the *P. bavaricum* Zone corresponds to the *S. semiforme* Zone, lower Middle Tithonian. The beds with *Isterites* (Barthel and Geyssant, 1973) and the ammonite-free beds (117 through 237) underlying the *Calpionella* A Zone of the Oberhausen Member may correspond to the rest of the Middle Tithonian (*Fallauxi* and *Ponti* Zones). Barthel (1975) also recorded forms similar to *Zaraiskites,* from the upper Unterhausen Member (beds 102 through 116). Thus, the Panderi Zone presumably corresponds to the upper part of the *P. bavaricum* Zone; and the Pseudoscythicus Zone, to the *palatinum* and lower *P. bavaricum* Zones. This correlation is confirmed by *Ilowaiskya* cf. *pseudoscythica* (Ilov. et Flor.) (Zeiss, 1968, p. 177) in the upper Rennertshofen Beds (Palatinum Zone), and conversely, by *Franconites vimineus* (Schneid) in the Sokolovi Zone of the Sukhaya Peschanka section (Trans-Volga area) (Mikhailov, 1964, p. 56, Pl. XI, Fig. 1). The Klentnize beds would then find their place not above, but below the Middle Tithonian* (Fig. 19).

The third level, useful for correlating the Tithonian with the Volgian, lies beyond the limits of these stages as presently understood. This level corresponds to the lower part of the Ryazanian horizon, which yields the Berriasselidae, *Riasanites,* and *Euthymiceras.* In accordance with finds of *Euthymiceras* in the lower Paramimounum Subzone of the Boissieri Zone in the Berriassian stratotype (Le Hegarat, 1973), the base of the Ryasanian is commonly made coincident with the base of the Boissieri Zone (Saks, 1972; Sazonova and Sazonov, 1979). However, Drushchits (Drushchits and Mikhailova, 1966; Drushchits and Vakhrameev, 1976) showed that the stratigraphic range of *Euthymiceras* in the sections of the Crimea and the northern Caucasus is more extensive than in the Vocontian Basin; he also distinguished the *Euthymiceras euthymi* and *Dalmasiceras dalmasi* Zones, corresponding to the Upper Occitanica–lower Boissieri Zone. In the northeastern Caucasus, according to Sakharov (1976, 1979), *Euthymiceras* spp. have a slightly different range: the *euthymi* and the *rjasanensis* Zones together correspond to the Boissieri Zone. In Mangyshlak (Luppov and others, 1979), the range of beds with *Euthymiceras* corresponds to the upper Occitanica Zone (Dalmasi Subzone) and the lower Boissieri Zone (Paramimounum Subzone). It is noteworthy that in all sections in the southern USSR, including Crimea (Kvantaliani and Lysenko, 1979)†, *Riasanites* occur higher than *Euthymiceras,* whereas in the Oka Basin they are found together, and *Euthymiceras* is more frequent in

---

*Zeiss illustrated *"Pavlovia iatriensis* Ilov." emend Michl. from the Klentnize beds of Niederfallabrunn, northeast Austria (Zeiss, 1977a, p. 376, Pl. 2, Fig. 1). This small specimen can hardly be identified reliably and certainly does not belong to *P. iatriensis* because of its comparatively coarse, distinct sculpture and inflated whorls.

---

†*Tauricoceras* I. V. Kvantaliani et N. I. Lysenko is rather close to *Riasanites.*

		VOLGA BASIN		POLAND			FRANCONIA			
Stage		**Zones**		**Zones**	**Lithol.**	**Lithol.**		**Zones**		**Stage**
VOLGIAN	M					Neuburg Beds	Oberhausen Member	*Paraulacosph. transitorius*	U	**TITHONIAN**
								Isterites		
		Dorsopl. panderi	*Z. zarajskensis*	*Zarajskites zarajskensis*	Limestones, marls b-1, b-2, a-3, a-4		Unterhausen Member	*Pseudolioceras bavaricum*	M	
			P. pavlovi	*Z. scythicus*						
	L	*Ilowaiskya pseudoscythica*		*I. pseudoscythica*	a-1, a-2 Marls, clays		Rennertshofen Beds, Usseltal Beds	*Danub. palatinum Franc. vimineus Neoch. mucronatum*	L	
		I. sokolovi								
		I. klimovi		*I. klimovi*			Altmultal Beds	*Hyb. hybonotum*		

Figure 19. Correlation of the Volgian and Tithonian of the Volga Basin, central Poland, and Franconia (southern Germany).

the upper *rjasanensis* Zone than *Riasanites*. Thus, there is good evidence that the *Euthymiceras* ranges (teil zones) in the southeastern USSR exceed that in France. The association of *Riasanites, Berriasella* ex gr. *privanzensis* (Pict.), and *Euthymiceras* in the Oka Basin suggest that the lower boundary of *Rjasanensis* Zone corresponds to the lower Occitanica Zone (the base of Privarensis Subzone). Furthermore, the gradual transition from the Upper Volgian to Ryazanian beds, recorded by Pavlov (1895), has been more recently confirmed (Mesezhnikov and others, 1979). Thus it can be assumed that some part of the Upper Volgian corresponds to the Grandis (s.l.) and lower Occitanica Zone.

In conclusion, it can be said provisionally that the Lower Volgian corresponds to the Lower Tithonian and part of the Bavaricum Zone; the Middle Volgian, to the remainder of the Middle Tithonian; and the Upper Volgian, to the Upper Tithonian and the Grandis Zone, and possibly to the lower half of the Occitanica Zone.

Indeed, if lower Berriassian ammonites occur in the Upper Volgian, there is apparently no need for distinguishing the Ryazanian horizon from that of the Berriassian. Also, the introduction of any additional stage names, e.g., Gorodishchian and Kashpurian (Sazonova and Sazonov, 1979), makes the terminology of the Jurassic/Cretaceous boundary even more complicated and does not add anything new to a solution. The possible correspondence of part of the Upper Volgian to the Lower Berriassian, of course, introduces the prospect of significant corrections to geological maps for rather extensive areas of the USSR. Thus, in discussing the Jurassic/Cretaceous boundary, the suggestion of Casey (1962, 1973) is worthy of attention, that is, to draw the lower boundary of the Berriassian at the top, rather than the base, of the Grandis s.l. Zone. Although this suggestion was most un-

popular, it does allow the present-day Jurassic/Cretaceous boundary within the entire Boreal Realm to be retained.

SOVIET UNION

The Tithonian, and particularly the Volgian, occurrences are extremely extensive in the USSR (Fig. 20; marine facies alone not less than 5×10^6 km^2).

Russian Platform

The marine Volgian is recorded in the Baltic, Moscow and Pechora Synclinoria, the Voronezh and Volga-Ural Anticlinoria, the Caspian Depression, and the Ul'yanovsk-Saratov Trough, but the development of several substages differs.

The Lower Volgian occurs mainly in the eastern Russian Platform, the Middle and Lower Volga area, and the Ural Basin. In the Pechora Basin, only its uppermost zone is present, the Pseudoscythica Standard Zone (Mesezhnikov and others, 1973). On the central Russian Platform, the Middle Volgian rests on the Upper Kimmeridgian or Oxfordian (Krymholts, 1972b).

The Middle Volgian is most extensive, but the area extent of some zones differs and generally decreases upward. The Panderi Zone has the largest distribution, coinciding with that of the entire Volgian. Its faunal assemblage varies, with the most typical development in a broad belt from the Moscow area to Orenburg, whereas the diversity and abundance of the Dorsoplanitinae gradually decrease east of the Volga. In the extreme southeast, in the Caspian Depression, the zonal assemblage is dominated by *Zaraiskites;* northward, the Doroplanitinae become most abundant, *Zaraiskites* are relatively rare in the Sysola Basin; in the

Stage	European Standard Zones		Northern Caucasus Beds		Stage	Russian Platform		
TITHONIAN U	"DURANGITES" (- - -) / TRANSITORIUS		400 m — Dolomites, limestones: *Paraulacosph. transitorius* (U)		**VOLGIAN** U	5–25 m — Sands, sandst.: *Craspedites nodiger* / *C. subditus* / *Kashpurites fulgens*		U
M	PONTI / FALLAUXI / SEMIFORME | BAVARICUM		180–300 m — Limestones: *Lithacoceras albulus* (M)		M	10–100 m — Clays, sands, sandstones: *Paracraspedites oppressus*; *Epivirg. nikitini* (*E. nikitini* / *Lom. blakei*); *Virgat. virgatus* (*V. rosanovi* / *V. virgatis*); *Dorsoplanites panderi* (· *zarajskensis* / *Pavlova pavlovi*)		M
L	PALATINUS / VIMINEUS / PARVINODOSUM / TRIPLICATUS / TAGMERSHEIMENSE / HYBONOTUM		350–380 m — Dolomites: *Lithacoc. ulmense & Glochiceras nimbatum* (L)		L	*Ilowaiskya pseudoscyhtica* / *I. sokolovi* / *I. klimovi*		L

Figure 20. The Tithonian and Volgian of the major regions of the U.S.S.R. (continued on facing page).

southern Pechora Synclinorium, only a few specimens have been found; and *Zaraiskites* is unknown farther north. Mikhailov (1962a, 1964) noted the shifting areal extent within the Panderi Subzones: the lower, the Pavlovi Subzone, occurs mainly in the east and is absent in the Moscow area, and the upper, the Zaraj-skensis Subzone, is ubiquitous. The Virgatus Zone is most complete in the western part of the region, in the Moscow area, and the Volga area at Jaroslavl. Eastward, its thickness is usually reduced, but thickness again increases in the Volga area. As in the Panderi Zone, *Dorsolpanites* dominate in sandy facies, and Virgatitinae predominate in calcareous-clayey facies. Northward, *Virgatites* gradually disappears; in the Pechora Basin, they are replaced by Dorsoplanitinae, characterizing the *D. maximus*

Zone (Mesezhnikov and others, 1979). Significantly, directly west of Timan in the Sysola Basin, the Virgatus Zone also yields *Dorsoplanites* ex gr. *flavus* Spath, a mixed fauna of the Virgatus and *D. maximus* Zones. The Nikitini Zone has the most limited areal extent, and the most diverse fauna. As already noted, beds with *Epivirgatites nikitini* and beds with *E. bipliciformis* should be distinguished within the Nikitini Zone. The latter beds are most widespread, including the Pechora Basin. However, in the extreme northwestern Timan (Lower Vollonga River), beds with diverse *Laugeites,* resembling Greenland forms (Donovan, 1964), possibly correspond to the Nikitini Zone. The upper Volgian occurs mostly in the central Russian Platform, from the Moscow area to the Middle Volga areas and in the Pechora Basin.

	WEST SIBERIAN		SIBERIAN PLATFORM		NORTH-EAST		FAR EAST	
U	25–700 m	Subcraspedites Beds	150–300 m	Chetaites chetae	800–13000 m	Buchia terebratuloides, B. tenuicollis	800–8000 m	Beds w. Buchia terebratuloides
		Craspedites subditus		Craspedites taimyrensis				
				C. okensis: C. originalis				
		Kashpurites fulgens		C. okensis: C. okensis				
				C. okensis: V. exoticus				
M	Cent.: argill. & bit. shales 30–90 m; East: siltst. & sandst.	Epilaugeites vogulicus	Katangu Rv. Basin: siltst. & clays 50–100 m; Lena Rv. Basin: siltst. & sandst.	Epivirgatites variabilis	Siltstones and sandstones	Buchia fischeriana, B. piochii	Argillites, siltstones, sandstones and tuffits	Beds with Buchia fischeriana
		Laugeites groenlandicus						
		Crendonites spp.		Taimyr. excentricum / Dorsop. sachsi				
		Dorsopianites maximus		D. maximus				
		D. ilovaiskii		D. ilovaiskii				
		iatriensis: S. strajevskyi		Pavlovia iatriensis				
		iatriensis: P. iatriensis						
L		Pectinatites lideri		Pectinatites pectinatus		Buchia mosquensis, B. piochii		B. mosquensis Zone
		Subdichotom. subcrassum						
		Eusphinctoceras magnum						

FAR EAST — L & M TITHONIAN: 30 m; Sandstones and limestones; Beds with Berriasella; Beds with Prymoryites.

The lithofacies of the Volgian is relatively diverse. The Lower Volgian in the Middle Volga area consists of clay, frequently calcareous (8 m); in the Ural-Ilek confluence, of calcareous sandstone (6 m); and in the North Caspian area, of calcareous clay and marl (20 m). Finally, in the Pechora Basin near Timan, the upper Lower Volgian consists of clayey silt (1 m); and in the Cis-Uralian area, of siltstone and sandstone members (20 m). Middle Volgian deposits of the Panderi Zone are clay, often calcareous, with oilshale interbeds (6–40 m); and in the Moscow area, commonly thin glauconitic sands (1 m). Higher horizons (Virgatus and Nikitini Zones) are almost ubiquitously sand and sandstone, reaching 8 m in the Volga area at Yaroslavl (Ivanov, 1979). In the Trans-Volga area, the Virgatus Zone is represented by calcareous sandstone (4–6 m), and in the north Caspian area, by calcareous clay and marl (20 m). In the Pechora Basin, the *D. maximus* and Nikitini Zones are calcareous clay (20 m). The Upper Volgian on the central Russian Platform consists also of sand and glauconitic sandstone (6–8 m), and in the Pechora Basin, of calcareous, in places silty, clay (15–20 m). The total thickness of the Volgian on the central Russian Platform is less than 30 m, but it increases rapidly north and eastward, attaining 100 m in the Pechora Basin and around Lake Inder, and exceeding 350 m in the Novouznensk test hole.

Mediterranean Geosynclinal Belt

Quite different deposits with Tithonian fauna occur in the northern Caucasus (Krymholts, 1972b; Khimshiashvili, 1976;

Beznosov, 1973; Resolutions, 1984). They are widespread along the entire northern slope of the Caucasus and have a highly variable facies. In the Fiagdon-Asa area (central northern Caucasus), the Lower-Middle Tithonian is represented by the upper part of the Balta Formation. Below is dolomite (350–380 m), which on the Terek River yields *Glochiceras nimbatum* (Opp.), *Taramelliceras disceptatum* Font., *T.* cf. *prolithographicum* (Opp.), *Neochetoceras praecursor* Zeiss, *Lithacoceras ulmense* (Opp.), and *Usseliceras* (*Subplanites*) *tajmerschimense* Zeiss, indicating the Lower Tithonian. The superjacent limestone (300 m) is assigned to the upper Lower and Middle Tithonian and yields *Lithacoceras albulum* (Qu.), *L. siliceum paraboliferum* Berkch., *Paradiceras bicornutum* Pcel., and *Heterodiceras skeliense* Pcel. The Upper Tithonian comprises limestone and dolomite of the Matlam Formation (400 m) with foraminiferal fauna.

In most of the northern Caucasus, the Tithonian (Gandalbos Formation) is represented by lagoonal anhydrite, gypsum, clay, and locally, limestone and breccias. West of Fiagdon, the lower part of the Tithonian consists also of gypsiferous clay, sandstone, dolomite, or variegated lagoonal sediments (Mezmai Formation), and the upper part of limestone (Matlam Formation). In the northwestern Caucasus, the Tithonian is represented by thick (1,000 m) subflysch, with alternating mudstone, siltstone, and sandstone. The upper part yields the Upper Tithonian *Paraulacosphinctes* cf. *transitorius* (Opp.).

On the southeastern Turan Plate (Kugitang), the Tithonian is represented by the upper part (30–40 m) of the gypsiferous Gaurdak Formation and the red terrigenous Karabil Formation (200 m). On the northern Turan Plate, in southern Mangyshlak, probable Volgian is widespread and consists of gray clay and marl with foraminifers.

Western Siberia Plate

The Volgian is extremely widespread, and the areal extent exceeds 2×10^6 km^2. The lithofacies is rather uniform. On the eastern slope of the Subpolar Urals, the section (90 m) begins with clayey silt, grading into calcareous quartz–glauconitic siltstone with numerous carbonate interbeds and nodules, and is crowned by oolitic ferruginous sandstone and gritstone. Eastward, in the West Siberian Lowland proper, the Volgian has two facies: (1) dark gray to black mudstone of the upper Mar'yanovka Formation (30–100 m) developed around the periphery, which encircles (2) the bituminous Bazhenovo Formation (25–30 m) and equivalents, underlying all of central western Siberia, and consists of brownish and black siliceous clay and sapropelic mudstone. In the extreme northeast part of western Siberia, Lower Yenisei, Volgian (150–450 m) is represented by the Yanov Stan Formation with black mudstone and clayey siltstone. The most complete and fossiliferous Volgian is described below from the eastern slope of the Subpolar Urals (Zakharov and Mesezhnikov, 1974).

LOWER VOLGIAN

1. *Eosphinctoceras magnum* Zone. *Eosphinctoceras triplicatum* (Mesezhn.), *E. magnum* Mesezhn., *E. gravesiforme* Mesezhn., and *Gravesia* cf. *polypleura* Hahn, G. sp.

2. *Subdichotomoceras subcrassum* Zone. *Eosphinctoceras gravesiforme* Mesezhn., *Subdichotomoceras subcrassum* Mesezhn., *S. praeinflatum* Mesezhn., *S. michallovi* Mesezhn., and *Ilowaiskya* sp.

3. *Pectinatites lideri* Zone. *Pectinatites federovi* Mesezhn., *P. lideri* Mesezhn., *P.* aff. *devillei* (Lor.), and *P.* spp.

MIDDLE VOLGIAN

4. *Pavlovia iatriensis* Zone. Below, *P. iatriensis* Subzone, characterized by index species, *Pavlovia hypophantica* Ilov., *Strajevskya strajevskyi* (Ilov.), rare *Pavlovia raricostata* Ilov. Above, *Strajevskya strajevski* Subzone, characterized by *Strajevskya*, e.g., *strajevskyi*, *S. hoffmanni*, *Pavlovia raricostata* Ilov., and first *Dorsoplanites antiquus* Spath; rare *Pavlovia iatriensis* Ilov.

5. *Dorsoplanites ilovaiskii* Zone. *D. ilovaiskii* Mesezhn., *D. ovalis* Mesezhn., *D. antiquus* Spath, *D.* aff. *gracilis* Spath, *D. crassus* Spath, *Pavlova* aff. *jubilans* Spath, and *Strajevskya* cf. *strajevskyi* (Ilov.).

6. *Dorsoplanites maximus* Zone. *D. maximus* Spath, *D. flavus* Spath, *D. gracilis* Spath, *D. panderiformis* Michlv, *D. sibirakovi* Michlv, *D. subdorsoplanus* Mesezhn., *D. crassus* Spath, and *Pavlovia ponomarevi* Michlv.

7. *Credonites* spp. Beds. *C. subleslie* Mesezhn., *C.* cf. *irregularis* Spath, and *Laugeites* sp.

8. *Laugeites groenlandicus* Zone. *L. borealis* Mesezhn., *L. groenlandicus* Spath, *L. lambecki* Ilov., and *L. biplicatus* Mesezhn.

9. *Epilaugeites vogulicus* Zone. *E. iatriensis* Mesezhn., *E. vogulicus* (Ilov.), and *Laugeites* aff. *borealis* Mesezhn.

UPPER VOLGIAN

10. *Kachpurites fulgens* Zone. *Craspedites okensis* (Orb.), *C.* cf. *leptus* Spath, *Kachpurites* cf. *subfulgens* (Trd.).

11. *Craspedites subditus* Zone. *C. okensis* (Orb.), *C. fragilis* (Trd.), and *Garniericeras* sp. indet.

The uppermost Volgian of the Subpolar Urals has rather diverse ammonites; on the Yatriya River, there is *Craspedites* ex gr. *nodiger* (Eichw.) (=*C.* cf. *taimyrensis* (Bodyl.) of Golbert and Klimova, 1979); somewhat higher, *Subcraspedites* sp. South, in the Tol'ya Basin, *Subcraspedites* (*Volgidiscus*) *pulcher* Casey was recorded (Casey and others, 1977).

West Siberian Lowland

Most of the above zonal units are found here also (Mesezhnikov, 1978). The Volgian is discordant on different Kimmeridgian and Oxfordian horizons, with the Lower Volgian almost entirely missing (except local beds with *Pectinatites*). In the Middle Volgian, the *P. iatriensis, D. maximus,* and *L. groenlandicus* Zones are established; and in the Upper Volgian, the beds contain *Craspedites okensis* and *Craspedites taimyrensis.*

Siberian Platform (Fig. 20)

In the north and east, the Volgian (50–110 m) is reported from the Kheta Basin (Saks and others, 1969), the Taimyr (Basov and others, 1965; Strat. Jur. Syst., 1976), the Anabar Basin (Osipova and Basov, 1965; Krymholts, 1972b), and the Lower Lena River (Bidzhiev and Mikhailov, 1966; Strat. Jur. Syst., 1976), and is mainly represented by silt and sandstone. Only in the Chelyuskin Peninsula is sand dominant; sandstone and gritstone occur along the right bank of the Anabar River (Udzha Basin). In the central Khatanga Depression (Pakhsa Peninsula), clays predominate. The Volgian of the Taimyr and Anabar-Khatanga areas has numerous breaks. The section begins with the upper *Pectinatus* Zone, although the earlier *Eosphinctoceras* and *Subdichotomoceras* are found in talus; in the Kheta Basin, the *Variabilis* Zone rests on beds with *Pectinatites;* whereas the Middle Volgian is most widespread in the Taimyr. Nevertheless, the well-preserved abundant fauna allows us to distinguish several regional zones.

LOWER VOLGIAN

1. *Pectinatites pectinatus* Zone. *P. bojarkensis* Mesezhn. and *Pavlovia* (?) aff. *lydianites* (Buckm.).

MIDDLE VOLGIAN

2. *Pavlovia iatriensis* Zone, known only from Lower Bikada-Nguoma River, east of Lake Taimyr.

3. *Dorsoplanites ilovaiskii* Zone. *D. subovalis* Mesezhn., *D. byrrangensis* Mesezhn., *D.* cf. *antiquus* Spath, and *D. dainae* Mesezhn.

4. *Dorsoplanites maximus* Zone. *D. maximus* Spath, *D.* cf. *panderiformis* Michlv., *D.* cf. *triplex* Spath, *Epipallasiceras costatus* Spath, and *Taimyrosphinctes* spp.

5. *Taimyrosphinctes excentricus* Zone. *T. excentricus* Mesezhn., *T. trikraniformoides* Mesezhn., *T. elegans* Mesezhn., and *Virgatosphinctes subtenuicostatus* Mesezhn.

6. *Epivirgatites variabilis* Zone. *E.*(?) *variabilis* Schulg., *Virgatosphinctes bicostatus* Schulg., *V.* cf. *subtenuicostatus* Mesezhn. Known from Kheta Basin. To the north, in Taimyr, talus deposits yield *Laugeites parvus* Dononvan and *Epilaugeites arcticus* Schulg., indicating a different fauna in the upper Middle Volgian.

UPPER VOLGIAN

7. *Craspedites okensis* Zone. Below, *Virgatosphinctes exoticus* Subzone, mainly with *Virgatosphinictes* spp., and *Craspe-*

dites okensis Subzone, mainly with index species. Above, *Craspedites originalis* Subzone, with index species, *C. okensis* (Orb.), and *Virgatosphinictes.*

8. *Craspedites taimyrensis* Zone. *C. taimyrensis* (Bodyl.), *C. laevigatus* (Bodyl.), *Virgatosphinctes exoticus* Schulg., and *Chetaites* sp.

9. *Chetaites chetae* Zone. *C. chetae* Schulg., *Virgatosphinctes,* and *Schulginites margaritae* (Schulg.).

At the Lower Lena River, thick Volgian (170 m) is mainly sand and silt, with clay above. On the Lena River, only the Lower Volgian, characterized by *Ilowaiskya pavida* (Ilov.) and *Ilowaiskya* cf. *sokolovi* (Ilov.), and the Middle Volgian are recorded, the latter with the *P. iatriensis, D. maximus, D. sachsi,* and *D. groenlandicus* Zones. The important *Dorsoplanites sachsi* Zone, characterized by *D. molodonensis* Michlv, *D. sachsi* Michlv, *D. gracilis* Apth, and *Taimyrosphinctes* sp., can be traced northwestward from the Molodo Basin to Olenek.

Northeast

Volgian deposits are mainly marine and very widespread: the Yana Indigirka, Kolyma, Anadyr, and Penzhina Basins, north and east Chukotka, Koryak Highland, and Northern Okhotsk area. Biostratigraphy of the remarkably thick Volgian is mainly based on *Buchia* (Paraketsov and Paraketsova, 1979; Zakharov, 1979, 1981). The lithofacies varies at the Yana-Indigirka interfluve, and is mainly sandstone with siltstone, less frequently, mudstone (1,100–2,000 m); in the Momo-Zyryznka Depression, lagoonal siltstone and sandstone (1,000–8,000 m) with some marine sedimentary volcanics in the lower part. The upper coal-bearing mudstone and sandstone yields *Raphaelia diamensis* Sew. and *Cladophlebis aldanensis* Vachr.

In the Alazeya Upland and northeastern Kolyma area, Volgian deposits are tuff, tufogenic sandstone, and limestone (1,000 m). In the Bolshoi Anyui Basin, the Volgian (1,200 m) consists of alternating sediments and tuffs, and lavas. Similar to the Momo-Zyryanka Depression, the upper part of the section may contain coal measures. In Chukotka, the lower part of the Volgian is missing, and the remainder consists of mudstone, sandstone, siltstone, and tufogenic rocks (300–500 m). In the Koryak Highland are siltstone, sandstone, and conglomerates with flint, jasper, andesite, basalt, and tuff interbeds (900 m); and in the Northern Okhotsk area are andesite and dacite, and sedimentary and tufogenic rocks (1,500–2,000 m).

The Volgian of the northeastern USSR is divisible into several biostratigraphic units.

1. Beds with *Buchia mosquensis* (Buch) and *B. piochii* (Gabb). On the Pezhenka River, these beds yield the ammonite *Ilowaiskya*(?), suggesting the Lower Volgian.

2. Beds with *Buchia fischeriana* (Orb.), *B. piochii* (Gabb), and *B. russiensis* Pavl. They yield *Dorsoplanites,* including *D.* cf. *transitorius* Spath, the Middle Volgian.

3. Beds with *Buchia tenuicollis* (Pavl.) and *B. terebratuloides* (Lah.). With *Chetaites*(?) sp. and *Craspedites* sp., the Upper Volgian.

Far East

The Volgian is widespread and mainly characterized by *Buchia*. Tithonian ammonites are found only in the extreme south. The most complete sections are recorded in the Uda, Torom, and South Primorye Troughs.

The Uda and western Torom Troughs have similar sections. The Volgian is discordant on Kimmeridgian(?), with basal conglomerates (1,500 m). The Lower Volgian is characterized by *Buchia mosquensis* (Buch) and *B. rugosa* (Fisch.). Middle Volgian is most widespread, and possibly thickest; it yields a varied assemblage of *Buchia* and other bivalves, dominated by *Buchia fischeriana* (Orb.), *B. russiensis* (Pavl.), and *B. piochii* (Gabb). Middle Tithonian *Durangites* sp. is also found here. Up-section, marine facies grades into continental. The facies of the Upper Volgian is not fully known. In the eastern Torom Trough (Tugur Bay coast), the Volgian consists of siltstone, and less frequently, sandstone (800 m), which yields below *Buchia mosquensis* (Buch), *B. rugosa* (Fisch.), and *B. stantoni* (Pavl.); in and above the middle, it contains *B. fischeriana* (Orb.) and *B. russiensis* (Pavl.), and above, *B. terebratuloides* (Lah.). All three substages appear to be present. The section grades upward into the Berriassian.

In the South Primorye Trough, the Volgian, sandstone with limestone interbeds, siltstone, and conglomerate (800 m) rest with disconformity on the Middle Jurassic. They comprise all three substages and contain approximately the same *Buchia* sequence as in northern areas. Lower and Middle Tithonian deposits can be distinguished only in the southernmost part of the territory, mainly the islands. Khudolei (1960) assigned sandstone with limestone interbeds, containing *Aulacosphinctes* sp., *Subplanites contiguus* (Zitt.), *Partschiceras schetuchaense* Chud., *Virgatosphinctes* aff. *ruppelianus* (Qu.), and *Primoryites primoryensis* to the Lower Tithonian. The Middle Tithonian consists of sandstone with siltstone interbeds, yielding *Berriasella* sp. indeter. and "*Perisphinctes*" sp. The total thickness is about 30 m.

SUMMARY

A rather reliable zonation has been worked out for the Tithonian and Volgian deposits of most of the USSR. Exceptions are only the Far East and northeast, where rare ammonites have made it necessary to use mainly *Buchia* zones. An immediate task is to draw a common upper boundary for the Tithonian and Volgian, i.e., the Jurassic/Cretaceous boundary.

SUBDIVISION OF THE CONTINENTAL JURASSIC BASED ON PLANTS

V. A. Vakhrameev, V. I. Iljina, and N. I. Fokina

INTRODUCTION

In the Soviet Union, most of the continental Jurassic is in central and eastern Siberia and in the east part of middle Asia, where they sometimes make up the entire (or almost entire) Jurassic. In both territories, the lateral transition from continental to marine facies can be traces throughout the major part of the Jurassic section, and the age of plant macrofossils and microfossils (spores and pollen) can be derived from the correlation between these deposits. A direct comparison of the marine, mostly shallow-water, deposits with the continental deposits can be made by palynology, because all deposits normally contain a considerable number of spores and pollen grains.

During the Jurassic, in the two regions mentioned, the change in the floral composition can be traced in the warm-temperate climate belt that covered central and eastern Siberia, and in the subtropical belt that covered middle Asia. The floras of central and eastern Siberia were a part of the Siberian (Siberian-Canadian) paleofloristic area, whereas the floras of middle Asia belonged to the European-Sinean subarea of the Indo-European area (Vakhrameev and others, 1970).

The difference in climate determined the difference in the floras of the two areas. The Jurassic flora of the Siberian area, which grew in the warm-temperate climate with well-defined seasons, is poorer and lacks (completely or almost) dipteridacean, matoniacean, and marattiacean ferns, most of the Bennettitales, and some of the Conifera. These differences make direct correlation by plant remains between the continental deposits of Siberia and middle Asia rather difficult. Thus indirect correlation by means of fauna-bearing deposits may be advisable, because Jurassic marine invertebrates showed less provincialism than did the flora.

For the third region studied, the Caucasus, only the plant macrofossil sequence is given, and the continental deposits are not as common as in the other two areas. Many marine sections in the Caucasus, however, contain layers of continental, usually coal-bearing, rocks with plant remains, so that the plant assemblages can be dated by marine faunas, mostly ammonites. These plant assemblages can be traced to middle Asia with only slight changes in composition (Vakhrameev, 1969).

The Jurassic palynozones are, on the whole, more detailed than the macrofloral zones, owing to the substantial content of spores and pollen in the deposits. Palynological analysis establishes not only qualitative but also quantitative differences. Frequency estimation is also currently being introduced as a technique for researching macroflora.

We listed from the macrofossil data only those species and genera of plants which characterize particular intervals of selected Jurassic assemblages. Such commonly observed plant groups as the equisetaceans, the ferns of the form genus *Cladophlebis,* the ginkgoes, czekonowskias, podozamitacans, and certain conifers (*Pityophyllum*) were not included in the lists. Although the remains of these plant groups are abundant, their species vary slightly through the Jurassic and they can seldom be used for dating. This is due to the low rate of phenetic evolution of their leaves and shoots, despite the intraspecific variation of some (e.g. ginkgoaceans), which may be fairly large.

It is hoped that a more extensive study of the epidermis cell structure will improve the systematics of the ginkgoes, czekanowskias, podozamitaceans, and conifers for better use in stratigraphy. Sudden changes of the ecosystem due to aridization, such as during middle late Jurassic time, and the consequent reductions or almost complete disappearances of taxa adapted to mostly humid environments, are important for correlation.

At the beginning of the short list of spore-pollen assemblages are the dominating forms; these forms usually have extensive vertical distribution and visibly prevail within one stratum. They are followed by rare forms with narrow range being restricted to the stratum.

MIDDLE ASIA AND ADJACENT REGIONS

The Jurassic flora of middle Asia and of the adjacent regions of Kazakhstan (Mangyshlak, the Emba basin, Tashkent Karatau) belong to the Middle Asia Province, which, together with the European Province, is a part of the European-Sinaean subarea.

The boundary between the provinces runs approximately along the latitude of the Caspian Sea. Our subdivision of the Jurassic continental deposits according to macroflora is based on the materials described by M. I. Brik and A. T. Burakova (unpublished data), Vakhrameev (1969), Doludenko and Orlovskaya (1970), Genkina (1966, 1977, 1979), Gomolitskii (1968), Kirichkova (*in* Kalugin and Kirichkova, 1968; Baranova and others, 1975), Luchnikov (1963), V. M. Mikishova, E. R. Orlovskaya, Z. P. Prosviryakova, L. I. Savitskaya, T. A. Sikstel, and A. I. Turutanova-Ketova (unpublished data), among others.

The Early Jurassic flora is distinctly divided into the Hettangian-Sinemurian and the Toarcian assemblages; a Pliensbachian assemblage is less obvious.

1. The Hettangian-Sinemurian flora is best developed in the eastern regions: Issyk-Kul and Kavak depressions, southern Ferghana (Shurab, Sulyukta), Darvaz, and southern slope of the Gissar Range (Tashkutan). The deposits of this age were named by Genkina (1979) as the Tashkutan Phytostratigraphic Regional Stage; they are not as common as the Toarcian, and especially the Middle Jurassic deposits (Genkina, 1979). The sequence is missing in some sections (northern Ferghana, Mangyshlak, Tuarkyr) where the Toarcian is discordant on Triassic or older rocks.

The relation between Late Triassic and Early Jurassic floras is most obvious in the Issyk-Kul and Kavak depressions, where the system boundary is marked by the disappearance of *Danaeopsis* sp., *Dictyophyllum exile, Cladophlebis schensiensis,* and *Yuccites* spp.; and by the appearance of *Thaumatopteris schenkii, Osmundopsis plectophora, Phlebopteris,* and *Dictyophyllum.*

2. Pliensbachian continental deposits are, doubtless, present in a number of sections (southwestern end of the Gissar Range, Darvaz), but they are as yet poorly characterized by the flora. We believe that this floristic assemblage is close to the Hettangian-Sinemurian assemblages, and therefore date the Tashkutan regional Stage as Hettangian to Pliensbachian, instead of Hettangian-Sinemurian. We assign the overlying Shargun Regional Stage to the Toarcian. This view is based on the presence of two species of *Coniopteris* in the latter stage, a genus practically unknown from the Pliensbachian of the Caucasus and Europe.

3. The Toarcian assemblage is characterized by the persistent presence of one or two species of *Coniopteris,* the appearance of *Sagenopteris,* a larger diversity of *Nilssonia,* a fairly extensive distribution of *Pagiophyllum,* and, to a lesser extent, of *Brachyphyllum,* and by a higher proportion of *Classopollis* pollen produced by these conifers. The number and species diversity of *Neocalamites* and dipteridacean ferns are visibly reduced.

The Middle Jurassic floras are more amply represented than the Early Jurassic ones, because the Middle Jurassic continental deposits cover larger areas. In many Jurassic sections (Tuarky, Mangyshlak, northern Ferghana, the southern slope of the cissar Range), the Toarcian, or Middle Jurassic, directly overlies pre-Jurassic formations. The transgressions during the Middle Jurassic permitted establishment of a correlation between marine and continental deposits for many regions of middle Asia, revealing the age of continental deposits and of the plant remains in them.

The characteristic feature of the Middle Jurassic floras is the abundance and diversity of *Coniopteris* (ferns) and *Milssonis* (cycads) and the great amount of *Ptilophyllum* (Bennettitales) and *Sagenopteris* (Caytoniales). Concurrently, the amount of dipteridaceous and matoneaceous ferns decreases, and *Cycadorcarpidium* disappears altogether. Among the Middle Jurassic floras of middle Asia, three assemblages of different ages are distinguished; they have different species composition of *Coniopteris* ferns and *Nilssonia* cycads. The middle and the upper assemblages contain *Klukis* and *Otozamites.* These assemblages tentatively identify three Middle Jurassic stages in the continental deposits of middle Asia.

During the Middle Jurassic, the assemblages succeeded one another gradually. The Aalenian and Bajocian floras are represented by associations which appear in humid environments; only in the Bathonian flora are indications of starting aridization by the appearance of most localities of considerable conifer remains (*Brachyphyllum* and *Bagiophyllum*). It should also be noted that the Bajocian flora of the Yakkabag Mountains (Gomolitskiy, 1968), although varied, shows no signs of aridization.

An earliest Bathonian age is indicated by the overlying coal-bearing member with plants and early Bathonian marine fossils. Aridization in that region perhaps started later, owing to the immediate vicinity of the sea.

Based on the succession of these three assemblages, Genkina (1979) distinguished three phytostratigraphic regional stages (Vandob, Sherdjan, and Shelkan), which approximately correspond to the Aalenian, Bajocian, and Bathonian. Coeval deposits are also traced farther west, in Tuarkyr, Mangyshlak, and the Caspian depression.

Aridization of the climate, starting at the end of the Middle Jurassic, caused the substitution of gray rocks with poor coal content, by multicolored and red deposits with practically undefinable macrofloral remains. This change occurred approximately at the boundary of the Middle and Upper Jurassic. In the region studied, we know of only one area with early Late Jurassic flora. The localities are in the south of Tashkent Karatau (southern Kazakhstan) and expose a limnic sequence of lamellated clay, dolomitic limestones, and marls. The assemblage (Doludenko and Orlovskaya, 1976) is characterized by an abundance of Bennettitales (including *Otozamites, Ptillophyllum, Pseudocycas,* and *Zamites*) and conifers (*Brachyphyllum* and *Pagiophyllum*). *Classopollis* pollen from these conifers increases sharply (>50 percent). Flora of humid environments (ferns, *Nilssonia,* ginkgoaceans, and czekonowskias) are represented by single impressions. The deposits of the uppermost Jurassic yielded no identifiable plant remains.

The palynological studies of the Jurassic in middle Asia were summarized by Fokina (Barash and Fokina, 1970; Renzhina and Fokina, 1978; Rozanov and Fokina, 1972) and supplemented by workers including Aliev and Barkhatnaya (*in*

MACROFLORAL ASSEMBLAGES

Callovian-Kimmeridgian

Conifers prevail: mostly *Brachyphyllum* (5 spp.), *Pagiophyllum* (5 spp.), and *Elatocladus* (3 spp.); rare ferns, including *Coniopteris* (2–3 spp.) and first *Stachypteris turkestanica* Tur.-Ket.; fairly varied Bennettitales; *Ptilophyllum, Otozamites, Pterophyllum, Sphenozamites, Zamiophyllum,* single *Nilssonia,* and *Paracycas.*

Bathonian

Abundant conifers: *Brachyphyllum, Pagiophyllum, Elatocladus;* diversity of *Coniopteris* reduced (<10 spp.), mostly small pinnules; among *Nilssonia, N. brevis* Brongn., *N. tenuicaulis* (Phill.) Fox-Strang., *N. polymorpha* Schenk, and *N. vittaeformis* Pryn. dominate; *Otozamites, Ptilophyllum,* and *Pseudocycas* present; and *Ferganiella* appears again.

Bajocian

Coniopteris ferns reach maximum diversity (15 spp.); small pinnules abundant, including *Cagnustiloba* Brick, *C. furssenkoi* Pryn., *C. nerifolia* Genkina, *C. pulcherrima* Brick, and *C. vialovae* Tur.-Ket. In middle Asia, *Klukia* is restricted to stage; rare *Eboracia* and *Gonatosorus; Sagenopteris phillipsi* (Brongn.) Presl. quite common; *Nilssonia* numerous and diverse; Bennettitales with reduced diversity; *Ptilophyllum acutifolium* Morr. and *P. cutchense* Morr. common; and a few conifers.

Aalenian

Increased diversity of *Conopteris: C. hymenophylloides* (Brogn) Sew., *C. latifolia* Brick, *C. spectabilis* Brick, and *C. an-* *gustiloba* Brick with small pinnules appear; *Nilssonia* numerous and diverse (15 to 20 spp.); Bennettitales almost same as in Torcian; *Ferganiella* abundant; certain neocalamites, dipteridaceans (*Clathropteris obovata*), and matoneacean still present.

Toarcian

Abundance and diversity of Neocalamites and dipteridacean ferns decrease notably; while equisetums increase; rare *Coniopteris* ex gr. *hymenophylloides* (Brongn.) Sew., and *Sagenopteris* spp.; abundant *Nilssonia* and Bennettitales, i.e., *Nilssoniopteris, Pterophyllum,* and rare *Ptilophyllum;* abundant conifers *Pagiophyllum* and also *Brachyphyllum.*

Pliensbachian

Leaf flora poor; close to older assemblage.

Hettangian-Sinemurian

Diverse and abundant *Neocalamites* and ferns, dipteridaceans, and matoniacean dominate; among the dipteridaceans, *Clathropteris elegans* Oishi, *C. menisciodes* Brongn., *Dictyophyllum muenstri* (Goepp.) Nathn., *D. nilssonii* (Brongn) Goepp., *Thaumatopteris schenkii* Nath., and *T. hissarica* Brick et Sixt.; among the matoniaceans, with *Phlebopteris braunii* (Goepp.) Hirm. et Hoerh., and *P. muensteri* (Schenk) Hirm. et Hoerh; in Darvaz, *Antrophyopsis* sp. and various *Pterophyllum;* also *Cycadocarpidium* spp. and rare *Stachyotaxus elegans* Nath. and *Swedenborgia major* Harris.

Barkhatnaya, 1975); K. V. Vinogradova, L. S. Pozemova, M. A. Petrosiants, and L. I. Tarasova (unpublished data); and Dubrovskaya (1973) and Kuzichkina and Khachieva (1973).

The study of cores from the deep boreholes in western Uzbekistan and central and eastern Turkmenia revealed a fairly complete pattern of the change of pollen assemblages from latest Early to Late Jurassic, and made it possible to distinguish pollen assemblages for the Jurassic stages (see following section).

The oldest Hettangian-Sinemurian pollen assemblage was discovered in the Kavak and Issyk-Kul depressions and on the southern slope of the Gissar Range. The conditions of sedimentation changed quite often during this time, due to the instability of the mostly small fresh-water basins. This is observed in the changing quantitative relations between spore and pollen taxa, i.e., the change of the dominating forms. The gymnosperms, though abundant in the Triassic, still occurred locally, and produced the occasionally observed *Florinites* and *Striatopinites* pollen.

The *Kyrtome* spores provide the background of the early Liassic assemblage, and sometimes give way to the spores of the *Cyathidites* and *Leiotrilites* type and to the asaccate gymnosperms. The proportion of bisaccate pollen increases toward the east and southeast of middle Asia.

The Pliensbachian assemblage covers a larger area: Ustyurt, Amu Darya, and Gissar-Zeravshan regions, Ferghana. The conditions of sedimentation were relatively stable. The pollen of the conifers, including *Paleoconiferus variabilis* (Mal.) M. Petr., *P. asaccatus* Bolch., and *Paleopicea,* almost universally prevail. Sometimes, the asaccate *Chasmatosporites major* T. Nils., *C. crassus* T. Nils., *C. apertus* (Rog.) T. Nils., and *Cycadopties deterius* Pocock, etc. dominate over the bisaccate pollen. On the southern slope of the Gissar Range (Kosenkova, 1975) the pollen assemblage differs somewhat by the dominance of *Cyathidies minor* Couper. The proportion of bisaccate pollen seldom rises in this region, resembling the older Hettangian-Sinemurian assemblage.

The Toarcian pollen assemblage is ubiquitously present in middle Asia, from Tuarkyr in the west to Ferghana in the east. This time was marked by a notable warming of the climate and possibly by slight aridization. In western middle Asia, and partly in the east (Zeravshan), the proportion of *Classopollis* pollen increases, in extreme cases to more than 50 percent (Kuzichkina and Khachieva, 1973), a reliable indication of climate change at the end of the Early Jurassic. Abundance of spores of *Cyathidites, Leiotriletes,* and *Osmundacidites wellmanii* Couper increases occasionally.

In the Pitnyak region, the proportion of *Perinopollenites elatoides* Couper and *Araucariacites* reaches 30 percent (Barash and Fokina, 1970), at a level with *Classopollis.* In the east and northeast (Ferghana and Issyk-Kul region), *Classopollis* increases less, ranging from 0 to 1.5 percent, below, to 6 to 8 percent in the Toarcian.

In middle Asia, continentality reaches its maximum in the Middle Jurassic, and spores and pollen abound. The pollen assemblages change greatly from those of the Lower Jurassic.

Among the spores, *Cyathidites* and *Leiotrileles* become increasingly numerous, whereas the number of kyrtome spores (*Torvisporites* and *Matonisporites*) is greatly reduced. Among the pollen, the Lower Jurassic gymnosperms (*Chasmatosporites* and *Disaccites* with undifferentiated sacs) are replaced by more complicated forms: *Podocarpidites, Cedripites,* and *Inaperturopollenites dubis* (Pot. et Ven.) Th. et Pf. Diverse spores *Ischiosporites, Neoraistrickia rotundiforma* (K.-M.) Tar., *Contiguisporites fornicatus* Dettm., and *Converrucosisporites disparituberculatum* Vin., characteristic of the Middle Jurassic, are common but not dominant.

The Aalenian climate was cooler, as evident from the sharp decrease of *Classopollis* and the considerable increase of spores in number and diversity.

The limnic swamp and alluvial facies are mostly Bajocian. Fresh-water basins were shallow, with inadequate water circulation. Occasionally, river drainage increased. Both continental and marine facies contain spores, represented primarily by *Cyathidites minor* Couper and *Leiotrileles* in maximum proportion (90–95%). Compared to the Aalenian, the proportion of spores of *Converrucosisporites disparituberculatum* Vin. increases to 31 percent, *Contignisporites fornicatus* Dettm. to 13 percent, and *Neoraistrickia rotundiforma* (K.-M.) Tar. to 11 percent. Spores of *Gleicheniidites* are persistenly present. The Amu Darya region is characterized by more abundant *Caytonipollenites pallidus* (Reiss) Couper (21–50%).

Continental facies lasted through the Bathonian in the east of middle Asia (Ferghana) and a somewhat shorter time on the southern slope of the Gissar Range. In continental, and particularly marine Bathonian, the proportion of *Classopollis* pollen increases irregularly (from 10 to 82%); this happened before in the Toarcian. *Cycadopites* and *Disaccites* decrease gradually. Spores of *Cyathidites* and *Leiotrileles* sometimes still dominate (80%), but usually diminish slowly, similar to *Neorairstrickia rotundiforma* (K.-M.) Tar., *Contiguisporites fornicatus* Dettm., *Sphagnumsporites,* and other plants held over from the Bajocian. Compared to the Bajocian, a somewhat larger proportion of *Cedripites* pollen is persistently present. Abundance of *Classopollis* and *Cedripites* pollen and reduction of spores indicate a change from the warm and humid climate of the Bajocian to hot and dry Bathonian climate.

In western and central parts of middle Asia, the Upper Jurassic is represented by the marine carbonate; only in the east (Ferghana) do continental, mostly varigated deposits occur. Pollen assemblages are known from Tuarkyr in the west to Ferghana in the east. All are characterized by a considerable, but variable, proportion of *Classopollis* pollen.

In the marine Lower Callovian, the proportion of *Classopollis* increases notably (40–70%) without reaching its maximum. Besides the spores of *Cyathidites,* those of *Gleicheniidites* sp. and *Heliosporites kemensis* (Chlon.) Sriv., are persistently present. *Classopolis* pollen becomes completely dominant in the Middle–Upper Callovian, and particularly in the Oxfordian (100%). The continental Callovian deposits of the Zeravshan River Basin and in Ferghana show *Classopollis* pollen increasing slowly and irregularly, as compared to the rapid rate in coeval marine deposits. Many spores still occur, of which *Cyathidites* is the most frequent. Locally, *Dissacites* and *Cycadopites* pollen are fairly numerous.

The limnic Oxfordian-Kimmeridgian Karabastaus Formation (Karatau in southern Kazakhstan) (Doludenko and Orlovskaya, 1976), however, has predominant *Classopollis* pollen (80%).

In carbonates, spores and pollen are replaced by peridinians. The Lower Callovian marls contain cysted tabulate *Gonyaulax* (e.g., *G. cladophora, C. jurassica*) and *Litodinium jurassica* Eis. Oxfordian limestones have numerous coarse-cyst, nontabulate, and tabulate forms: *Endoscrinium luridum* Khem., *Scriniodinium crystallinum* (Detl.) Khem., *Scriniosaccus reticulatus* Pocock, *Gonyaulax cladophors* Khem., and *G. jurassica* Eis. In the uppermost Oxfordian, the thick-walled forms occasionally change to the soft, naked *Pareodinia* (*P. brevicornis*) indicating desalting and undisturbed hydrodynamic conditions.

THE CAUCASUS

The Jurassic flora of the Caucasus is in the southeastern part of the European Phytogeographic Province. As noted earlier, marine Jurassic dominates in the Caucasus; the continental facies is less frequent. The floras were studied by workers including R. A. Vasina, V. A. Vakhrameev, V. A. Krassilov, A. N. Kryshtofovich, A. F. Lesnikova, E. M. Loladze, and V. D. Prinada; and, during the last two decades, mainly by G. V. Delle, M. P. Doludenko, and Ts. I. Svanidze.

Early Jurassic floras are not as well represented as Middle Jurassic ones. The Hettangian-Sinemurian assemblage was found in Georgia (Lok and Dziruli crystalline massifs). Its age is indicated by stratigraphic position and by the presence of *Dictyophyllum nilssonii,* and particularly by *Anthrophyopsis narulensis* (Svanidze, 1965).

A typically Pliensbachian flora occurs in the northern Caucasus (Baksan and Kuban River Basins) in coal measures discordant on Paleozoic; it is overlain by marine Upper Pliensbachian (Domerian). A similar flora was found in a volcanic layer along the Eshkakon, Tarakul-tyube, and Chechek-Tokhakasu Rivers. The diversity of the Pliensbachian flora is poor; most characteristic are *Neocalamites, Thaumatopteris schenkii, Marattiopsis muensteri,* and *Phlebopteris polypodioides.* Toarcian flora is also known from the Knukh River (Kuban River Basin), where *Coniopteris hymenophylloides* and two species of *Ptilophyllum* have now been found (see following section).

Middle Jurassic floras of the Caucasus are much more diverse and better studied than Early Jurassic floras, particularly the Bathonian floras of Georgia (Tkvarcheli, Tkibuli) (Delle, 1967; Svanidz, 1965). An incompletely described Aalenian flora occurs in Dagestan (Vasina and Doludenko, 1968), in a paralic sequence of coal measures with marine interbeds containing ammonites. It contains such typical Middle Jurassic species as *Dico-*

tylophyllum rugosum, Coniopteris spp., and several *Nilssonia* and *Ptilophyllum* spp. Ginkgoaceans and czekanowskias are sharply reduced compared to Early Jurassic floras.

Bajocian flora occurs only in the upper part of the stage (region of Speti, Georgia) (Svanidze, 1965). Its composition is close to the Bathonian flora. At Tkvarcheli, Tkibuli (Georgia), the floras occur in coal measures above a porphyritic formation. Unlike Aalenian, these floras contain *Otozamites, Klukia exilis, Pachypteris lanceolata,* and the more abundant *Brachyphyllum* and *Pagiophyllum.*

The coastal marine Callovian with ammonites at Tsesi (Rioni River and Bzyb River Basin) yields a flora (Doludenko and Svanidze, 1969) distinctly different from earlier Middle Jurassic flora, found primarily in coal measures. Equisetaceans, ferns, and czekanowskias are almost completely absent. Bennettitales are extremely diverse, and the conifers with shoots covered by scaly or awl-like needles (*Brachyphyllum* and *Pagiophyllum*) are numerous. Pteridosperms (*Pachypteris*) and Caytoniales (*Sagenopteris*) are frequent. Recurrent assemblages indicate a sudden change in the ecosystem. The known Bathonian flora comes predominantly from swampy lowlands of very humid climate, whereas the Callovian habitat consisted of drained coastal slopes washed by the sea, and a more arid climate.

CENTRAL AND EASTERN SIBERIA

The Jurassic floras of this vast territory belong to the Siberian Phytogeographic Area, within the warm–temperate seasonal climate belt and probably with temperate climate in the northern extremity of Asia. Comparison of the Jurassic floras of middle Asia from the subtropical belt with coeval floras of Siberia shows the considerable impoverishment of the latte, with diversity reduced to one-half or one-third. In particular, analysis of only Early and Middle Jurassic floras shows that Bennettitales and Caytoniales have almost entirely disappeared. Their absence is already manifest in northern Ferghana and the Issyk-Kul depression. Marattiaceans, dipteridaceans, matoneaceans, and cycads are rare and have few species; *Klukia* is absent; and the proportion of thermophilic conifers is sharply reduced (e.g., *Brachyphyllum, Pagiophylum*).

The low diversity of the slightly higher clades, such as ginkgos, czekanowskias, and podozamitacean conifers, renders difficult the macrofloral zonation of the continental Jurassic of Siberia. Yet spores and pollen do permit some subdivision of Jurassic deposits. The next section, on continental macrofloral assemblages of central and eastern Siberia, is based on the research by A. V. Askarin, Batyaeva and Bystritskaya (Bystritskaya, 1974), Vakhrameev (1964), Kirichkova (1976), Markovich and Prinada (Prinada, 1962), and Samylina and Teslenko (Teslenko, 1970). The most important source is "The regional stratigraphic scheme of the Jurassic deposits of the south of Central Siberia," which was adopted at the Interdepartmental Stratigraphic Conference in Novosibirsk in 1979.

Two distinct assemblages of the Early Jurassic leaf floras are

SPORE-POLLEN ASSEMBLAGES

Callovian-Kimmeridgian

SPA composition remains practically unaltered from the middle Callovian to the Kimmeridgian. Pollens of *Classopollis* (ranging from 85 to 95 to 100 percent) are absolutely dominant, with *C. classoides* (Pflug) Pocock et Jans., *C. minor* Pocock et Jans., *C. itunensis* Pocock and *C. pflugii* Pocock et Jans.; also single pollen of *Disaccites* and *Cycadopites* in association with rare spores of *Leiotriletes, Gleicheniidites, Ischyosporites, Heliosporites kemensis* (Chlon.) Sriv., etc. In the marine Oxfordian, peridinialean algae sometimes dominate. *Classopollis* pollen often dominate (50–70%); other pollen taxa decrease notably; among spores still prevailing are *Cyathidites* and *Leiotriletes;* variable spore proportions of *Osmundacidites, Gleicheniidites,* and *Ischyosporites,* etc., occur.

Bathonian

Classopollis is notably more abundant (30–50%); among spores, *Cyathidites* and *Leiotriletes* prevail; also much pollen of *Disaccites* (*Pinuspollenites, Podocarpidites,* etc.) and *Cycadopites;* sometimes increasing abundance of *Osmundacites* and *Ischysporites;* reduction of *Inaperturopollenites dubious* (Pot. et Ven.) Th. et Pf., *Matonisporites, Contignisporites, Converrucosisporites, Neoraistricia,* and *Cyatonipollenites.*

Bajocian

Abundant, sometimes dominating, spores with smooth exine (*Cyathidites, Leiotriletes*); occasionally, the numbers of spores with exine sculpturing increase, e.g., *Neoraistrickia, Contignisporites, Converrucosisporites, Gleicheniidites,* and *Osmundacidites;* single *Ischiosporites.* Pollen content is irregular; the proportions of *Disaccites, Cycadopites,* and *Inaperturopollentis dubious* (Pot. et Ven.) Th. et Pf. often increases, whereas *Retinopollenites elatoides* Couper decreases; regionally sharp increases in proportion

of *Caytonipollenites pallidus* (Reiss) Coupter occur; *Classopollis* is minimal.

Aalenian

Spores with many *Cyathidites* and *Leiotriletes,* variable abundance, often dominating; regionally, abundance of *Marattisporites, Osmundacidites* increases. Among numerous disacctic pollen, proportion of grains with poorly differentiated sacs decreases; abundance of *Cycadopites, Inaperturopollenite dubious,* and sometimes, of *Eucommiidites,* increases; abundance of *Classopollis* decreases sharply.

Toarcian

Persistently high abundance of *Classopollis* (30–50%), locally, abundance of *Chasmatosporites, Cycadopites, Disaccites* increases, less often in *Perinopollenites* and *Araucariacites.* Spores, with numerous *Cyathidites* and *Leiotriletes;* also present, *Converrucosisporites, Contignisporites, Ischiosporites, Marattisporites,* and *Neoraistricia.*

Pliensbachian

Mostly large pollen of *Disaccites, Chasmaosporites,* and *Cycadopites* dominate. Abundance and diversity of spores of *Auritulinasporites, Matonisporites, Toroisporis,* and *Cyathidites* are reduced. Triassic relics disappear (*Florinites, Cordaitales, Striatites*).

Hettangian-Sinemurian

Spores of *Cyathidites, Auritalinasporites, toroisporis,* and *Matonisporites* prevail. Persistent presence of *Osmundacites* and *Calamotriletes,* and of pollen of *Chasmatosporites, Cycadopites,* and *Disaccites* with undifferentiated sacs. Triassic relics are *Florinites, Striatites,* and *Cordaitales.*

MACROFLORAL ASSEMBLAGES
(CONTINENTAL AND LITTORAL)

Callovian-Kimmeridgian

Ferns rare; equisetaceans absent. Common are Pteridosperms (*Pachypteris bendukidzei* Dolud. et Svan., *P. lanceolata* Brongn., and *Ctenozamites usnadzei* Dolud. et Svan.) and Caytoniales (three spp. of *Sagenopteris*). Bennettitales are abundant and diverse (*Nilssoniopteris, Otozamites, Pterophyllum, Ptilophyllum, Pseudocycas,* and *Cycadolepsis*). The most frequent cycads are *Paracycas* and *Pseudoctenis,* but *Nilssonia* is rare; *Brachyphyllum* and *Pagiophyllum* are numerous. Ginkgoaceans and Podozamites are infrequent and czekanowskias are absent.

Bathonian

Contains *Osmundopsis prynadae* Delle, *Klukia exilis* (Phill.) Racio., *Coniopteris* ex gr. *hymenophylloides* (Brongn.) Sew., *C. murrayana* Brongn., *Dictyophyllum rugosum* L. et H., *Sagenopteris phillipsii* (Brongn.) Presl, *S. heterophylla* Dolud. et Svan., and *Pachypteris lanceolata* Brongn. Also contains *Otozamites* (four spp.), *Ptilophyllum* (four spp.), *Nilssonia* (five spp.), *Paracycas brevipinnata* Delle, and *P. cteis* (Harris) Harris. Czekanowskias are rare. Conifers *Brachyphyllum* and *Pagiophyllum* are frequent.

Bajocian

Only known from upper Bajocian of Georgia (Speti region); identical to Bathonian assemblage.

Aalenian

Equisetum beanii (Bunb.) Sew., *E. columnare* Brongn., *Coniopteris* ex gr. *hymenophylloides* (Brongn.) Sew., *C. murrayana* Brong., *Dictyophyllum rugosum* Lindll. et Hut, *Pachypteris* Presl., and *Ptilophyllum,* which are more frequent than *Pterophyllum.* Also various *Nilssonia* (seven spp.). Czekanowskias only with *Phoenicopsis angustifolia* Heer.

Toarcian

With *Coniopteris* ex gr. *hymenophylloides* (Brongn.) Sew., *Ptilophyllum acutifolium* Morr., *P. cutchense* Morr.; *Nilssonia* ex gr. *orientalis* Heer, poorly known.

Pliensbachian

With *Neocalamites kssykkulensis* Tur.-Ket., *Phlebopteris polypodioides* Brongn., *Thaumatopteris schenkii* Nath., *Taeniopteris tenuinvervis* Brauns., and *Nilssonia* spp.

Hettangian-Sinemurian

With *Neocalamites hoerensis* (Schimper) Halle, *Dictyophyllum nilssonii* (Brongn.) Goepp., *Anomozamites minor* (Brongn.) Nath., *Anthrophiopsis narulensis* Dolud. et Svan., various Pterophyllum, *Stachyotaxus* sp., czekanowskias, and *Pityophyllum latifolium* Tur.-Ket.

distinguished. The lower flora characterizes the Hettangian-Pliensbachian, and is as yet poorly known. It contains *Schizoneura, Neocalamites,* and the large pinnule fern *Cladophlebis suluctensis.* The upper assemblage is Toarcian and Upper Pliensbachian. It is marked by the appearance of *Coniopteris* spp. and *Phlebopteris polypodioides* and also contains *Raphaelia diamensis,* practically unknown in older deposits. The occurrence of *Phlebopteris polypodioides,* a species common in the Lower Jurassic of more southern regions, is perhaps related to Toarcian warming (Ilyina, 1985). This is indicated by the appearance in the Siberian Toarcian of moderately abundant *Classopollis* pollen and of fern spores normally found farther south.

The undivided Aalenian-Bathonian assemblage has a number of species of *Coniopteris,* a large amount of equisetums, and *Raphael diamensis;* however, it almost completely lacks such thermophilic plants as dipteridaceans (*Clathropteris obovata*) and matoneacean (*Phlebopteris polypodioides*) from the upper Lower Jurassic of Siberia.

In central Siberia, the Callovian-Volgian is known only from the Chulymo-Enisei Basin, represented by the variegated Tyazhin Formation without identifiable macroflora. Coal measures occur in the Vilyui Depression, which is part of eastern Siberia. Until recently, only a single assemblage with *Cladophlebis aldanensis, C. orientalis, C. serrulata, Raphaelia diamensis,* and *R. stricta,* was known.

Kiritchkova (1976) determined two assemblages. The older one (Callovian-Oxfordian?), at sites including Cape Dzhaskoi (Lena River), contains the new species *Raphalelia kirinae* and also *R. diamensis* and *R. stricta. Cladophlebis* is missing. The latter species is abundant in the upper assemblage in the Vilyui Depression (Markhinsk Formation) and in the Priverkhoyanye region. Later Jurassic coal measures with plant remains are also found in the South Yakutia Basin (Vlasov and Markovich, 1979) and contain an assemblage similar to that of the Vilyui Depression.

Palynology provides not only comparison of coal-measures between different basins, but also direct correlation of marine with continental facies. Ilyina (1978a) subdivided and correlated the marine Jurassic of northern Central and Eastern Siberia with the continental Jurassic in the south. The marine deposits were zoned by ammonites and other invertebrates as well as by pollen assemblages at Anabar Bay, on the Anabar and Lena rivers, in Eastern Taimyr, in the Vilyui synclinorium and elsewhere. The continental deposits of the central syncline, Doronin Depression of Kuzbass, and the Kansko-Achinskiy and Irkutsk basins in the south, were analyzed and their characteristic pollen assemblages determined.

The pollen assemblages of marine and continental sequences were also studied in different regions of central and eastern Siberia (Ilyina, 1976, 1978b, 1980; Odintsova, 1977). The palynologic zonations and correlation schemes of the Jurassic deposits of central Siberia were adopted at the Interdepartmental Stratigraphic Conference on the Mesozoic and Cenozoic of Central Siberia.

The list of pollen assemblages contains only stratigraphically useful taxa, dominant and characteristic forms. All features controlled by facies were disregarded. Microphytoplankton was also used for subdivision of marine sections. The biostratigraphy for central and eastern Siberia was based on the evolution of the pollen assemblages, which reflects floral evolution and migration caused by climatic variations. Three floral intervals were traced in northern and southern continental facies.

1. The first floral interval is Hettangian-Late Pliensbacian. The pollen assemblages gradually changed, reflecting the slow evolution of the mesophytic flora in a warm-temperature climate. The pollen assemblages indicate the beginning and flourishing (?Pliensbachian) of the Siberian Early Jurassic flora, which changed little throughout Siberia. The assemblages differ by the appearance, acme, and extinction of certain floral groups and individual taxa. The characteristic feature of the Hettangian-Sinemurian pollen assemblages is the maximum proportion of ancient conifer pollen with poorly differentiated sacs, and spores of *Camptotriletes cerebriformis* Naum. et Jarosch. The Early Pliensbachian assemblages differ only by gradual reduction of ancient conifer pollen; the Late Pliensbachian assemblages show the maximum abundance and diversity of sphagnoid spores of *Stereisporites* and cf. *Selaginella.*

2. The second floral interval is latest Pliensbachian-Aalenian. Frequent changes in the pollen assemblages reflect repeated floral renewal due to considerable climatic changes, i.e., a sudden warming in the Early Toarcian followed by gradual cooling from the middle Toarcian to a minimum in the Aalenian. Early Toarcian warming is indicated by a pollen assemblage with maximum abundance of *Tripartina variabilis* Mal., spores of *Cyathidites minor* Coup., rare *Marattisporites scabratus* Coup., and Bennettitales pollen. The pollen assemblage with various spores of Indo-European ferns and pollen of *Classopollis* is characteristic for all of Siberia; it coincides with the maximum of early Toarcian warming. Against the background of Siberian forms, the pollen assemblage with rare *Marattisporites scabratus* Coup. and *Dipteridaceae* characterizes the interval of reduced warming in the latest Toarcian; the relatively poor Aalenian assemblages—primarily represented by *Osmundacidites* spp., *Cyathidites minor* Coup., and *Piceapollenites* and *Ginkgoales*—indicate a change to a cooler climate.

Identification and comparison of these pollen assemblages are based on climate-stratigraphic peculiarities, i.e., the appearance, maximum, and disappearance of spores and pollen of plants, which migrated into Siberia from the Indo-European phytogeographic area at the time of the Early Toarcian warming.

3. Pollen assemblages of the Late Aalenian, Bajocian, and Bathonian reflect the gradual development of the Jurassic flora in the humid warm-temperature climate of the third floral interval. These assemblages show the appearance and flourishing of the Siberian Middle Jurassic flora, which is remarkable for the variety and dominance of fern-like plants. The pollen assemblages are confined to large lithostratigraphic units with indistinct boundaries, reducing the accuracy of zonations and correlation. The features most useful for correlation, and common to marine and

continental facies, are present in the (?)Bajocian: acme of *Neorai-strickia rotundiforma* (K.-M.) Taras., spores of *Dicksonia densa* Bolch., *Lycopodium intortivallus* Sach. et Iljina, and *Pinus divul-gata* Bolch. The appearance of *Lophotriletes torosus* Sach. et Iljina and *Gleicheniidites* appears to mark the Bathonian in ma-rine and continental deposits.

At the end of the Bathonian, a warming of climate begins anew in southern Siberia. Apparently, however, it did not reach the northern regions, or was insignificant there. This warming trend is reflected in the Late Bathonian pollen assemblages of the Kansko Achinskiy Basin by the appearance of rare *Classopollis* pollen and by increased abundance of *Quadraeculina limbata* Mal. The floral differentiation between northern and southern Siberia also began at this time, but became marked in the Late Jurassic.

During the later Jurassic* evolution of mesophytic flora, the north and south parts of central Siberia belonged to different phytogeographic areas. The floras of southern Siberia, which con-stituted a part of the Indo-European area, developed in subtropi-cal semi-arid climate, whereas the floras of northern regions, as earlier, mostly grew in humid warm climate.

The later Jurassic pollen assemblage of the Tyazhin Forma-tion of the Kansko-Achinskiy Basin shows parallel floral and climatic changes. This assemblage has a high proportion of *Clas-sopollis* pollen and some spores of *Klukisporites variegatus* Coup., resembling the Callovian-Oxfordian assemblages of the Indo-European Phytogeographic Area. In the later Jurassic, its boundary moved much farther north, to northern Siberia. Com-pared to the Bathonian, the climate was perhaps somewhat warmer and milder due to the vast transgression of the sea. In northern Siberia, the Callovian pollen assemblages are similar to basic Bathonian assemblages, but contain *Densoisporites velatus* Weyl. et Krieg., rare *Classopollis,* and some *Gleicheniidites.* The temperature and aridity maxima of Eurasia in the Oxfordian affected the climate of northern Siberia. The Oxfordian pollen assemblage of the west coast of Anabar Bay definitely indicates some climatic warming by the presence of *Cardioceras percaela-tum* and *Classopollis* (10–12%). The Kimmeridgian and Volgian assemblages are poorly known and their description is tentative.

The analysis of pollen assemblage sequences in marine and continental facies in central and eastern Siberia shows that the accuracy of Jurassic palynozones greatly depends on the rate of floral evolution and the frequency of floral changes, which were caused by variations in the physico-geographic environments, mostly by climate.

The boundaries of the pollen zones in marine and continen-tal facies of southern central Siberia do not always coincide with the ammonite standard zones. Correlation is therefore largely tentative, especially of boundaries that were established conven-tionally. The accuracy of detailed subdivision is also reduced by the incompleteness of palynologic data, e.g., for Volgian-Kimmeridgian, Upper and Middle Callovian and Lower Pliens-bachian times. Most distinct and reliable are the subdivision and correlation of the Toarcian and Upper Pliensbachian.

The phytostratigraphic correlations between the continental Jurassic of middle Asia and Siberia are fairly good. This is due primarily to large-scale climatic changes that caused coeval changes in floral composition in both areas. The extent and char-acteristics of these changes, however, differ in each region. Two warming phases are clearly recognized in the Jurassic. The less intense one was Toarcian. It is manifested by the increase of *Classopollis* pollen in the Caucasus and middle Asia, and by the expansion of this pollen and of the spores of thermophilic ferns into northern Asia. The second, stronger, phase was later Jurassic, and was concurrent with high aridity indicated by peculiar xero-phytic vegetation of conifers, producing *Classopollis* pollen and various bennettites in the Caucasus, middle Asia, and southern Kazakhstan. In the north, this phase apparently caused only cli-matic warming; coal measures were still being formed there. The Middle Jurassic had a more humid climate, with smaller thermal gradient and reduced latitudinal differentiation of vegetation.

---

*A term used purposely to include the Callovian (Westermann, ed.).

CONTINENTAL MACROFLORAL ASSEMBLAGES

Volgian-Kimmeridgian

With *Equisetites tschetschumensis* Vassilevsk., *Coniopteris burejensis* (Zal.) Sew., *Cladophiebis aldanensis* Vachr., *C. orientalis* Pryn., *C. serrulata* Samyl., *Raphaelia diamensis* Sew., *R. stricta* Vachr., *Hausmannia leeiana* Sze, *Coniferites marchaensis* Vachr., *Pseudotorellia longifolia* Dolud., and *Pagiophyllum kryshtofovichii* Samyl.

Callovian-Oxfordian

With *Equisetites beanii* (Bunb.) Sew., *E. tschetschumensis* Vass., *Osmundopsis acutipinnula* Vass., *Coniopteris burenjensis* (Zal.) Sew., *Gleichenites jacutensis* Vass., *Cladophlebis serrulata* Samyl., *Raphaelia diamensis* Sew., *R. kirinae* Kiritchk., *R. stricta* Vachr., *Sphenobaiera uninervis* Samyl., and *Baiera ahnertii* Krysht.

Aalenian-Bathonian

With *Equisetites lateralis* Phill., *E. asiaticus* Pryn., *Coniopteris hymenophylloides* (Brongn.) Sew., *C. burejensis* (Zal.) Sew.,

C. maakiana (Heer) Pryn., *C. jurensis* (Gol.) Tesl., *C. snigirevskiae* Tesl., *Cladophlebis haiburnensis* (L. et H.) Sew., *C. denticulata* (Brongn.) Font., *Raphaelia diamensis* Sew., *Sphenobaiera longifolia* (Pomp.) Flor., and *Podozamites lanceolatus* (L. et H.) Schimp.

Toarcian

Neocalamites pinitoides (Chachl.), *Equisetites lateralis* Phill., *E. beanii* (Bunb.) Sew., *Coniopteris hymenophylloides* (Brongn.) Sew., *C. spectabilis* Brick, *C. angustiloba* Brick, *C. angarensis* Pryn., *Phlebopteris polypodioides* Brongn., *Clathropteris obovata* Oishi, and *Raphaelia diamensis* Sew.

Pliensbachian-Hettangian

Schizoneura sp., *Neocalamites pinitoides* (Chachl.), *Equisetites sokolowskii* Eichw., *Clathropteris obovata* Oishi, and *Cladophlebis haiburnensis* (L. et H.) Sew., *C. suluctensis* Brick, *C. nebbensis* Brick, *Sphenobaiera longifolia* (Pomel) Flor., *S. czekanowskiana* (Heer) Flor., *Ferganiella urjanchaica* Neub., *Schizolepis moelleri* Sew., and *Samaropsis rotundata* Heer.

CONCLUSION

G. Ya. Krymholts and M. S. Mesezhnikov

Based on the analysis of the Jurassic zonal scheme useful for the Soviet Union, conclusions can be drawn that may be of general significance. The elaboration of basic notions and methods of stratigraphy were not accidentally based largely on studies of Jurassic deposits. In the course of studies over a hundred and fifty years, a stable system of stage subdivision has been established. The number and the names of the stages of this system cause no objections. Only one problem is cause for further consideration: the Jurassic/Cretaceous boundary.

The problem of the upper boundary of the Jurassic, the Jurassic/Cretaceous boundary, is very important. At present, most specialists draw this boundary between the Tithonian and the Berriassian, although some workers prefer it higher up, i.e., within or at the top of the Berriassian. Without analyzing the arguments, we note only that, in case of disagreement, stratigraphic boundaries should be drawn in the original way. Displacements of boundaries should be based on convincing arguments, and these are lacking in the case of the Upper Jurassic boundary. For Soviet scientists, however, the problem of system boundaries is complicated even more by the fact that the Volgian cannot yet be entirely correlated with the Tithonian.

The second problem is the boundary between the Middle and Upper Jurassic, which Soviet geologists solved differently from most foreign specialists. Prior to the publication of Arkell's synthesis (1956), the Callovian was placed in the Upper Jurassic in England, France, the USSR, and some other countries. Mapping and other geological studies were carried out on this basis. The analysis of ammonite evolution shows that it is preferable to drawn the boundary at the base of the Callovian. To accept Arkell's viewpoint would mean we must reject tradition, and we should review the extensive evidence available from our large territory where a significant paleogeographic rearrangement took place in the early Callovian. Yet the International Subcommission on Jurassic Stratigraphy has placed the boundary according to priority, i.e., between the Callovian and Oxfordian (see the preface, by Westermann, ed.).

A specific feature of the Soviet Jurassic is the extensive presence of the Volgian in the Boreal biogeographic area. We consider that it is only temporarily retained as a stage, beside the Tithonian; but much time may pass until the Tithonian zonation

is worked out and the complete zonal correlation between the Tithonian and Volgian can be accomplished.

Concerning the Standard, or International Stage Scale, of the Jurassic, founded in the middle of the last century by d'Orbigny, it is emphasized that opinions on all stages and their range and boundaries differed greatly at that time. In some cases, reexamination of the original sections for the stages has shown that they do not conform to the present-day requirements of stratotypes. These sections are frequently more or less incomplete, with breaks, condensed intervals, and the like. It should be acknowledged, therefore, that the Jurassic stages now in use are synthetic notions; they result from studies of entire type areas, amplified by data on coeval formations in other areas, and are characterized by their zonal fossil assemblages.

For zones, several of which make up a stage, type sections are also significant. The stratotypes of zones, distinguished in the type area of the stage, allow establishment of zonal boundaries and are, as a rule, characterized by fossils. In the Jurassic case, these are the ammonites of certain phyletic clades, which often pass from one zone into the next, indicating continuity of sections, and enhancing the precision of zonal boundaries. A zone should be characterized by an assemblage of species, usually with different ranges. Their areal extent also differs, which helps in the intercontinental recognition of zones, after the vicariants have been established. Arkell (1956) has shown that, where sufficient paleontological material exists, some Jurassic zones acquire a global range.

Subzones, defined in the zonal stratotypes, are commonly much more limited in area than zones, and are restricted to a basin or its parts. Local zonal units are therefore required at this level much more frequently than zones; these local units are the lonas of Krymholts (1972). This term, included into the Stratigraphic Code of the USSR (Stratigraphic Code, 1977), allows for easy recognition of the assemblage of a certain minute unit, which is named after the index species.

Western Europe is a type area for Jurassic stages. Although Jurassic deposits have long been studied and subdivided there in detail, the task of distinguishing zones, and particularly subzones, has not been completed. This is evident in some of our figures where the column labeled "subzones" is empty. Only further studies of sections and their ammonites by Western European specialists will securely establish subzones in the general scale.

Detailed studies of distribution of ammonites have shown that in certain cases the range zone of the index species does not coincide with the formal zone or subzone. Zones should therefore be based on the assemblage, not on single species, and the type of zone should be clearly defined, such as range zone or assemblage zones.

As expected, zonal correlation within the USSR of some Jurassic stages is influenced by paleogeographic setting. Faunal and floral evolution is modified by regional conditions, e.g., that weakening of geographic links produces variants. This is particularly pronounced in the case of climatic differentiation, and produces different fauna in separate sedimentary basins.

At the beginning of the Jurassic, global marine zoogeographic differentiation was at its minimum. Hettangian standard zones can therefore be traced from the stratotype area of Western Europe to the northeast part of the USSR. Subsequently, seas transgressed, covering ever larger areas in the north and south of the Soviet Union. In the Mediterranean Belt, i.e., the Crimea, Caucasus, and southern middle Asia, faunal assemblages were similar to those in Western Europe, and the Standard Zonal Scale is usually applicable, though certain boundaries are less distinct. But in northern areas, beginning in the late Pliensbachian, the peculiarities of ammonite assemblages become pronounced. All Northern Hemisphere seas were dominated by Amaltheidae, but the species of *Amaltheus* differed markedly. Among 15 of them known from northern Siberia, the Northeast, and Far East USSR, only three species are the same as in Western Europe. However, even at this time of high endemism, morphologic trends are similar, so that local units can be correlated with the standard zones.

At the end of the Early and the beginning of the Middle Jurassic, Boreal and Tethyan faunas diverged less, possibly due to some reduction of climatic differences. Since the end of the Middle Jurassic, and particularly in later Jurassic time, the areal extent of marine deposits on Soviet territory increased, mainly due to the transgression from the north in the European part of the USSR, Western Siberia, and the eastern USSR. Northern transgression also took place in western Europe. The Bathonian to Kimmeridgian standard zones established there (mainly in England), can therefore be recognized in most regions of the USSR.

The Tithonian standard zonation, associated with the Submediterranean area of Western Europe, is applicable only to a small southern part of the Soviet Union. This resulted more than 100 years ago in the distinction of the Volgian stage, which has retained its significance. Its standard zonal units can be correlated with local biostratigraphic units over extensive areas of the USSR.

General and continuing studies we are involved in concern basic problems of the Jurassic, such as the detailed stratigraphy of sections in type areas, ammonite taxonomy of zonal assemblages, and their succession. Here, the coordinating role of the International Subcommission on Jurassic Stratigraphy is fruitful. Attention should be paid to the present discrepancies in the names of certain zones and subzones, on the one hand, and to range zones of their index species on the other. Sometimes, traditional names of index species (and zones) differ from the present names of the species; this conflict should be taken into account.

Soviet investigators have their own particular tasks. For each of the seven regions of the USSR, independent Jurassic zonations should be distinguished and correlated with the Standard Scale, which should reflect the peculiar regional character. Special emphasis should be placed on the stratigraphic correlation of different biogeographic belts, i.e., Boreal and Tethyan, based on the above-mentioned procedure.

ILLUSTRATIONS OF INDEX AND GUIDE AMMONITES OF THE SOVIET UNION

REPOSITORY OF SPECIMENS

CNIGR—Central Scientific-Research Geological Exploration Museum, Leningrad

VNIGRI—Geological Museum of the All-Union Science Research Petroleum Geological Prospecting Institute, Leningrad

LGU—Geological Museum of the Cathedra of Historical Geology of Leningrad State University

MM—Mining Museum, Leningrad

GIN—Geological Institut of the Academy of Science of the U.S.S.R., Moskwa

GM M—Geological Museum of the Geological Survey of Northeastern U.S.S.R., Magadan

IGG—Geological Museum of the Institute of Geology and Geophysics, Siberian Branch of the Academy of Science of the U.S.S.R., Novosibirsk

GM—Geological Museum of the Ministry of Geology of the Usbekskoi S.S.R., Tashkent

All figures at natural size.

Plate 1. Hettangian and Sinemurian

Figure 1. *Psiloceras viligense* Chud. and Polub. Northeast of USSR, Viliga River; Hettangian, Planorbis Zone (Coll. Polubotko and Repin).

Figure 2. *Angulaticeras (Gydanoceras) kolymicum* Repin. Holotype. GM Magadan, N 362/12. Northeast of USSR, Korkodon River Basin; Sinemurian, *A. kolymicum* Zone (Polubotko and Repin, 1972, Pl. 7, Fig. 4).

Figure 3. *Waehneroceras frigga* (Waehner). Northeast of USSR, Yana River Basin; Hettangian, Liasicus Zone (Coll. Repin).

Figure 4. *Schlotheimia ex gr. angulata* (Schloth). GM M, N 362/9. Omolon River Basin; Hettangian, Angulata Zone (Polubotko and Repin, 1972, Pl. 2, Fig. 4).

Figure 5. *Primapsiloceras primulum* (Repin). Holotype. GM M, N 362/1. Omolon River Basin; Hettangian, *P. primulum* Zone (Polubotko and Repin, 1972, Pl. 1, Fig. 1).

Figure 6. *Alsatites?* sp. indet. GM M, N 362/24. Omolon River Basin; Hettangian (Polubotko and Repin, 1972, Pl. 1, Fig. 6).

Figure 7. *Waehneroceras armanense* Repin. Holotype. GM M, N 362/34. Arman River; Hettangian, Liasicus Zone. (Field atlas . . ., 1968, Pl. 12, Fig. 1).

Figure 8a, b. *Arietites libratus* Repin. Paratype. GM M, N 344/2. Omolon River Basin; Sinemurian, Bucklandi Zone (Polubotko and Repin, 1972, Pl. 4, Fig. 1). X 0.84.

Figure 9. *Coroniceras (Primarietites) reynesi* (Spath). GM M, N 362/19. Omolon River Basin; Sinemurian, *C. siverti* Zone (Polubotko and Repin, 1972, Pl. 6, Fig. 1).

Plate 2. Sinemurian and Upper Pliensbachian

Figure 1a, b. *Amaltheus (Amaltheus) stokesi* (Sowerby). GM M, N 400/39. Sededema River Basin; Upper Pliensbachian, Stokesi Zone (Field atlas . . ., 1968, Pl. 36, Fig. 2).

Figure 2a, b. *Amaltheus (Amaltheus) talrosei* Repin. Paratype. GM M, N 344/7. Korkodon River Basin; Upper Pliensbachian, *A. talrosei* Zone (Repin, 1972, Pl. 3, Fig. 3).

Figure 3a, b. *Amaltheus (Amaltheus) subbifurcus* Repin. Holotype. GM M, N 344/6. Omolon River Basin; Upper Pliensbachian, Stokesi Zone (Field atlas . . ., 1968, Pl. 34, Fig. 1).

Figure 4. *Arieticeras japonicum* Matsumoto. CNIGR, N 1-205/1. Southern Sikhote-Alin, Isvilinka River Basin; Upper Pliensbachian (Sey and Kalacheva, 1980, Pl. 2, Fig. 4).

Figures 5, 6. *Amaltheus (Amaltheus) margaritatus* (Monft.). 5. CNIGR 11511/111. Bureya River Basin; Upper Pliensbachian, Margaritatus Zone (Sey and Kalacheva, 1980, Pl. 1, Fig. 12). 6. Lena River Basin; Upper Pliensbachian, Margaritatus Zone (Coll. Repin).

Figure 7. *Amaltheus (Nordamaltheus) viligaensis* (Tuchkov). Paratype. GM, N 400/72. Viliga River; Upper Pliensbachian, *A. viligaensis* Zone (Coll. Repin).

Figure 8. *Coroniceras (Paraconiceras) siverti* (Tuchkov). Lectotype. GM, N 362/21. Omolon River Basin; Sinemurian, *C. siverti* Zone (Field atlas . . ., 1968, Pl. 15, Fig. 1), X0.63.

Plate 3. Toarcian

Figure 1. *Grammoceras thouarsense* (Orb.). LGU N 235/62. Northern Caucasus, Cuban River Basin; Thouarsense Zone (Krymholts, 1961, Pl. 2, Fig. 8).

Figure 2. *Dumortieria gundershofensis* Haug. LGU N 235/159. Northern Caucasus, Bol. Zelenchuk River Basin; Levesquei Zone (Krymholts, 1961, Pl. 4, Fig. 10).

Figure 3a, b. *Grammoceras quadratum* (Haug). LGU N 235/69. Northern Caucasus, Baksan River Basin; Thouarsense Zone (Krymholts, 1961, Pl. 2, Fig. 7).

Figure 4a, b. *Zugodactylites braunianus* (Orb.). Korkodon River Basin; *Z. monestieri* Zone (Coll. Repin).

Figure 5. *Pseudogrammoceras fallaciosum* (Bayle). LGU N 235/133. Northern Caucasus, Urup River Basin; Thouarsense Zone (Krymholts, 1961, Pl. 4, Fig. 4).

Figure 6. *Pseudolioceras rosenkrantzi* A. Dagis. GM M, N 318/18. Omolon River Basin; *P. rosenkrantzi* Zone (Polubotko and Repin, 1966, Pl. 4, Fig. 3).

Figure 7. *Harpoceras falcifer* (Sowerby). Omolon River Basin; Falcifer Zone (Coll. Repin).

Figure 8. *Harpoceras exaratum* (Y. and B.). GM M, N 318/5. Omolon River Basin; Falcifer Zone (Polubotko and Repin, 1966, Pl. 3, Fig. 7).

Figure 9a, b. *Porpoceras polare* (Frebold). Paren River Basin; *Porpoceras spinatum* Zone (Coll. Repin).

Figure 10a, b. *Zugodactylites monestieri* A. Dagis. Korkodon River Basin; *Z. monestieri* Zone (Coll. Repin).

Figure 11. *Eleganticeras elegantulum* (Y. and B.). Omolon River Basin; *E. elegantulum* Zone (Coll. Repin).

Figure 12. *Dactylioceras athleticum* (Simps.). Omolon River Basin; *D. athleticum* Zone (Coll. Repin).

Figure 13a, b. *Tiltoniceras propinquum* (Whit.). GM M, N 400/142. Omolon River Basin; *T. propinquum* Zone (Field atlas . . ., 1968, Pl. 44, Fig. 1).

Figure 14. *Porpoceras spinatum* (Frebold). GM M, N 400/143. Omolon River Basin; *Porpoceras spinatum* Zone (Field atlas . . ., 1968, Pl. 50, Fig. 1).

Plate 4. Aalenian and Bajocian

Figure 1, 3. *Pseudolioceras (Pseudolioceras) beyrichi* (Schloeb.). 1. CNIGR, N 9546/4. Western Okhotsk area, Tugur Bay; Aalenian, *P. maclintocki* Zone (Sey and Kalacheva, 1980, Pl. 5, Fig. 5). 3. LGU, N 235/177. Northern Caucasus, Belaja River; Opalinum Zone (Krymholts, 1961, Pl. 8, Fig. 4).

Figure 2. *Pseudolioceras (Tugurites) whiteavesi* (White). CNIGR, N 10045/91. Western Okhotsk area, Tugur Bay; Aalenian, *P. tugurensis* Zone (Sey and Kalacheva, 1980, Pl. 6, Fig. 7).

Figure 4. *Staufenia (Costilioceras) sinon* (Bayle). Northern Caucasus, Cuban River, Aalenian, Murchisonae Zone (Coll. Rostovtsev).

Figure 5a, b. *Leioceras costosum* (Quenst.). Northern Caucasus, Cuban River; Aalenian, Murchisonae Zone (Coll. Rostovtsev).

Figure 6. *Erycitoides (Kialagvikes) spinatus* Wester. CNIGR, N 9706/10. Western Okhotsk area, Tugur Bay; Aalenian, *Erycitoides howelli* Beds (Sey and Kalacheva, 1980, Pl. 6, Fig. 5).

Figure 7. *Ludwigia bradfordensis* Buckm. Northern Caucasus. Belaja River; Aalenian, Murchisonae Zone (Coll. Rostovtsev).

Figure 8. *Pseudolioceras (Tugurites) tugurensis* Kalach. and Sey. CNIGR, N 10045/5. Western Okhotsk area, Tugur Bay; Aalenian, *P. tugurensis* Zone (Sey and Kalacheva, 1980, Pl. 6, Fig. 9).

Figure 10a, b. *Arkelloceras elegans* Frebold. CNIGR, N 10814/4. Bureya River Basin; Bajocian, *A. tozeri* Zone (Sey and Kalacheva, 1980, Pl. 8, Fig. 2).

Figure 11. *Pseudolioceras (Tugurites) fastigatum* Wester. CNIGR, N 10335/251. Bureya River; Bajocian, *P. fastigatus* Zone (Sey and Kalacheva, 1980, Pl. 8, Fig. 4).

Figure 12. *Pseudolioceras (Tugurites) maclintocki* (Haught.). Lena River Basin; Aalenian, *P. maclintocki* Zone (Coll. Repin).

Figure 13a, b. *Dorsetensia tessoniana* (Orb.). Northern Caucasus, Bol. Zelenchuk River, Bajocian, Humphriesianum Zone (Coll. Rostovtsev).

Figure 14. *Leioceras opalinum* (Rein.). Northern Caucasus, Bol. Zelenchuk River, Aalenian, *Opalinum* Zone (Coll. Rostovtsev).

Figure 15. *Toxolioceras mundum* Buckm. LGU, N 235/308. Northern Caucasus, Andian Kojsu River; Bajocian, Discites Zone (Krymholts, 1961, Pl. 6, Fig. 1).

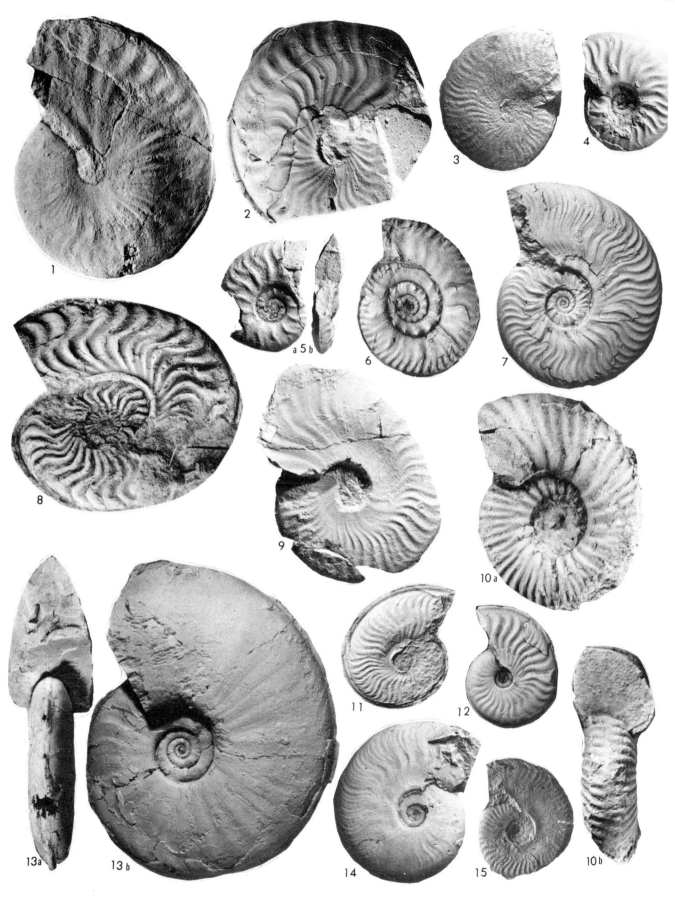

Plate 5. Bajocian

Figure 1a, b. *Parkinsonia rarecostata* Buckm. Trans-Caucasus, Dzharychai River; Parkinsoni Zone (Coll. Rostovtsev).

Figures 2, 3, 4. *Umaltites era* (Krymholz). 2. CNIGR, N 11511/179. Bureya River Basin; *Umaltites era* Beds. 3, 4. Same area (Sey and Kalacheva, 1980, Pl. 10, Fig. 17).

Figure 5a, b. *Cranocephalites vulgaris* Spath. IGG, N 311/69. Anabar Bay; Vulgaris Zone (Meledina, 1973, Pl. 3, Fig. 1).

Figure 6a, b. *Bradfordia alaseica* Repin. GM M, N 374/1. Sededema River; *A. tozeri* Zone (Repin, 1972, Pl. 2, Fig. 1).

Figures 7a, b. *Boreiocephalites borealis* (Spath). IGG, N 311/1. Anabar Bay; *B. borealis* Zone (Meledina, 1973, Pl. 1, Fig. 1).

Figure 8a, b. *Strenoceras niortense* (Orb.). Northern Caucasus, Bol. Zelenchuk River; Subfurcatum Zone (Coll. Rostovtsev).

Figure 9. *Leptosphinctes asinus* (Zatworni.). Northern Caucasus, Cuban River; Subfurcatum Zone (Coll. Rostovtsev).

Figure 10. *Parkinsonia parkinsoni* (Sow.). CNIGR, N 161/12284. Trans-Caucasus, Negram Section; Parkinsoni Zone (Coll. Rostovtsev).

Figure 11. *Garantiana (Garantiana) garantiana* (Orb.). CNIGR, N 1205/12284. Trans-Caucasus, Asnabjurt-II Section; Garantiana Zone (Coll. Rostovtsev).

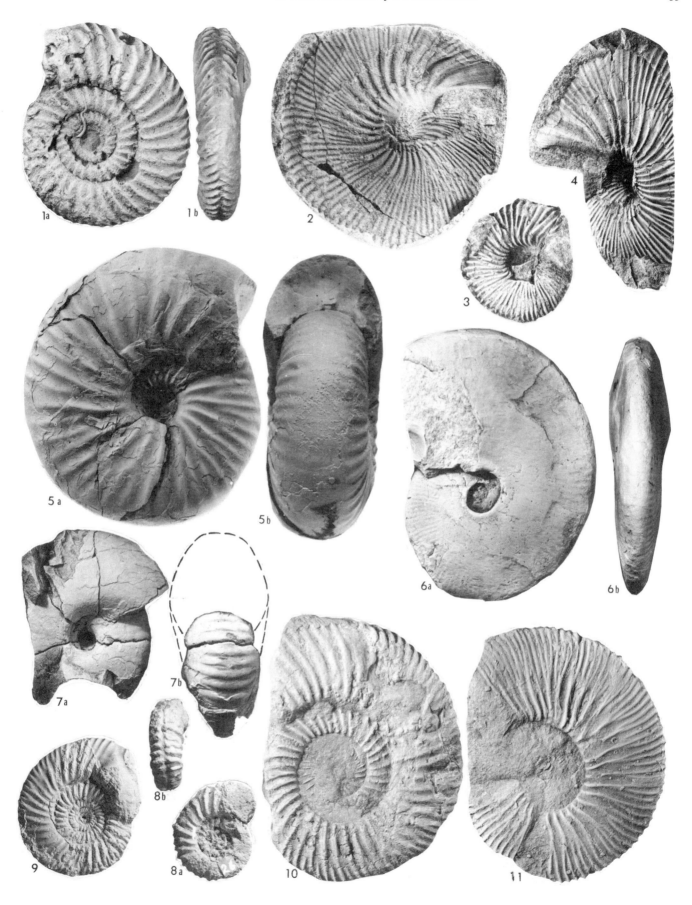

Plate 6. Bathonian and Callovian

Figure 1a, b. *Arcticoceras ishmae* (Keyserling). Holotype. MM. Petchora River; Bathonian, *A. ishmae* Zone (Stratigraphy . . ., 1976, Pl. 9, Fig. 1a, b).

Figure 2. *Macrocephalites ex gr. macrocephalus* (Schloth.). Volga River near Saratov, Malinowy ravine; Callovian, *C. elatmae* Zone (Coll. Alexeeva and Repin).

Figure 3a, b. *Macrocephalites* c.f. *macrocephalus* (Schloth.). CNIGR, N 32/1344. Oka River; Callovian, Macrocephalus Zone (Nikitin, 1888, Pl. X, Fig. 18).

Figure 4. *Pseudocosmoceras michalskii* (Boriss.). LGU, N 282/2. Northern Caucasus, Avarskian Cojsu River; Bathonian, *P. michalskii* Zone (Coll. Krimholts).

Figure 5. *Arctocephalites elegans* Spath. IGG, N 311/146. Anabar Bay; Bathonian, *A. elegans* Zone (Meledina, 1973, Pl. 18, Fig. 1).

Figure 6a, b. *Cadoceras elatmae* (Nikitin). IGG, N 489/213. Anabar Bay; Callovian, *C. elatmae* Zone (Stratigraphy . . ., 1976, Pl. 11, Fig. 1).

Figure 7. *Clydoniceras discus* (Sowerby). GM T, N 434/2. Kugitang, Airibaba; Bathonian, Discus Zone (Krymholts and Zahkarov, 1971, Pl. 1, Fig. 3.

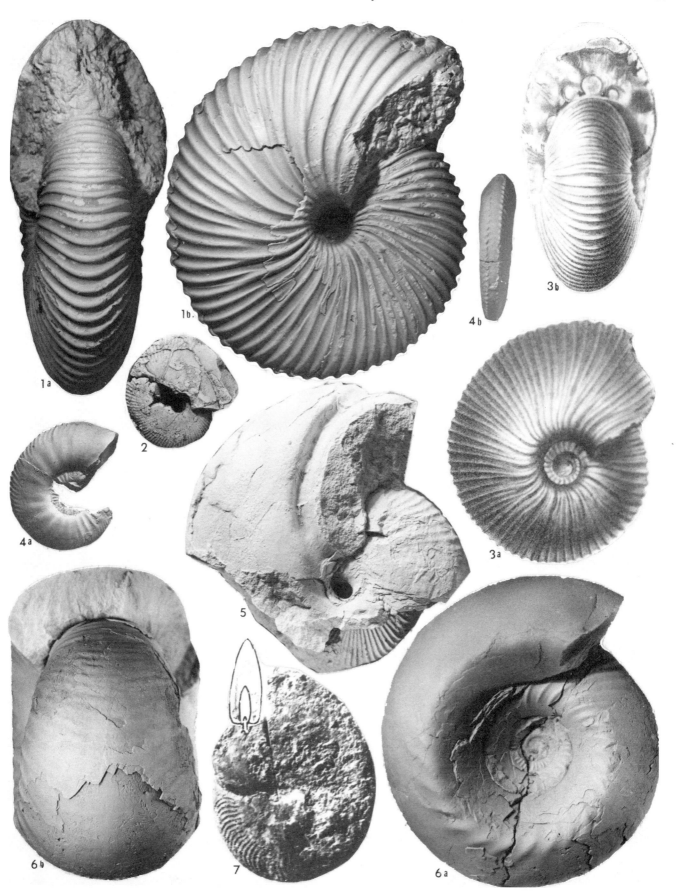

Plate 7. Callovian

Figure 1a, b. *Cadoceras emelianzevi* Vor. Holotype. Anabar Bay; *C. emelianzevi* Zone (Stratigraphy . . ., 1976, Pl. X, Fig. 1a, b).

Figure 2a, b. *Eboraciceras subordinarium* Buckm. IGG, N 489/7; Big Begitchev Island; *E. subordinarium* Zone (Meledina, 1977, Pl. 43, Fig. 1a, b).

Figure 3. *Quenstedtoceras lamberti* (Sowerby). IGG, N 579/264. Volga River near Saratov, Malinowy ravine; Lamberti Zone.

Figure 4. *Peltoceras* aff. *tuarkyrensis* Amann. IGG, N 579/101. Oka River near Elatma; Athleta Zone.

Figure 5a, b. *Longaeviceras keyserlingi* (Sok.). CNIGR, N 10/1370. Petchora River Basin, Usa River; *L. keyserlingi* Zone (Sokolov, 1912, Pl. II, Fig. 2a, b).

Figure 6. *Rondiceras milaschevici* (Nik.). IGG, N 489/302; Big Begitchev Island; Middle Callovian (Meledina, 1977, Pl. 20, Fig. 2).

Plate 8. Callovian

Figure 1. *Kosmoceras jason* (Rein). IGG, N 579/43; Oka River near Elatma; Jason Zone.

Figures 2a, b. *Sigaloceras calloviense* (Sowerby). IGG, N 579/22; Unzha River; Calloviense Zone.

Figure 3. *Longaeviceras keyserlingi* (Sok.). CNIGR, N 2/1-939. East Siberia, Preobrazhenia Island; *L. keyserlingi* Zone.

Figure 4a, b. *Erymnoceras coronatum* (Orb.). IGG, N 579/281; Oka River, Elatma; Coronatum Zone.

Plate 9. Oxfordian

Figure 1. *Cardioceras (Scarburgiceras) praecordatum* R. Douv. IGG, N 460/73. East Siberia, Anabar River; *C. percaelatum* Zone (Knyazev, 1975, Pl. IV, Fig. 4).

Figure 2. *Cardioceras (Scarburgiceras) gloriosum* Arkell. IGG, N 460/32. East Taimyr, Chernohrebetnaja River; *C. gloriosum* Zone (Knyazev, 1975, Pl. V, Fig. 5).

Figure 3a, b. *Cardioceras (Cardioceras) cordatum* (Sowerby). IGG, N 460/94. East Siberia, Anabar River; Cordatum Zone (Knyazev, 1975, Pl. XIII, Fig. 9).

Figures 4, 5. *Cardioceras (Subvertebriceras) zenaidae* Ilovaisky. 4. Holotype. Miatschkovo near Moskva, bed 13 (Ilovaisky, 1903, Pl. X, Fig. 35). 5. CNIGR, N 34/12525. Petchora River Basin, Ishma River; *C. densiplicatum* Zone.

Figure 6a, b. *Cardioceras (Subvertebriceras) densiplicatum* Boden. CNIGR, N 29/12525. Petchora River Basin, Ishma River; *C. densiplicatum* Zone.

Figure 7a, b. *Cardioceras (Plasmatoceras) tenuicostatum* (Nikitin). CNIGR, N 8/12525. Petchora River Basin, Ishma River; *C. densiplicatum* Zone.

Figure 8a, b. *Amoeboceras (Amoeboceras) alternoides* (Niki.). Holotype. CNIGR, N 1/5247. Miatchkovo (near Moskva), *A. alternoides* Zone (Nikitin, 1916, Pl. 1, Fig. 1).

Figure 9a-c. *Amoeboceras (Amoeboceras) tuberculatoalternans* (Niki.). CNIGR, N 17/5247. Mnevniki near Moskva, uppermost Oxfordian.

Figure 10. *Cardioceras (Miticardioceras) tenuiserratum* (Oppel). CNIGR, N 37/12525. Volga River Basin, Unzha River, South Makarjev Section; *C. tenuiserratum* Zone.

Figure 11. *Amoeboceras (Amoeboceras) koldeweyense* Sykes and Callomon. CNIGR, N 69/12525. Volga River Basin, Unzha River, North Makarjev Section, *A. serratum* Zone, *A. koldeweyense* Subzone

Figure 12. *Amoeboceras (Paramoeboceras) ilovaiskii* (M. Sokilov). CNIGR, N 12/12490. Volga River Basin, Unzha River, South Makarjev Section; *A. alternoides* Zone, *A. ilovaiskii* Subzone.

Figure 13. *Ringsteadia marstonensis* Salfeld. CNIGR, N 109/12525. Ural River Basin, Berdjanka River, Hanskaja Gora Section; *R. pseudocordata* Zone.

Figure 14. *Amoeboceras (Amoeboceras) ravni* Spath. VNIGRI, N 20/686. East Siberia, Chatanga River Basin, Levaja Bojarka River; *A. ravni* Zone (Mesezhnikov, 1967, Pl. 1, Fig. 1).

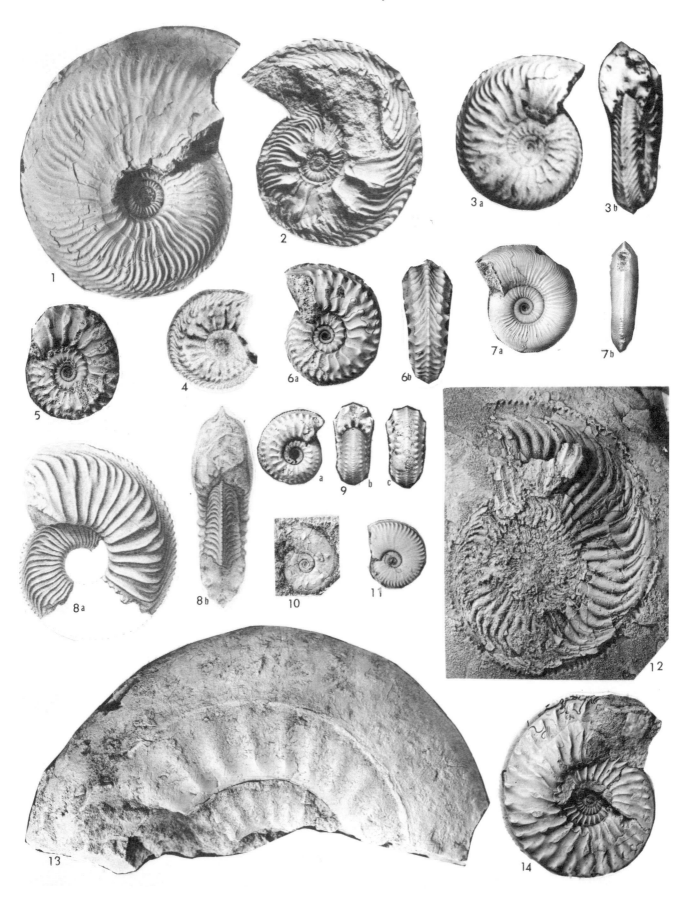

Plate 10. Oxfordian

Figure 1a, b. *Amoeboceras (Prionodoceras) serratum* (Sowerby). CNIGR, N 2/12490. Petchora River Basin, Adzva River; *A. serratum* Zone and Subzone.

Plate 11. Lower Kimmeridgian

Figure 1. *Pictonia (Pictonia) involuta* Mesezhn. VNIGRI, N 93/686. Chatanga River Basin, Levaja Bojarka River; *P. involuta* Zone (Mesezhnikov, 1968, Pl. 4, Fig. 1).

Figures 2. *Amoeboceras (Amoebites) kitchini* (Salfeld). VNIGRI, N 1424/686. Chatanga River Basin, Cheta River; *R. evoluta* Zone (Mesezhnikov, 1968, Pl. 1, Fig. 1).

Figure 3a, b. *Zonovia (Zonovia) uralensis* (Orbigny). Neotype. VNIGRI, N. 1180/633. Eastern slope of Subpolar Ural, Tolja River. *R. evoluta* Zone, *Z. uralensis* Subzone (Meszhnikov, 1984, Pl. 31, Fig. 1).

Figure 4. *Rasenia (Rasenia) optima* Mesezhn. Holotype. VNIGRI, N 482/686. Chatanga River Basin, Levaja Bojarka River. *R. evoluta* Zone (Meszhnikov, 1984, Pl. 18, Fig. 1).

Plate 12. Upper Kimmeridgian

Figure 1. *Aulacostephanus (Aulacostephanoides) mutabilis* (Sowerby). VNIGRI, N 47/636. Chatanga River Basin, Levaja Bojarka River. Mutabilis Zone (Mesezhnikov, 1984, Pl. 21, Fig. 10.

Figure 2. *Aulacostephanus (Aulacostephanoceras) undorae* (Pavlov). VNIGRI, N 189/767. Petchora River Basin, Pishma River. Eudoxus Zone (Mesezhnikov, 1984, Pl. 21, Fig. 3).

Figure 3. *Virgataxioceras dividuum* Mesezh. Paratype. VNIGRI, N 1521/633. Eastern slope of Subpolar Ural, Dolja River. Autissiodorensis Zone, *V. dividuum* Subzone.

Figure 4. *Aulacostephanus (Aulacostephanoceras) autissiodorensis* (Cotteau). VNIGRI, N 412/767. X0.5. Petchora River Basin, Pishma River. Autissiodorensis Zone (Mesezhnikov, 1984, Pl. 34, Fig. 1).

Figure 5. *Aulacostephanus (Aulacostephanoides) sosvaensis* (Sasonov). VNIGRI, N 3172/633, East slope of subpolar Ural, Lopsia River. *A. sosvaensis* Zone (Mesezhnikov, 1984, Pl. 39, Fig. 1).

Figure 6. *Oxydiscites taimyrensis* (Mesezh.). Holotype. VNIGRI, N 3001/686. Chatanga River Basin, Cheta River. Uppermost Kimmeridgian (Mesezhnikov, 1984, Pl. 6, Fig. 1).

Plate 13. Lower Volgian

Figure 1. *Ilowaiskya pseudoscythica* (Ilovaisky). Ilek River Basin, Vetlianka River; *I. pseudoscythica* Zone (Ilovaisky and Florensky, 1941, Pl. 15, Fig. 32).

Figure 2. *Ilovaiskya klimovi* (Ilovaisky). Ural River Basin, Berdjanka River; *I. klimovi* Zone (Ilovaisky and Florensky, 1941, Pl. 21, Fig. 40).

Figure 3. *Ilovaiskya sokolovi* (Ilovaisky). Ilek River Basin, Suchaja Pestschanca River; *I. sokolovi* Zone (Ilovaisky and Florensky, 1941, Pl. 13, Fig. 27).

Figure 4. *Pectinatites (Pectinatites) fedorovi* Mesezhnikov. VNIGRI, N 759/686. Chatanga River Basin, Cheta River.

Plate 14. Lower-Middle Volgian

Figure 1. *Pavlovia pavolovi* (Michalsky). CNIGR, N 177/300. Moskva. Panderi Zone (Michalsky, 1890, Pl. XI, Fig. 6).

Figure 2. *Laugeites borealis* Mesezhnikov. VNIGRI, N 570/634. Eastern slope of Subpolar Ural, Iatria River. Groenlandicus Zone (Zakharov and Mesezhnikov, 1974, Pl. 22, Fig. 6).

Figure 3. *Epilaugeites vogulicus* (Ilovaisky). VNIGRI, N. 1647/634. Eastern slope of Subpolar Ural, Iatria River; *E. vogulicus* Zone (Zakharov and Meszhnnikov, 1974, Pl. 22, Fig. 1).

Figure 4. *Subdichotomoceras (Sphinctoceras) subcrassum* Mesezhn. Holotype. VNIGRI, N 1121/634. Eastern slope of Subpolar Ural, Iatria River; *S. subcrassum* Zone (Zakharov and Mesezhnikov, 1974, Pl. 7, Fig. 1).

Figure 5. *Eosphinctoceras magnum* Mesezhn. VNIGRI, N 1131/634, X 0.5. Eastern slope of Subpolar Ural, Iatria River; *E. magnum* Zone (Zakharov and Mesezhnikov, 1974, Pl. 9, Fig. 1).

Figure 6. *Dorsoplanites ilovaiskii* Meszhn. VNIGRI, N 1914/634. Eastern slope of Subpolar Ural, Iatria River; *D. ilovaiskii* Zone (Zakharov and Mesezhnikov, 1974, Pl. 16, Fig. 3).

Plate 15. Middle Volgian

Figure 1. *Epivirgatites nikitini* (Michalsky). Volga River, Kachpir Section near Syzran (Coll. Mesezhnikov).

Figure 2. *Vigatites virgatus* (Buch). CNIGR, N 1/300. Moskva; Virgatus Zone (Michalski 1890, Pl. 1, Fig. 1).

Figure 3. *Strajevskya strajevskyi* (Ilovaisky). Eastern slope of Subpolar Ural, Iatria River; *P. iatriensis* Zone, *S. strajevskyi* Subzone (Coll. M. S. Mesezhnikov).

Figure 4. *Pavlovia iatriensis* (Ilovaisky). Eastern slope of Subpolar Ural, Iatria River; *P. iatriensis* Zone and Subzone (Coll. M. S. Mesezhnikov).

Figure 5. *Laugeites biplicatus* Mesezhn. Holotype. VNIGRI, N 655/634. Eastern slope of Subpolar Ural, Iatria River; Groenlandicus Zone (Zakharov and Mesezhnikov, 1974, Pl. 21, Fig. 1).

Figure 6. *Dorsoplanites panderi* (Orbigny). CNIGR, N 161/300. Moskva; Panderi Zone (Michalski, 1890, Pl. 12, Fig. 2).

Plate 16. Middle Volgian

Figure 1. *Dorsoplanites sachsi* Mikhailov. GIN, N 3561/814. Lena River Basin, Molodo River; *D. sachsi* Zone (Mikhailov, 1966, Pl. 13, Fig. 1).

Figure 2. *Taimyrosphinctes (Taimyrosphinctes) excentricum* Mesezhn. Holotype. VNIGRI, N 749/686. Taimyr, Debjaka-Tari River; *T. excentricum* Zone (Stratigraphy . . ., 1976, Pl. 24, Fig. 1).

Figure 3. *Dorsoplanites maximus* Spath. VNIGRI, N 3008/634. Eastern slope of Subpolar Ural, Iatria River; *D. maximus* Zone (Zakharov and Mesezhnikov, 1974, Pl. 17, Fig. 1).

Figure 4. *Zaraiskites zaraiskensis* (Michalsky). CNIGR, N 73/300. Moskva; Panderi Zone, *zarajskensis* Subzone (Michalsky, 1890, Pl. 6, Fig. 1).

Plate 17. Upper Volgian

Figure 1a, b. *Craspedites nodiger* (Eichwald). Volga River near Kineshma; *C. nodiger* Zone (Gerasimov, 1969, Pl. 23, Fig. 1).

Figure 2. *Kachpurites fulgens* (Trautschold). Volga River near Rybinsk; *K. fulgens* Zone (Greasimov, 1969, Pl. 32, Fig. 3).

Figure 3. *Craspedites subditus* (Trautschold). Moskva; *C. subditus* Zone (Gerasimov, 1969, Pl. 22, Fig. 4).

Figure 4. *Virgatosphinctes exoticus* Schulgina. Chatanga River Basin, Levaja Bojarka River; *C. okensis* Zone, *V. exoticus* Subzone (Coll. N. I. Schulgina).

Figure 5a, b. *Subcraspedites (Volgidiscus) pulcher* Casey, Mesezhn. and Schulgina. Holotype. VNIGRI, N 1857/634. Eastern slope of Subpolar Ural, Volja River, borehole 255; Uppermost Volgian (Casey and others, 1977, Pl. 1, Fig. 2).

Figure 6a, b. *Craspedites (Taimyroceras) taimyrense* (Bodylevsky). CNIGR, N 69/9565. Chatanga River Basin, Cheta River; *C. taimyrense* Zone (Schulgina, 1969, Pl. 34, Fig. 3).

Figure 7. *Craspedites originalis* Schulgina. Holotype. Chatanga River Basin, Leevaja Bojarka River; *C. okensis* Zone, *C. originalis* Subzone (Schulgina, 1969, Pl. 35, Fig. 1).

Figure 8. *Chetaites chetae* Schulgina. Chatanga River Basin, Cheta River; *Ch. chetae* Zone (Coll. N.I. Schulgina).

Figure 9. *Craspedites okensis* (Orbigny). CNIGR, N 47/9565. Chatanga River Basin, Levaja Bojarka River; *C. okensis* Zone (Schulgina, 1969, Pl. 26, Fig. 3).

REFERENCES

Following is a list of many of the abbreviations found in the references:

BIN	Botanical Institute of the Academy of Sciences USSR, Leningrad
GIN	Geological Institute of the Academy of Sciences USSR, Moscow
IGIG	Institute of Geology and Geophysics, Siberian Branch of the Academy of Sciences USSR, Novosibirsk
MGU	Moscow State University
MOIP	Moscow Society of Natural History
NIIGA	Research Institute of Arctic Geology, Lenigrad
ONTI VIEMS	Department of Scientific Information of the All-Union Institute of Economic Geology, Moscow
SevKavNIPI	North-Caucasian Research Project Institute, Grozhny
SNIIGGIMS	Siberian Research Institute of Geology, Geophysics, and Mineral Resources, Novosibirsk
SVKNII	Northeast Complexes Research Institute of the Academy of Sciences USSR, Magadan
VGRO	All-Union Geological Prospecting Trust
VNIGNI	All-Union Research Geological Petroleum Institute, Moscow
VNIGRI	All-Union Petroleum Research Geological Institute, Leningrad
VSEGEI	All-Union Research Geological Institute, Leningrad

Arkell, W. J., 1933, The Jurassic System in Great Britain: Oxford, Clarendon Press, 681 p.

——, 1939, The ammonite succession at the Woodham Brick Company's pit, Akeman Street Station, Buckinghamshire, and its bearing on the classification of the Oxford Clay: Quarterly Journal of the Geological Society, v. 95, pt 2, p. 135–221.

——, 1941, The Upper Oxford Clay at Purton, Wiltshire, and the zones of the Lower Oxfordian: Geological Magazine, v. 78, no. 3, p. 161.

——, 1946, Standard of the European Jurassic: Geological Society of America Bulletin, v. 57, p. 1–34.

——, 1947, The geology of the country around Weymouth, Swanage, Corfe, Lulworth: Oxford, Geological Survey of Great Britain, Memoir, 287 p.

——, 1956, Jurassic geology of the world: Edinburgh and London, Oliver and Boyd, 806 p.

——, 1951–1958, A monograph of English Bathonian ammonites: London, Palaeontographic Society Monograph, v. 104–112, 264 p.

Baranova, Z. E., Kiritchkova, A. I., and Zauer, V. V., 1975, Stratigraphy and flora of Jurassic deposits in the eastern Caspian depression: VNIGRI Transactions, issue 332, 190 p. (in Russian).

Barsh, B. P., and Fokina, N. J., 1970, Jurassic stratigraphy of the Pitnjak region: Moscow, Soc. Imp. Nat. Bulletin, v. 45, no. 3, p. 119–128 (in Russian).

Barkhatnaya, I. N., 1975, Supplementary data on the palynological characteristics of the Jurassic deposits of the Greater Balkhan, *in* Besnosov, N. V., ed., New data on the Mesozoic stratigraphy of petroleum-bearing regions in the south U.S.S.R.: VNIGNI Transactions, issue 1971, p. 112–116 (in Russian).

Barthel, K. W., 1962, Zur Ammonitenfauna und Stratigraphie der Neuburger Bankkalke: Abh. Bayer. Acad. Wissensch., Math.-Naturw. Reihe, N.F., Heft. 105, 30 s.

——, 1969, Die obertithonische, regressive Flachwasser-phase der neuburger Folge in Bayern: Abh. Bayer, Akad. Wissensch., Math.-Naturw. K1, N.F., v. 142, 174 p.

——, 1975, The Neuburg area (Bavaria, Germany) as prospective reference region for the middle Tithonian; Colloque sur la limite Jurassique-Cretace, Lyon-Neuchatel, 1973: Paris, Memoires du Bur. des Récherches Géol. et Mineraux, France, no. 86, p. 332–336.

Barthel, K. W., and Geyssan, J. R., 1973, Additional Tethydian ammonites from the lower Neuburg formation (Middle Tithonian, Bavaria): Neues Jahrbuch für Geologie und Palaeontologie Monatshefte 1, p. 18–36.

Basov, V. A., Zakharov, V. A., Mesezhnikov, M. S., and others, 1963, New data on the Jurassic stratigraphy of eastern Taimyr.: Science Letters of NIIGA, Regional Geological Series, issue 1, p. 157–164 (in Russian).

Basov, V. A., Zakharov, V. A., and Mesezhnikov, M. S., 1965, On the Jurassic stratigraphy of the Leningradskaya River Basin (Northern Taimyr), *in* Saks, V. N., ed., Mesozoic stratigraphy and paleontology of northern Siberia: Moscow, Institute of Geology and Geophysics, Academy of Sciences, p. 61–66 (in Russian).

Beznosov, N. V., ed., 1973, Explanatory notes for the stratigraphic scheme of the Jurassic deposits of northern Caucasus: Moscow, Nedra, 194 p. (in Russian).

——, 1978, On the boundaries of the Middle series of the Jurassic system, *in* Leonov, G. P., ed., Problems of stratigraphy and historical geology: Moscow University Press, p. 38–43 (in Russian).

Beznosov, N. V., and Kutuzova, V. V., 1972, On the boundaries and subdivision of the Bathonian in western central Asia: VNIGNI Transactions, issue 114, p. 20–43 (in Russian).

Bidzhiev, R. A., 1965, First finds of Kimmeridgian ammonites in the Cis-Verkhoyanye Trough: Science Letters of NIIGA, Regional Geological Series, issue 5, p. 193–195 (in Russian).

Bidzhiev, R. A., and Mikhailov, N. P., 1966, Volgian stage in the north Cis.-Verkhoyanye Trough: MOIP Bulletin, Geological Series, no. 3, p. 3114 (in Russian).

Birkelund, T., Thusa, B., and Virgan, J., 1978, Jurassic-Cretaceous biostratigraphy of Norway, with comments on the British Rasenia Cymodoce Zone: Palaeontology, v. 21, no. 1, p. 31–63.

Bogoslovsky, N. L., 1897, L'horizon de Riazan: Mater. Géol. Ross., v. 18, St. Petersburg, 157 p.

Bolkhovitna, N. A., and Fokina, N. E., eds., 1971, Jurassic and Early Cretaceous spores and pollen of Central Asia: VNIGRI Transactions, issue 104, 176 p. (in Russian).

Bonarelli, G., 1894, Contribuzione alla conoscenza del Giuralias lombardo: Atti R. Accad. Sci. Torino, v. 30, p. 81–96.

Brasil, L., 1986, Rémarques sur le constitution du Toarcien supérieur de Calvados: Bulletin Société Linné Normandie, v. 4, no. 9, p. 147.

Buch, L., 1837, Ueber de Jura in Deutschland: Königliche Akademie der Wissenschaften Berlin, p. 47–135.

Buckman, S. S., 1913, The Kelloway Rock of Scarborough: Quarterly Journal of the Geological Society, v. 69, p. 152–168.

——, 1909–1930, Type ammonites: London, Published by the author, 1055 tables.

Bystritskaya, L. I., 1974, Plant assemblages in the Jurassic deposits of the Kuznets Basin: Tomsk State University Transactions, v. 227, p. 31–49 (in Russian).

Callomon, J. H., 1955, The ammonite succession in the Lower Oxford Clay and Kellaways Beds at Kidlington, Oxfordshire, and the zones of the Callovian stage: Philosophical Transactions of the Royal Society, series B. 239, no. 664, p. 215–264.

——, 1964, Notes on the Callovian and Oxfordian Stages; Compte Rendu, Colloque du Jurassique à Luxembourg, 1962: Luxembourg, Mem. Inst. grand-ducal, Sect. Sci. nat. phys. math., p. 269–292.

Casey, R., 1962, The ammonites of the Spilsby Sandstone, and the Jurassic-Cretaceous boundary: Geological Society of London Proceedings, no. 1598, p. 95–100.

——, 1967, The position of the Middle Volgian in the English Jurassic: Geological Society of London Proceedings, no. 1467, p. 128–133.

——, 1973, The ammonite succession at the Jurassic-Cretaceous boundary in eastern England, *in* Casey, R., and Rawson, P. F., eds., The Boreal lower Cretaceous: Liverpool, Seet House Press, p. 193–266.

Casey, R., Mesezhinikov, M. S., and Shulgina, N. I., 1977, Comparison of the Jurassic-Cretaceous boundary of England, Russian Platform, subpolar Ural, and Siberia: Proceedings of the USSR Academy of Science, Geological Series, no. 7, p. 14–33 (in Russian).

Choffat, P., 1885–1888, Description de la faune Jurassique du Portugal: Lisbon, Comm. Travaux Géologie Portugal.

Collenot, J. J., 1869, Description géologique de l'Auxois: Bull. Soc. Sci. Hist. Nat., v. 5, p. 57–204.

Conze, R., Ernst, Ch., and Mensink, H., 1984, Die Ammonite des Ober-Callovium bis Unter-Kimmeridgium in der Nordwestlichen Keltiberischen Kette: Palaeontographica, Abt. A 183, Lif. 4-6, p. 162–211.

Cope, J.C.W., 1967, The palaeontology and stratigraphy at the lower part of the Upper Kimmeridge Clay of Dorset: Bulletin of the British Museum of Natural History, v. 15, no. 1, p. 3–79.

——, 1978, The ammonite faunas and stratigraphy of the upper part of the Upper Kimmeridge Clay of Dorset: Palaeontology, v. 21, no. 3, p. 469–533.

Cope, J.C.W., and Zeiss, A., 1964, Zur Parallelisierung des englischen Oberkimmeridge mit dem frankischen Untertithon: Geol.-Bl. NO Bayernrlangen, band 14, hefte 1, seite 5–14.

Cope, J.C.W., Getty, T. A., Howarth, M. K., Morton, N., and Torrens, H. S., 1980a, A correlation of Jurassic rocks in the British Isles; Part 1, Introduction and Lower Jurassic: Geological Society of London Special Report 14, 73 p.

Cope, J.C.W., Duff, K. L., Parsons, C. F., Torrens, H. S., Wimbledon, W. A., and Wright, J. K., 1980b, A correlation of Jurassic rocks in the British Isles; Part 2, Middle and Upper Jurassic: Geological Society of London Special Report 15, 190 p.

Corro, G., 1932, Le Callovien de la bordure orientale du bassin de Paris: Paris, Mem. Carte géol. det. France, 263 p.

Cox, B. M., 1979, Distribution of ammonites of the genus *Gravesia* in England and its relation with the Kimmeridgian, *in* Saks, V. N., ed., The Upper Jurassic and its boundary with the Cretaceous system: Novosibirsk, Nanka, p. 54–60 (in Russian).

Cox, B. M., and Gallois, B. W., 1981, The stratigraphy of the Lower Kimmeridge Clay of the Dorset type area, London: London, Institute of Geological Sciences Annual Report, no. 80 (4), 44 p.

Cox, L. B., and Arkell, W. J., 1949, A survey of the Mollusca of the British Great Oolite Series, pt. 2: Palaeontological Society of London Monograph, v. 103, no. 449, p. 49–105.

Dagis, A. A., 1975, Zonal subdivision of Upper Pliensbachian and Toarcian in northern Siberia, *in* Koshelkina, Z. V., ed., Mesozoic of the northeast USSR: SVKNII Transactions, p. 61–63 (in Russian).

Dagis, A. A., and Vozin, V. F., 1972, New data on the oldest Jurassic layers in northern Central Siberia, *in* Saks, V. N., Problems of paleozoogeography of Siberia: Moscow, Nanka, p. 56–67 (in Russian).

Dagis, A. A., Dagis, A. S., Kazakov, A. M., and others, 1978, Discovery of the Lower and Middle Liassic deposits in the Buur, Siberia, *in* Saks, V. N., ed., New data on the Jurassic and Cretaceous stratigraphy and fauna of Siberia: IGIG, p. 6–13 (in Russian).

Davies, A. M., 1916, The zones of the Oxford and Anthill Clays in Buckinghamshire and Bedfordshire: Geological Magazine, v. 53, no. 9, p. 395–408.

Davitashvili, L. C., 1926, On the zoning of the Upper Oxfordian of the Middle Russia: Bull. Soc. Nat. Imp. Moscow, v. 34, no. 3–4, p. 282–293 (in Russian).

Dean, W., Donovan, D., and Howarth, M., 1961, The Liassic ammonite zones and subzones of the northwest European province: Bulletin of the British Museum of Natural History, v. 4, no. 10, p. 437–505.

Delle, G. V., 1967, Middle Jurassic flora of the Tkvarcheli coal basin: BIN, series 8, Paleobotany, v. 6, p. 51–132 (in Russian).

Deslongchamps, E., 1864, Etudes sur les étages jurassiques inferieurs de la Normandie: Memoires de la Société Géologique de France, 296 p.

Dietl, G., 1977, The Braunjura (Brown Jurassic) in southwest Germany: Stuttgart, Stuttgarter Beitrage zur Naturkunde, series B, no. 25, 41 p.

——, 1981, On the systematic position of *Ammonites sugfurcatus* Zieten and its significance for the subfurcatum Zone (Bajocian, Middle Jurassic): Stuttgart, Stuttgarter Beitrage zur Naturkunde, Serie B, v. 81, p. 1–11.

Dietl, G., and Etzold, A., 1977, The Aalenian at the type locality: Stuttgart, Stuttgarter Beiträge zur Naturkunde, series B, no. 30, 13 p.

Doludenko, M. P., and Orlovskaya, E. P., 1970, Jurassic flora of the Karatau: GIN Transactions, v. 284, 160 p. (in Russian).

Doludenko, M. P., and Svanidze, Js.I., 1969, Late Jurassic flora of Georgia: GIN Transactions, v. 178, 116 p. (in Russian).

Donovan, D. T., 1956, The zonal stratigraphy of the Biue Lias around Keynsham, Somerset: Geological Society of London Proceedings, v. 66, p. 182–212.

——, 1964, Stratigraphy and ammonite fauna of the Volgian and Berriasian rocks of East Greenland: Meddelelser om Grønland, v. 154, no. 4, 34 p.

Donze, P., and Enay, R., 1961, Les Cephalopodes du Tithonique inférieur de la Croix de Saint-Conors près de Chambéry (Savoie): Trav. Lab. Géol. Fac. Sci. Lyon, n.s., no. 7, 236 p.

Druschitz, V. V., and Vakhrameev, V. A., 1976, Jurassic-Cretaceous boundary, *in* Keller, B. M., ed., Boundaries of geological systems: Moscow, Nauka, p. 185–224 (in Russian).

Druschits, V. V., and Mikhailova, I. A., 1966, Lower Cretaceous biostratigraphy of the Northern Caucasus: Moscow University Press, 190 p. (in Russian).

Dubar, G., Elmi, S., Mouterde, R., and Ruset-Perrot, Ch., 1974, Divisions et limites de l'Aalenien (Sud-est de la France et quelques régions méridionales); Colloque du Jurassique à Luxembourg, 1967: Clérmont-Ferrand, p. 397–410.

Dubrovskaya, E. N., 1973, Subdivision of the Lower Mesozoic continental deposits in the Zeravshan-Gissar mountain area based on palynological data, *in* Chlonova, A. F., ed., Palynology of mesophytic era: Proceedings of the 3rd International Palynology Conference, p. 60–62 (in Russian).

Efimova, A. F., and others, 1968, Field atlas of the Jurassic flora and fauna in the northeast USSR: Magadan, District Publishing House, 379 p. (in Russian).

Elmi, S., and Mangold, C., 1966, Etudes de quelques *Oxycerites* du Bathonien inférieur: Trav. Lab. Géol. Fac. Sci. Lyon, n.s., no. 13, p. 143–182.

Elmi, S., and Mouterde, R., 1965, Le Lias inférieur et moyen entre Aubenas et Privos (Ardèche): Trav. Lab. Géol. Fac. Sci. Lyon, n.s. no. 12, p. 143–244.

Elmi, S., Guerin-Franiatte, S., and Mouterde, R., 1974, Les subdivisions biostratigraphiques de l'Hettangien en France; Colloque du Jurassique à Luxembourg, 1967; Clérmont-Ferrand, p. 513–520.

Enay, R., and Geyssant, J., 1975, Faunes tithoniques des chaînes bétiques (Espagne méridionale); Colloque sur la limite Jurassique-Crétace Lyon; Neuchâtel, Mem. Bur. Récherches Géol. et Min., no. 86, p. 39–55.

Enay, R., Tintant, H., and Cariou, E., 1974, Les Faunes oxfordiennes d'Europe méridionale, essai de zonation; Colloque du Jurassique à Luxembourg, 1967: Clérmont-Ferrand, p. 635–664.

Gabilly, J., 1964, Stratigraphie et limites de l'étage toarcien à Thouars et dans les regions voisines; Colloque du Jurassique à Luxembourg, 1962: Luxembourg, Mem. Inst. grand-ducal, Sect. Sci., nat. phys. math., p. 193–201.

Gabilly, J., Elmi, S., Maltei, J., Mouterde, R., and Rioult, M., 1974, L'étage toarcien, zones et sous-zones d'Ammonites; Colloque du Jurassique à Luxembourg, 1967; Clérmont-Ferrand, Mem. Bur. Récherches Géol. et Min., p. 605–634.

Galacz, A., 1980, Bajocian and Bathonian ammonites of Gyenespuszta Bokony Mts., Hungary: Budapestini, Geologica Hungarica, series Palaeontology, fasical 39, 227 p.

Gallois, R. W., and Cox, B. M., 1979, Stratigraphy of the Upper Kimmeridge Clay of the Wash area: Bulletin of the Geological Survey of Great Britain, no. 47, p. 1–28.

Genkina, R. Z., 1966, Fossil flora and stratigraphy of the Lower Mesozoic deposits of the Issyk-kul Depression: Moscow, Nauka, 148 p. (in Russian).

——, 1977, Stratigraphy of the continental Jurassic deposits of the Fergana Range and paleobotanical evidence of their age: Soviet Geology, no. 9, p. 61–79 (in Russian).

——, 1979, Subdivision of the Upper Triassic and Jurassic continental deposits in the eastern Central Asia: Soviet Geology, no. 4, p. 27–39 (in Russian).

Gerasimov, P. A., 1969, Upper substage of Volgian in the central Russian Platform: Moscow, Nauka, 144 p. (in Russian).

——, 1978, Two new ammonite species from Volgian deposits of the Moscow and Jaraslavl regions: MOIP Bulletin, geol. series, v. 53, no. 6, p.108–114 (in Russian).

Gerasimov, P. A., and Mikhailov, N. P., 1966, Volgian stage and a common stratigraphic scale for the Upper Series of the Jurassic system: Academy of Sciences USSR Geology series, no. 2, p. 118–138 (in Russian).

Geyer, O. F., 1969, The Ammonite genus *Sutneria* in the Upper Jurassic of Europe: Lethaia, v. 2, no. 1, p. 17–35.

Gignoux, M., 1950, Géologie stratigraphique: Paris, Masson, 735 p.

Golbert, A. V., and Klimova, I. G., 1979, Jurassic-Cretaceous boundary beds and marine Lower Cretaceous in the reference section of Neocomian, *in* Saks, V. N., ed., Upper Jurassic and its boundary with the Cretaceous system: Novosibirsk, Nauka, p. 35–40 (in Russian).

Gomolitskii, N. P., 1968, Contribution to the stratigraphy of Jurassic continental strata from the Yakkabug Mountains (Middle Asia): Academy of Sciences USSR, Geology Series, no. 2, p. 110–116 (in Russian).

Grigyalis, A. A., 1982, ed., Upper Jurassic biostratigraphy of the U.S.S.R. based on foraminifers: Moscow, H. Vilnius, 170 p. (in Russian).

Guerin-Franiatte, S., and Muller, A., 1978, Découverte de Psilophyllites (Ammonites) dans le Grès de Luxembourg (Hettangian): Bulletin d'information des géologues du Bassin de Paris, v. 15, p. 71–73.

Hahn, W., 1968, Die Oppelidae Bonarelli und Haploceratidae Zittel (Ammocoides) des Bathoniums (Brauner Jura) im südwestdeutschen Jura: Jahrbuch des Geologischen Landesamtes, Baden-Württemberg, Abh. 10, p. 7–72.

Hantzpergue, P., and Lafaurie, G., 1983, Le kimmeridgien Quercynois; Un complément biostratigraphique du Jurassique supérieur d'Aquitaine: Geobios, v. 16, p. 601–611.

Harland, W. B., Cox, A. V., Zlewellyn, P. G., and others, 1982, A geologic time scale: Cambridge University Press, 140 p.

Haug, E., 1892, Sur l'étage Aalenien: Bulletin de la Société Géologique de France, series 3, tome 20, p. 1524–1526.

——, 1894, Le System Jurassique, *in* La Grande Encyclopédie: Paris, v. 21, p. 322–331.

——, 1898, Portlandien, Tithonien et Volgien: Bulletin de la Société Géologique de France, series 3, tome 26, p. 197–228.

——, 1910, Traité de Geologie: Paris, Armand Collin, v. 2, fasical 2, p. 929–1396.

Hebert, E., 1857, Les mers anciennes et leurs rivages dans le basin de Paris; Première partie: Paris, Terrain Jurassique.

Hoffmann, K., 1962, Lias und Dogger im Untergrund der Niederrheinischen Bucht: Fortschritte in der Geologie von Rheinland-Westfalen, no. 6, p. 84–105.

——, 1964, Die Stufe des Lotharingien (Lotharingium) im Unterlias Deutschlands und allgemeine Betrachtungen ueber das "Lotharingien": Colloque du Jarassique à Luxembourg: Luxembourg, Mem. Inst. grand-ducal, Sect. Sci. nat. phys. math., p. 135–160.

Hölder, H., 1964, Jura; Handbuch der stratigraphischen Geologie: Stuttgart, Enke Verlag, Band 4, 603 p.

Hölder, H., and Zieger, B., 1958, Stratigraphische und faunistische Beziehungen im Weissen Jura (Kimmeridgien) zwischen Suddeutschland und Ardèche: Neues Jahrbuch fur Geologie und Palaeontologie Abhandlungen, Band 1958, v. 108, no. 2, p. 150–214.

Howarth, M. K., 1955, Domerian of the Yorkshire Coast: New York Geological Society Proceedings, v. 30, pt. 2, p. 147–175.

——, 1958–1959, The ammonites of the Liassic Family Amaltheidae in Britain: Palaeontographica, v. 111 and 112, 53 p.

——, 1973, The stratigraphy and ammonite fauna of the Upper Liassic Gray Shales of the Yorkshire coast: Bulletin of the British Museum of Natural History, Geology, v. 24, no. 4, p. 237–277.

——, 1978, The stratigraphy and ammonite fauna of the Upper Lias of Northamptonshire: Bulletin of the British Museum of Natural History, Geology v. 29, no. 3, p. 235–288.

Ilovaisky, D., 1903, L'Oxfordien et le Sequanien des gouvernements de Moscou et de Riasan: Bulletin Soc. Natur. Moscow, tome 17, no. 2-3, p. 222–292.

Ilovaisky, D. I., and Florensky, I. P., 1941, Upper Jurassic ammonites of the Ural and Ilek basins, *in* Janshin, A. L., ed., Materials on the geological structural pattern of the U.S.S.R.: Moscow, Soc. Nat. Moscow, issue 1, no. 4, 189 p. (in Russian).

Ilyina, V. I., 1976, A palynological characteristic, *in* Saks, V. N., ed., Jurassic stratigraphy of the North U.S.S.R., p. 326–343 (in Russian).

——, 1978a, On a possible correlation of the Jurassic in the north and south Central Siberia based on palynological data, *in* Saks, V. N., and Shurygin, B. N., eds., New data on the Jurassic and Cretaceous stratigraphy and fauna of Siberia: IGIG, p. 86–96 (in Russian).

——, 1978b, A palynological substantiation of stratigraphic subdivision of the Jurassic in northern Central Siberia: Geology and Geophysics, v. no. 9, p. 16–22 (in Russian).

——, 1980, A palynological substantiation of stratigraphy of the continental Jurassic strata of Central Siberia, *in* Khlonova, A. F., ed., Paleopalynology of Siberia: Moscow, Nauka, (in Russian).

——, 1985, Jurassic palynology of Siberia: Moscow, Nauka, v. 638, 175 p.

Ivanov, A. N., 1979, On the significance of the section of the Glebovo Village (Volga area at Jaroslavl) for studying the middle substage of Volgian and on the results of the revision of *Laugeites stachurowskyi* (Nitkitin) species, *in* Saks, V. N., ed., The Upper Jurassic and its boundary with the Cretaceous System: Novosibirsk, Nauka, p. 49–53 (in Russian).

Judd, J. W., 1875, The geology of Rutland and the parts of Lincoln, Leicester, Northampton, Huntingdon, and Cambridge: Geological Survey of Great Britain, England, and Wales Memoir, old series, sheet 64, 320 p.

Kalugin, A. K., and Kiritchkova, A. I., 1968, On the Jurassic stratigraphy of the continental strata of Mangyshlak, *in,* Problem of petroleum presence in Mangyshlak and Ustyurt: ONTI VIEMS, ser. geol. local miner. res. regional, issue 19, p. 15–23 (in Russian).

Kamysheva-Elpatievskaya, V. G., Nikolaeva, V. P., Troitskaya, E. A., and Khabarova, T. M., 1974, Callovian in the southeastern Russian Platform and its fauna, *in* Saks, V. N., ed., Problems of the Upper Jurassic stratigraphy: GIN Transactions, p. 20–29 (in Russian).

Kaplan, M. E., Knyazev, V. G., Meledina, S. V., and Masezhnikov, M. S., 1974, Jurassic deposits of the Cape Tsvetkov and Chernokhrebetnaya River (Eastern Taimyr), *in* Saks, V. N., ed., Mesozoic biostratigraphy of the Boreal Realm: Novosibirsk, Nauka, p. 66–83 (in Russian).

Kazakova, V. P., 1978, On the problem of the Aalenian Bajocian boundary, *in* Milanovsky, E. E., and Dobruskina, I. A., eds., Problems of stratigraphy and historical geology: Moscow, MGU, p. 43–56 (in Russian).

Khimshiashvili, N. G., 1976, Tithonian and Berriasian ammonites of the Caucasus: Tbilisi, "Mecneireba," 180 p. (in Russian).

Khudolei, K. M., 1960, Upper Jurassic strata of the southern and middle Sikhote-Alind: Soviet Geology, no. 2, p. 141–144 (in Russian).

Khydyaev, I. E., 1932, Upper Kimmeridgian fauna of Timan: VGRO Bulletin, issue 42, p. 635–653 (in Russian).

Kiparisova, L. D., 1937, Triassic fauna in the eastern soviet Arctic: Transactions of the Arctic Institute, v. 91, p. 135–250 (in Russian).

Kiritchkova, A. I., 1976, A paleobotanical characteristic and correlation of the Upper Jurassic continental deposits of western Jakutia: Geology and Geophysics, v. 11, p. 44–55 (in Russian).

Kirina, T. I., Mesezhnikov, M. S., Repin, Ju. S., 1978, On new local units in the Jurassic of western Jakutia, *in* Saks, V. N., and Shurygin, B. N., eds., New data on the Jurassic and Cretaceous stratigraphy and fauna of Siberia: IGIG, p. 70–85 (in Russian).

Knyazev, V. G., 1975, Lower Oxfordian ammonites and zonal stratigraphy of northern Siberia: Moscow, Nauka, 140 p. (in Russian).

Kosenkova, A. G., 1975, Jurassic miospores on the southern slope of the Gissar Range and their stratigraphic significance [abs.]: Dissertation, thes. Moscow, 27 p. (in Russian).

Koshelkina, Z. V., 1967, Correlation of the marine Middle Jurassic deposits of the northeastern U.S.S.R. with adjacent areas of the Arctic and Pacific Ring based on ammonoid remains: SVKNII Transactions, issue 30, p. 44–54 (in Russian).

——, 1975, A regional scheme of the Middle Jurassic stratigraphy of northeastern Siberia: SVKNII Transactions, issue 68, p. 85–97 (in Russian).

Krymholts, G. Ja., 1942, On the boundary of the Lower and Middle series of the Jurassic system: Reports of the Academy of Sciences USSR, v. 37, no. 7–8,

p. 265–268 (in Russian).

——, 1957, On the Aalenian stage and the boundary of the Lower and Middle series of the Jurassic system: Soviet Geology, v. 55, p. 115–123 (in Russian).

——, 1972a, "Lona"—A new term in stratigraphy: Vestnik Leningrad University, no. 18, p. 113–114 (in Russian).

——, ed., 1972b, Jurassic System; Stratigraphy of the U.S.S.R.: Leningrad, Nedra, 524 p. (in Russian).

——, 1974, Problems of studying the Jurassic deposits of the U.S.S.R., *in* Problems of the Upper Jurassic stratigraphy: GIN Transactions, p. 5–12 (in Russian).

——, 1978, Information about the Plenary Session of the Commission of the Jurassic system, *in* Resolutions of the Interdependent Stratigraphic Committee and its Standards Commission, issue 18, p. 32–34 (in Russian).

Krymholts, G. Ja., and Zakharov, E. V., 1971, Bathonian ammonites of Kugitang, *in* Shaykubov, T. Sh., ed., Paleontological substantiation of reference sections of the Jurassic system in Uzbekistan and adjacent areas: Leningrad, Nedra, p. 4–40 (in Russian).

Krystyn, L., 1972, Die Oberbajocium und Bathonium Ammoniten der Klaus-Schichten des Steinbruches Neumukhe bei Wien (Osterreich): Wien, Annalen des Naturhistori-Museums Wien no. 76, p. 195–310.

Kuhn, O., 1935, Die Fauna des unteren Lias (Gibbosus-Zone) aus dem Sendelbach im Hauptsmoorwald ostlich Bamberg: Neues Jahrbuch für Mineralogie, Geologie und Paläontologie, Stuttgart (B.-B.), band 73, p. 465–493.

Kutek, J., and Zeiss, A., 1974, Tithonian-Volgian ammonites from Brzostowka, near Tomaszow Mazowiecki, central Poland: Acta Geologica Polonica, v. 24, no. 3, p. 505–542.

——, 1975, A contribution to the correlation of the Tithonian and Volgian Stages; The ammonite fauna from Brzostowka, near Tomaszow Mazowiecki, central Poland; Colloque sur la limite Jurassique-Crétace, Lyon-Neuchâtel, 1973: Mem. Bur. Recherches Géol. et. Min., no. 86, p. 123–128.

Kutek, J., and Wierzbowski, A., 1979, Lower to Middle ammonite succession at Rogoznik in the Pieniny Klippen Belt: Acta Geologica Polonica, v. 29, no. 2, p. 195–204.

Kvantaliani, I. V., and Lysenko, N. I., 1979, A new Berriasian genus *Tauricoceras:* Reports Academy Sci. Georgia SSR, Tbilisi, v. 93, no. 3, p. 629–632 (in Russian).

Kuzichkina, Ju. M., and Khachieva, L. S., 1973, Lower Mesozoic spore-pollen assemblages of Uzbekistan and their significance for correlation, *in* Zaklinskay, N. D., ed., Palynology of the Mesophytic era: Proceedings of the 3rd International Palynology Conference, p. 49–53 (in Russian).

Lang, W. D., 1913, The Lower Pliensbachian—"Carixian"—of Charmouth: Geology Magazine, n.s., Dec. 5, v. 10, no. 9, p. 401–412.

——, 1936, The Great Ammonite Beds of the Dorset Lias: Quarterly Journal of the Geological Society, v. 92, pt. 4, p. 423–437.

Lange, W., 1941, Die Ammonitenfauna der Psiloceras-stufe Norddeutschlands: Palaeontographica Band 93A, 192 p.

——, 1951, Die Schlotheimiinae aus dem Lias Alfa Nordeutschlands: Palaeontographica, Band 100A, Hefte 1–4, 128 p.

Le Hegarat, G., 1973, Le Berriasien du Sud-Est de la France: Doc. Lab. Géol. Fac. Sci. Lyon, no. 43, 576 p.

Lahusen, J., 1883, Die Fauna der jurassischen Bildungen der Rjasanischen Gouvernements: Mém. Com. Géol v. 1, no. 1, SPb, 94 p.

Lissajous, M., 1923, Etude sur la faune du Bathonien des environs de Mâcon: Trav. Labor. Géol. Fac. Sci., Mem. 3, fasc. 3, 5, 286 p.

Leymerie, A., 1838, Memoire sur la partie inférieure du systeme secondaire du Département du Rhône: memoire de Société Geologie France, serie 1. tome 3, p. 313–378.

Luchnikov, V. S., 1963, Stratigraphy of the Darvaz Jurassic deposits: Soviet Geology, no. 6, p. 38–49 (in Russian).

Luppov, N. P., Bogdanova, T. N., and Lobacheva, S. V., 1979, Paleontological grounds for correlating Berriasian and Valanginian of Mangyshlak, southeastern France, northern Federal Republic of Germany, and the Russian Platform, *in* Saks, V. N., ed., Upper Jurassic and its boundary with the Cretaceous system: Novosibirsk, Nauka, p. 159–168 (in Russian).

Marcou, J., 1848, Récherches géologiques sur le Jura Salinois: Memoire Société Géologique France, v. 2, no. 3, p.1–151.

Mascke, E., 1907, Die Stephanoceras-Verwandten in den Coronaten-Schichten von Norddeutschland: Dissertation Gottingen, 38 p.

Maubeuge, P. L., 1964, La question de l'étage Aalenien et son stratotype; Colloque du Jurassique à Luxembourg, 1962; Luxembourg, Mem. Inst. grand-ducal Sect. Sci. Nat. phys. math., p. 203–215.

——, 1975, Catalogue des Ammonites du Jurassique supérieur (Callovien à Kimmeridgien) du Mûsée cantonal de Bâle-Campagne: Tâtigkeitsberichte der Naturforsch Ges. Baselland, Band 29, 338 p.

Mayer, Ch., 1874, Essai et proposition d'une classification naturelle, uniforme et pratique des terrains de sediment: Zurich, C. Schmidt, 23 p.

Mayer-Eymar, Ch., 1864, Tableau du synchronisation des terrains jurassiques: Zürich.

Mazenot, G., 1939, Les Palaeohoplitidae tithoniques et Berriasiens du Sud-Est de la France [Thèse]: Memoire Société Géologie France, v. 18, no. 41, 303 p.

Meledina, S. V., 1977, Ammonites and zonal stratigraphy of the Callovian in Siberia: IGIG Transactions, issue 356, 276 p. (in Russian).

Mesezhnikov, M. S., 1967, A new ammonite zone of the Upper Oxfordian and the position of Oxfordian and Kimmeridgian boundary in northern Siberia, *in* Saks, V. N., ed., Problems of paleontological substantiation of detailed stratigraphy of Siberia and Far East: Leningrad, Nauka, p. 11–130 (in Russian).

——, 1976, On a possible zonal subdivision of the Upper Kimmeridgian in northern Siberia, *in* Mesozoic and Cenozoic stratigraphy of central Siberia: Novosibirsk, Nauka, p. 79–85 (in Russian).

——, ed., 1977, The Jurassic/Cretaceous boundary beds in the Middle Volga area: Leningrad, VNIGRI, 26 p.

——, 1978, Supplements to the united stratigraphic scheme of western Siberia, *in* Rostovzev, N. N., ed., Stratigraphic glossary of Mesozoic and Cenozoic deposits of the West Siberian Lowland: Leningrad, Nedra, p. 122–124 (in Russian).

——, 1984, Kimmeridgian and Volgian on the North of the U.S.S.R.: Leningrad, Nedra, 166 p.

Meszhnikov, M. S., Kozlova, G. E., Kravets, V. S., and Jakovleva, S. P., 1973, On the Lower Volgian deposits in the Pechora Basin: Reports of the USSR Academy of Sciences, v. 211, no. 6, p. 1415–1418 (in Russian).

Mesezhnikov, M. S., Golbert, A. V., Zakharov, V. A., and others, 1979, New data in stratigraphy of the Jurassic Cretaceous boundary beds in the Pechora Basin, *in* Saks, V. N., ed., The Upper Jurassic and its boundary with the Cretaceous system: Novosibirsk, Nauka, p. 66–71 (in Russian).

Mesezhnikov, M. S., Zakharov, V. A., Shulgina, N. E., and Alekseev, S. N., 1979, Stratigraphy of the Ryazinian horizon on the Oka River, *in* Saks, V. N., ed., The Upper Jurassic and its boundary with the Cretaceous system: Novosibirsk, Nauka, p. 71–80, (in Russian).

Mesezhnikov, M. S., Zakharov, V. A., Braduchan, Ju. V., Meledina, S. V., Vyachkileva, N. P., and Lebedev, A. I., 1984, Zonal subdivision of the Upper Jurassic deposits of western Siberia: Geology and Geophysics, no. 8, p. 40–52 (in Russian).

Migacheva, E. E., 1957, On the problem of the Lower/Middle Jurassic boundary: Reports of the USSR Academy of Science, v. 113, no. 3, p. 653–656 (in Russian).

——, 1958, On the problem of the Lower/Middle Jurassic boundary in the northwestern Caucasus: Voronezh, Transactions of the Geology Department of the Voronezh State University, v. 48, p. 39–51 (in Russian).

Mikkailov, N. P., 1957, Mesozoic stratigraphy of the eastern slope of the Subpolar Urals, *in* Saks, V. N., ed., Proceedings of the Interdepartmental Meeting on the Stratigraphy of Siberia: Leningrad, Gostoptechizdat, p. 284–289 (in Russian).

——, 1962a, *Pavlovia* and related ammonite groups: Bull. Soc. Nat. Mosc., v. 37, no. 6, p. 3–30 (in Russian).

——, 1962b, The upper boundary of the Kimmeridgian: Reports of the USSR Academy of Science, v. 145, no. 6, p. 1366–1368 (in Russian).

——, 1964, Boreal Late Jurassic (Lower Volgian) ammonites (*Virgatosphincti-*

nae): GIN Transactions, issue 107, p. 7–88 (in Russian).

——, 1966, Boreal Jurassic amonites (*Dorsoplanitinae*) and zonal subdivision of the Volgian: GIN Transactions, issue 151, 151 p. (in Russian).

Michalski, A., 1890, Die Ammoniten der unteren Wolga-Stufe: Mém. Com. Géol., v. 8, no. 2, SPb, 330 p.

Moore, R. C., ed., 1957, Treatise on invertebrate paleontology; Part L, Mollusca 4, Cephalopoda, ammonoidea: Geological Society of America and University of Kansas, 490 p.

Morton, N., 1974, The definition of standard Jurassic stages; Colloque du Jurassique à Luxembourg, 1967: Clermont-Ferrand, p. 83–93.

Mouterde, R., 1961, Le problème de l'Aalenien et la limite Lias-Dogger; Colloque sur le Lias français, Chambéry, 1960: Paris, Masson, p. 407–410.

——, 1964, Suggestion pour la défense de l'Aalenien; Colloque du Jurassique à Luxembourg, 1962: Luxembourg, p. 217–220.

Mouterde, R., and Tintant, H., 1964, Variation du Sinemaurien dan la région du stratotype; Colloque du Jurassique à Luxembourg, 1962: Luxembourg, Mem. Inst. grand-ducal, Sect. Sci. nat. phys. math., p. 119–126.

Mouterde, R., Enay, R., Careou, E., and others, 1971, Les zones du Jurassique en France: C. r. Sommaire des Séances, fasical 6, p. 76–102.

Neumayr, M., 1871, Die Cephalopoden-Fauna der Oolite von Balin bei Krakau: Abhandlungen der Geologischen Reichsanstalt, Band 5, Heft 2, p. 20–54.

——, 1873, Die Fauna des Schichten mit *Aspidoceras acanthicum*: Abhandlungen der Kais.-Königl. Geologischen Reichsanstalt, Band 5, Heft 6, p. 141–257.

Nikitin, S. N., 1881, Jurassic formations between Rogbinsk, Mologa, and Myshkin, *in* Materials on the geology of Russia, volume X: SPb, Mineral. Soc., 194 p. (in Russian).

——, 1884, Allgemeine geologische Karte von Russland, Blatt 56: Mém. Com. Géol., v. 1, no. 2, SPb, 153 p.

——, 1885, Der Jura der Umgegend von Elatma: Mem. Soc. Natur. Moscow, tome 15, pt. 1, 51 p.

——, 1888, Allgemeine geologische Karte von Russland, Blatt 71: Mém. Com. Géol., v. 2, no. 1, SPb, 218 p.

Nutsubidze K., Sh, 1966, The Lower Jurassic fauna of the Caucasus: Tbilisi, Transactions of the Geological Institute of the Georgian SSR Academy of Science, n.s., issue 81, 212 p. (in Russian).

Odin, G. S., 1982, The Phanerozoic time scale revisited: Episodes, v. 3, p. 3–9.

Odintsova, M. M., 1977, Palynology of the Early Mesozoic of the Siberian Platform: Novosibirsk, Nauka, 115 p. (in Russian).

Oechsle, E., 1858, Stratigraphie und Ammonitenfauna der Sonninien; Schichten des Filsbebietes unter besonderer Berücksichtigung der *Sowerbyi*-Zone: Palaeontographica (A), band 111, p. 47–129.

d'Omalius d'Halloy, J. J., 1868, Précis élémentaire de Géologie: Paris, Bruxelles-Paris, 636 p.

Oppel, A., 1856-1858, Die Juraformation Englands, Frankreichs und sudwelchen Deutschlands: Württemberger Naturforschende Jahreshefte, Stuttgart, Hefte 12–14, 857 p.

——, 1862, Ueber Jurassiche Cephalopoden: Palaeontologische Mitteilungen des Museum des Koeniglich Bayerischen Staates, Stuttgart, Heft 2, p. 127–262.

——, 1863, Ueber Jurassiche Cephalopoden: Palaeontologische Mitteilungen des Museums des Koeniglich Bayerischen Staates, Hefta 3, p. 163–266.

——, 1865, Die Tithonische Etage: Zeitschrift der Deutschen Geologischen Gesellschaft, Jahrgang, 17, p. 535–558.

Orbigny, A. d', 1842–1851, Palaeontologie française, Terrains jurrassiques; Tome 1, Céphalopodes: Paris, Masson, 642 p.

——, 1850, Prodrome de Paléontologie stratigraphique universelle des animaux mollusques et rayonnés: Paris, Masson, v. 1, 394 p.

——, 1852, Cours élémentaire de Paléontologie et de Géologie stratigraphiques: Paris, Masson, v. 2, 847 p.

Osipova, Z. V., and Basov, V. A., 1965, Stratigraphy and lithology of Volgian deposits in the Anabar-Lena Interfluve in connection with diamond presence: Science Letters of NNIGA, Regional Geology Series, issue 7, p. 171–191 (in Russian).

Parsons, C. F., 1974, The *Sauzei* and "so-called" *Sowerbyi* Zones of the Lower Bajocian: Newsletters on Stratigraphy, v. 3, no. 3, p. 153–180.

Pavia, G., and Sturani, C., 1968, Etude biostratigraphique du Bajocien de Chaînes Subalpines aux environs de Digne (Basse-Alpes): Bollettino della Cocieta Geologica Italiana, v. 87, fascile 2, p. 305–316.

Pavlow, A., 1886, Les Ammonites de la zone à *Aspidoceras acanthicum*: Mém. Com. Géol., v. 2, no. 3, SPB, 91 p.

Pavlov, A. P., 1895, On the Mesozoic deposits of the Ryazan Province: Science Letters of the Natural History Department of the Moscow University, issue 11, p. 1–32 (in Russian).

Paraketsov, K. V., and Paraketsova, G. I., 1979, Volgian deposits of the northeast U.S.S.R. and their biostratigraphic characteristics, *in* Saks, V. N., ed., Upper Jurassic and its boundary with the Cretaceous system: Novosibirsk, Nauka, p. 81–86 (in Russian).

Paraketsov, K. V., and Polubotko, I. V., 1970, Jurassic system, *in* Geology of the U.S.S.R.; Northeast U.S.S.R.: Moscow, Nedia, v. 30, p. 309–376 (in Russian).

Paryshev, A. V., 1975, Evolutionary features of the Early Callovian ammonite fauna of the Middle Dnieper area, *in* Ivanov, A. N., ed., Problems of evolution, ecology, and taphonomy of the Late Mesozoic ammonites: Jaroslavl, p. 70–75 (in Russian).

Phillips, J., 1829, Illustration of the geology of Yorkshire; Part 1, The Yorkshire Coast: London, 184 p.

Pictec, J., 1867, Etudes paleontologiques sur la faune à Terebratula diphyoides de Berrias (Ardèche): Mélanges Paléontologiques, Géog. edit., Bâle, p. 43–130.

Polubotko, I. V., and Repin, Jr. S., 1972, Ammonites and zonal subdivision of the Lower Liassic in the northeast U.S.S.R., *in* Materials on geology and mineral resources of the northeast U.S.S.R., issue 20: SVKNII, p. 97–116 (in Russian).

——, 1974, Lower Jurassic biostratigraphy of the northeast U.S.S.R., *in* Major problems of biostratigraphy and paleogeography of the northeast U.S.S.R.: SVKNII Transactions, issue 63, p. 68–89 (in Russian).

——, 1981, On distinguishing a new ammonite zone at the base of the Jurassic system: Reports of the USSR Academy of Sciences, v. 261, no. 6, p. 1394–1398 (in Russian).

Polubotko, I. V., and Sey, I. I., 1981, Subdivision of the Middle Jurassic deposits in the eastern U.S.S.R. based on Mytiloceramus: Proceedings of the USSR Academy of Sciences, Geological Series, no. 12, p. 63–70 (in Russian).

Prinada, V. D., 1962, Mesozoic flora of eastern Siberia and Transbaikal area: Moscow, Gosgeolozdat, 368 p. (in Russian).

Quenstedt, F., 1843, Das Flozgebirge Wurttembergs: Tübingen, H. Laupp, 558 p.

——, 1858, Der Jura: Tübingen, H. Laupp, 842 p.

——, 1882–1885, Die Ammoniten des Schwäbischen Jura; 1. Der Schwarze Jura: Tübingen, H. Laupp, 440 p.

Rehbinder, B., 1912, Middle Jurassic ore-bearing clays from the southwestern side of the Krakow-Wielun Range: Geol. Comm., Transactions, issue 74, n.s., 209 p.

——, 1913, Die mitteljurassischen eisenerzfuhrenden Tone langs dem sudwestlichen Rande des Krakou-Wieluner Zuges in Polen: Zeitschr. Deutsch. geol. Ges., Band 65, Heft 2, p. 181–349.

Renevier E., 1864, Notices géologiques et palaéontologiques sur les Alpes vaudoises, et les régions environnantes; 1. Infra-Lias et zone à Avicula contorta: Lausanne, Bull. Soc. Vaud. Sci. Nat., v. 8, p. 39–97.

Renzhina, E. A., and Fokina, N. I., 1978, Terrigenous marine deposits and conditions of their sedimentation in western Uzbekistan: VNIGNI Transactions, issue 209, p. 76–90 (in Russian).

Repin, Ju. S., 1972, Bajocian ammonites of the northeast U.S.S.R., *in* Materials on geology and mineral resources of the northeast U.S.S.R., issue 20: SVKNII, p. 117–125 (in Russian).

——, 1983, Lower Jurassic ammonite standard zones and zoogeography in northeast Asia: IGCP Project 171, Circum-Pacific Jurassic, Report 2, 34 p.

Resolution du Colloque; Colloque du Jurassique à Luxembourg, 1964: Luxembourg, p. 77–80.

Resolution, 1970, du deuxième Colloque International du Jurassique; Colloque du Jurassique à Luxembourg, 1967: Nancy, p. 38.

Resolution, 1984, of the Second Interdepartmental Regional Stratigraphic Meeting on the Mesozoic of the Caucasus (Jurassic) held in 1977: 47 p. (in

Russian).

Resolution, 1963, of the Plenary session of the standing International Subcommission for the Jurassic System on the problem of recommendation of the First International Colloquium on the Jurassic System: Soviet Geology, no. 6, p. 146–149 (in Russian).

Resolutions, 1955, of the All-Union Meeting on the unified scheme of the Mesozoic stratigraphy for the Russian Platform: Leningrad, Gostoptechnizdat, 30 p. (in Russian).

Resolutions, 1962, of the All-Union Meeting on specifying the unified scheme of the Mesozoic stratigraphy for the Russian Platform: Leningrad, Nedia, 8 p., 15 tables (in Russian).

Resolutions, 1977, of the Interdepartmental Stratigraphic Meeting on the Mesozoic of central Asia, Samarkand, 1971: Leningrad, VSEGEI, 47 p. (in Russian).

Resolutions, 1978, of the Interdepartmental Regional Stratigraphic Meeting on the Precambrian and Phanerozoic of the northeast U.S.S.R., Magadan, 1974–1975: SVKII, 192 p. (in Russian).

Resolutions, 1984, of the Interdepartmental Stratigraphic Meeting on the Mesozoic of the Caucasus, Krasnodar, 1977: VSEGEI, 27 p. (in Russian).

Resultats de l'inquète sur la limite Jurassique-Crétace, 1975, Colloque sur la limite Jurassique-Crétace Lyon-Neuchatel, 1973: Paris, Mem. Burt. Recherches Géol. et Min., no. 86, p. 392–393.

Reynes, 1868, Essai de géologie et de paléontologie avayronnaises: Paris.

——, 1879, Monographie des ammonites (Atlas only): Marseilles and Paris.

Richardson, L., 1911, The Rhaetic and continuous deposits of west, mid-, and part of east Somerset: Quarterly Journal of the Geological Society, v. 67, p. 1–74.

Rieber, H., 1963, Ammoniten und Stratigraphie des Braunjura β der Schwäbischen Alb: Palaeontographica (A), Band 122, Heft 1–3, p. 1–89.

——, 1977, Remarks to the Aalenian of the Swabian Alb: Stutt., Beitr, Naturkunde, series B., no. 29, 5 p.

Rioult, M., 1964, Le stratotype du Bajocien; Colloque du Jurassique à Luxembourg, 1962: Luxembourg, Mem. Inst. grand-ducal, Sect. Sci. nat. phys. math., p. 239–258.

——, 1974, Observation sur le stratotype du Bajocien et sur l'étage bajocien de A. d'Orbigny; Colloque du Jurassique à Luxembourg, 1967: Clérmont-Ferrand, p. 375–383.

Rotkite, L. M., 1978, Distribution of the Kimmeridgian deposits in the Baltic area, *in* Grigelis, A. A., ed., Achievements and prospects of geological studies in the Lithuanian S.S.R.: Vilnius, Mokslas, p.27–29 (in Russian).

Rozanov, N. M., and Fokina, N. I., 1972, The Jurassic deposits of Fergana: VNIGNI Transactions, issue 83, p. 151–155 (in Russian).

Sakharov, A. S., 1976, The problem of substage subdivision of Berriasian in the northeastern Caucasus: Nalchick, SevKavNIPI Transactions, v. 25, p. 19–23 (in Russian).

——, 1979, A stratigraphic characteristic of the Berrasian deposits in northern Caucasus, *in* Saks, V. N., ed., The upper Jurassic and its boundary with the Cretaceous system: Novosibirsk, Nauka, p. 180–186 (in Russian).

Sakharov, A. S., and Khimshiashvili, N. G., 1967, New data about Kimmeridgian ammonites of the northeastern Caucasus: Reports of the Academy of Sciences USSR, v. 174, no. 6, p. 1406–1408 (in Russian).

Saks, V. N., ed., 1972, Jurassic-Cretaceous Boundary and Berriasian Stage in Boreal realm: Nauka, 371 p. (in Russian).

Saks, V. N., Ronkina, Z. Z., Shulgina, N. I., and others, 1963, Stratigraphy of the Jurassic and Cretaceous systems in the north U.S.S.R.: Moscow-Leningrad, Academy of Sciences USSR, 227 p. (in Russian).

Saks, V. N., Ronkina, Z. Z., Basov, V. A., and others, 1969, The reference section of the Upper Jurassic deposits in the Kheta Basin (Khatanga Depression): Leningrad, Naukaa, 208 p. (in Russian).

Saks, V. N., Meledina, S. V., Mesezhnikov, M. S., and others, 1976, Stratigraphy of the Jurassic system of the north U.S.S.R.: Moscow, Nauka 436 p.

Salfeld, H., 1913, Certain Upper Jurassic strata of England: Quarterly Journal of the Geological Society, no. 69, p. 423–430.

——, 1914, Die Gliederung des Oberen Jura in Nordwest Europa: Neues Jahrbuch für Mineralogie, Geologie und Palaeontologie, Beilage-Band 32, p. 125–246.

Sauvage, H. E., 1911, Sur quelques Ammonites du Jurassique Supérieur du Bulonnais: Bulletin de la Société Géologique de France, serie 4, tome 11, p. 455–462.

Sazonova, J. G., and Sasonov, N. T., 1979, The Jurassic-Cretaceous Boundary in the European Platform; Aspekte der Kreide Europas: JUGS, series A., no. 6, p. 487–496.

Sazonova, I. G., and Sazonov, N. T., 1979, The problem of distinguishing the upper stage of the Jurassic and the lower stage of the Cretaceous system on the East European Platform, *in* Saks, V. N., ed., The Upper Jurassic and its boundary with the Cretaceous system: Novosibirsk, Nauka, p. 86–93 (in Russian).

Sazonov, N. T., 1957, Jurassic deposits in central areas of the Russian Platform: Leningrad, Gostoptechnizdat, 155 p. (in Russian).

Schlatter, R., 1977, The biostratigraphy of the Lower Pliensbachian at the type locality (Pliensbach, Wurttemberg, southwest Germany): Stuttgarter Beitrage zur Naturkunde, Serie B, v. 81, p. 1–11.

Sherborn, C. D., 1899, On the dates of the "Paleontologie française" of D'Orbigny: Geology Magazine, n.s. Dec. 4, v. 6, p. 223–225.

Sey, I. I., and Kalacheva, E. D., 1972, Biostratigraphy of the Middle Jurassic in the Far East: Geology and Geophysics, no. 12, p. 111–119 (in Russian).

——, 1974a, Biostratigraphy of the Lower Jurassic in the Far East: Geology and Geophysics, no. 4, p. 11–18 (in Russian).

——, 1974b, Original finds of representatives of the genus *Arkelloceras* in the Far East of the U.S.S.R.: Geology and Geophysics, no. 7, p. 151–156 (in Russian).

——, 1977, Late Jurassic ammonites of the Far East: Geology and Geophysics, no. 6, p. 12–19 (in Russian).

——, 1979, An Ammonite assemblage of the boundary Middle–Upper Jurassic beds of the Soviet Far East: Geology and Geophysics, no. 8, p. 34–45 (in Russian).

——, 1980, Biostratigraphy of the Lower and Middle Jurassic in the Far East: VSEGEI Transactions, n.s. v. 285, 151 p. (in Russian).

——, 1985, Biostratigraphic chart for the Upper Jurassic marine deposits of the northern Far East: Geology and Geophysics, no. 5, p. 136–138 (in Russian).

Sey, I. I., and Polubotko, I. V., 1976, A review of fossil fauna and flora Inoceramids, *in* Saks, V. N., ed., Stratigraphy of the Jurassic system of the north U.S.S.R.: Moscow, Nauka, p. 281–287 (in Russian).

Sey, I. I., Kalacheva, E. D., and Westermann, G.E.G., 1986, The Jurassic ammonite *Pseudolioceras (Tugurites)* of the Bering Province: Canadian Journal of Earth Sciences, v. 23, p. 1042–1045.

Slastenov, Ju. L., 1978, On the Lower Jurassic stratigraphy of the central cis-Verkhoyanye Trough, *in* Saks, V. N., and Shurygin, B. N., eds., New data on the Jurassic and Cretaceous stratigraphy and fauna of Siberia: IGIG, p. 47–55 (in Russian).

Smith, W., 1815, Memoir to map of strata of England, Mather and Mason, 201 p.

Smorodina, N. I., 1926, On the genetic relations of ammonites of the Cardioceratidae family: Bulletin of the Association of Research Institutes of the Moscow State University, issue 3, 21 p. (in Russian).

Sokolov, D. N., 1901, On the geology of the vicinity of the town of Iletskaya Zashchita Orenburg: Bulletin of the Orenburg Branch of the Russian Geographical Society, issue 16, p. 37–78 (in Russian).

Spath, L. F., 1922, On the Liassic succession of Pally Inner Hebrides: Geological Magazine, v. 59, no. 12, p. 548–551.

——, 1923, Correlation of the Ibex and Jamesoni Zones of the Lower Lias: Geological Magazine, v. 60, no. 1, p. 6–11.

——, 1933, Revision of the Jurassic Cephalopod Fauna of Kachh (Cutch): Pal. Indica, v. 9, mem. 2, pt. 6, 249 p.

——, 1936, The Upper Jurassic Invertebrate Fauna of Cape Leslie (Milne Land); 2. Upper Kimmeridgian and Portlandian: Meddelelser om Grønland, band 99, no. 2, 180 p.

——, 1942, The ammonite zones of the Lias: Geological Magazine, v. 79, no. 5, p. 264–268.

Stankevich, E. S., 1964, Ammonites in the Jurassic sandy-clay deposits of the northwestern Caucasus: Moscow-Leningrad, Nauka, 99 p. (in Russian).

Stepanov, D. L., 1958, Principles and methods of biostratigraphic studies: VNIGRI Transactions, issue 113, 180 p. (in Russian).

Steuer, A., 1897, Doggerstudien; Beitrag zur Gliederung des Doggers in Nordwestlichen Deutschland: Habilitationschrit, University Jena, 48 p.

Stratigraphic Commission of the U.S.S.R., 1977, Stratigraphic code of the U.S.S.R.: Leningrad, VSEGEI, 79 p. (in Russian); 1979 (in English).

Sturani, C., 1967, Ammonites and stratigraphy of the Bathonian in the Digne-Barreme area (southeast France): Bolletino della Societa Paleontologica Italiana, v. 5, no. 1, p. 3–57.

Svanidze, Ts. I., 1965, Fossil flora in the Lower Jurassic deposits in the vicinity of Shrosha Village (western Georgia): Bulletin of the Geological Society of Georgia, v. 4, no. 2, p. 25–36 (in Russian).

Sykes, R. M., 1975, The stratigraphy of the Callovian and Oxfordian stages (Middle and Upper Jurassic) in northern Scotland: Scottish Journal of Geology, v. 11, p. 51–78.

Sykes, R. M., and Callomon, J. H., 1979, The *Amoeboceras* zonation of the Boreal Upper Oxfordian: Palaeontology, v. 22, pt. 4, p. 839–903.

Sykes, R. M., and Surlyk, F. A., 1976, A revised ammonite zonation of the Boreal Oxfordian and its application in northeast Greenland: Lethaia, v. 9, p. 421–436.

Tate, R., and Blake, J. F., 1876, The Yorkshire Lias: London, 475 p.

Teslenko, Yu, V., 1970, Jurassic stratigraphy and flora in western and southern Siberia and Tuva: SNIIGGIMS Transactions, paleontology and stratigraphy series issue 42, 270 p. (in Russian).

Thierry, J., 1978, Le Genre *Macrocephalites* au Callovien Inférieur (Ammonites, Jurassique moyen): mem. Géol. Univ. Dijon, v. 4, 449 p.

Tollmann, A., 1976, Analyse des klassichen Nordalpinen Mesozoikums; Stratigraphie; Fauna und Fazies der Nordlichen Kalkalpen: Wien, Monographie Nordlichen Kalkalpen, Teil 2, 580 p.

Torrens, H. S., 1965, Revised zonal scheme for the Bathonian stage of Europe: Sofia, Reports of the Seventh Carpato-Balkan Geological Association Congress, part 2, p. 47–55.

Toucas, A., 1890, Etude de la Faune de couches tithoniques de l'Ardèche: Bulletin Société Géologie France, v. 3, p. 560–629.

——, 1967, Standard zones of the Balhonian: Luxembourg, Colloque du Jurassique à Luxembourg, p. 581–604.

Trueman, A. E., 1922, The Liassic of Glamorgan: Proceedings of the Geological Association, v. 33, p. 245–284.

Tsagaerli, A. L., 1962, On the problem of stratigraphic boundaries of the Middle Jurassic, *in* Tsagareli, A. L., ed., Papers presented by the Soviet Geological at the First International Colloquium on the Jurassic System: Tbilisi, Academy of Sciences USSR, p. 121–135.

——, 1970, On the problem of boundaries of the Middle Jurassic in the light of materials of the Colloquia field in Luxemburg: Ann. Inst. Geol. Publ. Hungarici, v. 54, fasical 2, p. 335–344.

——, 1974, Brief information, *in* Problems of Upper Jurassic Stratigraphy: Moscow, GIN, p. 145–146 (in Russian).

Urlichs, M., 1977a, The Lower Jurassic in southwestern Germany: Stuttgarter Beitrage zur Naturkunde, series B, no. 24, 41 p.

——, 1977b, Stratigraphy, ammonite fauna, and some ostracoda of the Upper Pliensbachian at the type locality (Lias, southwest Germany): Stuttgarter Beitrage zur Naturkunde, series 13, no. 28, 13 p.

Vakhrameev, V. A., 1964, Jurassic and Early Cretaceous floras of Eurasia and paleofloristic provinces of this time: GIN, 260 p. (in Russian).

——, 1969, Stage subdivision of Middle Jurassic in the south U.S.S.R. based on paleobotanical evidence: Soviet Geology, no. 6, p. 8–18 (in Russian).

Vakhrameev, V. A., Dobruskina, I. A., Zaklinskaya, E. D., and Meyen, S. V., 1970, Paleozoic floras of Eurasia and phytogeography of this time: GIN Transactions, issue 208, 423 p. (in Russian).

Vasina, R. A., and Doludenko, M. P., 1968, Late Aalenian flora of Dagestan: Paleontological Journal, no. 3, p. 89–98 (in Russian).

Vlasov, V. M., and Markovich, E. M., 1979, Correlation of Jurassic and Lower Cretaceous deposits in central and eastern South Jakutsk Coal basin: Soviet Geology, no. 1, p. 72–80 (in Russian).

Welsch, J., 1897, Feuille de Saumur: Bull. Serv. Cart. Géol. Fr., v. 9, no. 59, p. 31–35.

Westermann, G.E.G., 1958, Ammoniten-Fauna und Stratigraphie des Bathonien nordwest Deutschlands: Beihefte zum Geologischen Jahrbuch, Heft 38, 103 p.

——, 1964, The ammonite fauna of the Kialagvik Formation of Wide Bay, Alaska Peninsula; Part 1, Lower Bajocian (Aalanian); Paleontological Bulletin, v. 47, no. 216, p. 229–496:.

——, 1967, Lexique stratigraphique International; Volume 1, Europe, Fascicul 5, Allemagne, Fascicul 5f; Volume 2, Jurassique moyen: Paris, Masson, 197 p.

——, 1969, The ammonite fauna of the Kialagvik Formation of Wide Bay, Alaska Peninsula; Part 2, *Sonninia sowerbyi* Zone (Bajocian): Paleontological Bulletin, v. 57, no. 255, p. 1–226.

——, 1979, Troublesome definition of the Lower/Middle Jurassic boundary: Canadian Journal of Earth Sciences, v. 16, no. 10, p. 2060–2062.

Wimbledon, W. A., and Cope, J.C.W., 1978, The ammonite fauna of the English Portland Beds and the zones of the Portlandian Stage: Journal of the Geological Society, v. 135, pt. 2, p. 183–190.

Woodward, H. B., 1894, The Jurassic rocks of England (Yorkshire excepted): Memoir of the Geological Survey of the United Kingdom, 628 p.

Wright, J. K., 1968, The stratigraphy of the Callovian rocks between Netondale and the Scarborough Coast, Yorkshire: Proceedings of the Geological Association, v. 79, pt. 3, p. 363–399.

Wright, T., 1860, On the zone of *Avicula contorta* and the Lower Lias of the south of England: Quarterly Journal of the Geological Society, v. 16, p. 374–411.

Zakharov, V. Z., 1979, Zonal subdivision of the Upper Jurassic and Neocomian strata based on *Buchia, in* Saks, V. N., ed., The Upper Jurassic and its boundary with the Cretaceous system: Novosibirsk, Nauka, p. 122–130 (in Russian).

——, 1981, *Buchia* (Bivalvia) and biostratigraphy of the Boreal Upper Jurassic and Neocomian: Moscow, Nauka, 271 p. (in Russian).

Zeiss, A., 1957, Die ersten *Cardioceraten*-Faunen aus dem oberen Unter-Oxfordien Suddeutschlands und einige Bemerkungen zur Dogger/Malm Grenze: Geologisches Jahrbuch, Band 73, p. 183–204.

——, 1968, Untersuchungen zur Palaeontologie der Cephalopoden des Unter Tithon der Südlichen Frankenalb: Bayerische Akademie der Wissenschaften, Math.-Naturw. Abh, N.F., Band 132, 192 p.

——, 1975, On the type region of the Lower Tithonian substage; Colloque sur limite Jurassic-Crétace Lyon-Neuchâtel: Mem. B.R.G.M., no. 86, p. 370–377.

——, 1977a, Some ammonites of the Kientnice Beds (Upper Tithonian) and remarks on correlation of the uppermost Jurassic: Acta Geologic Polonica, v. 27, no. 3, p. 269–386.

——, 1977b, Jurassic stratigraphy of Franconia:, Stuttgarter Beitrage zur Naturkunde, Serie B, no. 31, 32 p.

——, 1979, Problem of correlation in the Upper Jurassic and some ideas concerning the Jurassic/Cretaceous boundary, *in* Saks, V. N., ed., Upper Jurassic and its boundary with the Cretaceous system: Novosibirsk, Nauka, p. 14–27 (in Russian).

Zeiss, A., Bloos, G., Munk, Ch., Lang, B., Pluckebaum, M., 1984, Guidebook to excursions, Erlangen: University Erlangen–Nurnberg, 205 p.

Zhamoida, A. I., 1975, On the International Symposium on the stratigraphy of the Alpine-Mediterranean Triassic in Austria, Resolution of the Interdependent Stratigraphic Commission and its Standing Commissions: VSEGEI, issue 15, p. 35–43 (in Russian).

Ziegler, B., 1962, Die Ammoniten-Gattung *Aulacostephanus* im Oberjura (Taxonomie, Stratigraphie, Biologie): Palaeontolographica (A), Band 119, 172 p.

——, 1964, Das unteren Kimmeridgien in Europa; Colliquium Jurassic à Luxembourg, 1962: Luxembourg, Mem. Inst. grand-ducal Sect. Sci. nat. phys. math., p. 345–354.

Zinchenko, V. N., Kirina, T. I., and Repin, Ju. S., 1978, Jurassic deposits on the right bank of the Lena River (Zhigansk area), *in* Saks, V. N., and Shurygin, B. N., eds., New data on Jurassic and Cretaceous stratigraphy and fauna of Siberia: Novosibirsk, IGIG, p. 56–69 (in Russian).

Typeset by WESType Publishers Service, Inc., Boulder, Colorado
Printed in U.S.A. by Imperial Printing Co., St. Joseph, Michigan